Elizabeth Harris was born in Cambridge and brought up in Kent, where she now lives. After graduation she had a variety of jobs including driving a van, being a lifeguard and working in the Civil Service. She has travelled extensively in Europe and America and lived for some years in the Far East.

Elizabeth Harris was one of the finalists in the 1989 Ian St James Awards. She is also the author of *The Herb Gatherers* and *The Egyptian Years*.

Acclaim for *The Herb Gatherers*:

'Elizabeth Harris writes with sensitivity and skill and a spine-chilling eye for the sinister. I found it enormously enjoyable'
Barbara Erskine

'Unusual romance with a dramatic twist'
Woman

Acclaim for *The Egyptian Years*:

'It's easy to be swept up into the astonishing story'
Me

'A feast of mystery, romance and spine-chilling drama . . . impossible to put down'
Prima

By the same author

THE HERB GATHERERS
THE EGYPTIAN YEARS

ELIZABETH HARRIS

The Sun
Worshippers

Fontana
An Imprint of HarperCollins*Publishers*

With thanks to Joan and Geoffrey Harris,
travelling companions in Corfu;
and to Merric Davidson for letting me
raid his memory banks.

Fontana
An Imprint of HarperCollins*Publishers*,
77–85 Fulham Palace Road,
London W6 8JB

Published by Fontana 1993
9 8 7 6 5 4 3 2 1

First published in Great Britain by
HarperCollins Publishers 1993

ISBN 0 00 647 317 2

Set in Palacio by Avocet Typesetters, Bicester, Oxon

Printed in Great Britain by
HarperCollinsManufacturing Glasgow

For Jonathan and David, with my love

THE SUN WORSHIPPERS

'Everything may change in our demoralised
world except the heart, man's love, and his
striving to know the divine.'
Marc Chagall

As Time Began . . .

Even before her thought entered his mind, he knew that he could bear it no longer. They would never agree; they could go no further together.

He stood on the edge of the precipice. Level with his eyes a great eagle soared, sensitive wing tips trembling in response to the warm air currents. Down there on the plain was the world of men. A young, tentative species, like big strong children given wondrous toys whose control was beyond their wisdom. But there is good in them, he told himself. They strive, and they fail—make appalling mistakes, injure themselves and each other—but they go on striving.

The air was mild and full of birdsong. The sun was right above the earth's waist, dividing day and night into exact halves. On this island in the central land-circled sea, everything grew. Everything surged upwards and strived for the brilliant blue sky.

From behind him, she broke the peaceful sun-engendered spell.

—They are incorrigible, these people. Beyond hope.

He received her comment, although she had not put it into speech.

—They are young, he replied wearily, turning to her. Still finding their way. They must be given the chance to discover a system which . . .

—I gave them a system! Strident came her anger. I told them how it must be, what they shall and shall not do!

—You are not as they are. You cannot legislate for them.

—Some things must not be! she retorted. There must be no killing! No theft! No fornication! No . . .

He reached within himself for greater strength, for his thoughts must overpower hers.

—These things they will see for themselves! They will come to realise that if they are to live in harmony together, there must be laws which all men respect.

—We must give them laws! she flashed back. Impose order, make them . . .

—I AM TIRED!

It blasted out of him on a great wave of power and she was checked, the stern face suddenly doubtful.

—I am tired, he repeated more gently. I have done all that I think is wise. More than that, he thought, at your behest and against my own better judgement. But it was a thought he did not let her share.

—You must do as you see fit, he told her. Your ways are not my ways. We cannot go on together, for our perceptions of mankind are too different.

Her face went white.

—I did not mean . . .

But he did not want to hear. There was no point in any more argument.

He gathered his thoughts. Then he began to put them into her mind, quickly, forcefully, so that she would not interrupt.

—You look upon the earth's most wondrous evolution and you want it to develop your way. You want to curb the great ranging spirit of humanity before it has had the chance to know itself for what it is.

He paused, for the very thought of what she had been trying to do was abhorrent. Then he concluded:

—You must do as you will, for I cannot stop you.

He was sad, suddenly, for he saw what was ahead for her. An endless succession of systems she would thrust upon the world, some better than others, some lasting longer than others, but each in its turn ultimately failing.

Her thought spoke in his mind, an answering sadness in her voice as if she were looking into his future, too, and, like him, pitying:

—And you? What of you?

He gazed out over the wide valley, his eye catching the sparkle of distant sea and the brilliant rays of the sun pouring down benevolence on the land. Making crops grow. Making thrive the beautiful, frivolous flowers. Making the trees stand tall so that they gave shade in the heat of the day.

He saw in his mind's eye the people of the plain, struggling to make themselves at home in the world. He saw men and women working, squabbling. Hindering and helping each other. Being petty and being magnificent. Killing, and laying down their lives for each other.

Hating. And loving.

Discovering for themselves, eventually, the ultimate truths.

At last he answered. Aloud, for if he was to be with men he must learn to communicate as they did.

He said, 'I am going down the mountain.'

Part One

ONE

The House of the Twins

The first doubts broke through at Gatwick, when she realised the flight to Corfu was delayed by five and a half hours.

Five and a half hours. So where they should have been arriving in the late afternoon, in plenty of time to find accommodation and settle in before sauntering out for a lazy dinner, now they wouldn't even be landing till nearly midnight.

Would she be able to find them somewhere in Corfu town, in the small hours? Or was she doomed to spend a night with two young sons on some miserable park bench?

Fine start this is, she thought, trying to damp down the panic before either of the boys came back and noticed. Wonderful bloody holiday *this* is going to be.

'Hi, Mum.' She looked in the direction of the voice and saw Rupert approaching, sidestepping bits of luggage and baby buggies with a full back's ease. He must be in his Serge Blanco mode, she thought abstractedly.

'How long is it now?' Rupert threw himself into the seat she'd been saving for him by draping her jacket over it. Threw himself *on* her jacket, in fact, but she didn't think now was the moment to point it out.

13

Silently she nodded in the direction of the Departures board.

Oliver, arriving panting on her other side, spotted the ominous line before his elder brother. 'Five and a half *hours*!' he said, face screwing up in disgust. 'Shit!'

'Oliver!' she said. The reprimand was automatic, but more for form's sake, in case anyone else heard and thought her a poor mother for allowing a ten year old boy to say 'shit' and get away with it. Herself, she swore. Knew she shouldn't, but still did.

Rupert was up again. Restless, as always. 'Come on, Ol.'

Oliver fell into step behind him. 'Where?'

Rupert said something about looking for a Michael Jackson tape for his Walkman, then they were out of earshot.

They'd be back soon, she was well aware. What'll I do with them for five and a half hours? she wondered. The prospect was awful. We could eat, I suppose, go and sit in the cafeteria and order something we don't really want. But they'll bolt it down and we'll be through in half an hour, maximum. My sons have never lingered over food in their lives, and it's unrealistic to imagine they're going to start now.

We'll sit and read our books. Play Travel Trivial Pursuit. I-Spy. Whoopee. She wished she could summon some enthusiasm, convince herself it didn't really matter, delays were an integral part of travelling in the nineties and one just had to make the best of it. She glanced around her. Which other disappointed sun worshippers were on the Corfu flight? The miserable looking people, no doubt. That couple with the baby in the buggy, now, they look as if they've just had bad news. But then perhaps they always look like that. Perhaps the arrival of their bundle of joy has been as catastrophic for them as Rupert and

Oliver's advents were for Barry and me.

Barry. Would this be more tolerable if Barry were here? She tried to think. I can readily see that a certain type of husband could make all the difference. Regard this delay as a challenge, get busy entertaining the kids with games, plane-spotting, puzzles, drawing, organise all the children on the flight into a mammoth game of hide-and-seek. Wouldn't that kind of a husband be great?

Unfortunately my husband was as far removed from that as the sun from the moon. My husband would have said, 'Fay, you'll think of something.' And, sycophantically, 'you're so good with them, Fay, the perfect mother.' And then my husband would have slid off to the bar. Oh, he'd have gone on the pretext of getting us all a drink, would have come out with a lager for me and Cokes and crisps for the boys. But that would be that. Back he'd go, back to the corner he'd already have reconnoitred, to chat up the barmaid—or the barman, it didn't make any difference to Barry—and get into conversation with the first person who came to stand beside him. And there he'd stay, drinking his way through half a bottle, a bottle, moving from traveller's tales to rugby to women and eventually to blue jokes, until eventually I'd send one of the children in to tell him it was time to go.

Good old Barry.

She was cheered by realising how much worse she'd be feeling if he were there. Not cheered much, but a bit. Then she thought, we're here, me and the boys. Even if there is a five and a half hour delay, we're on our way. We're at the very start of a wonderful holiday, and it's entirely through my efforts.

That, now, that *is* worth smiling about.

And she opened her bag to get out the Travel Trivial Pursuit.

*

It was such a relief when they were finally on the aircraft—an extra hour's delay had crept on to the total from somewhere, but by then a mere hour was nothing—that she forgot to be afraid of the take-off. The boys' exhilaration, anyway, was catching. They'd fought, of course, over who should have the window seat, and she'd prised them apart and said that whoever didn't have it on the flight out would have it on the homeward journey. *Promise.*

The cabin crew came round with free drinks, in apology for the long wait. Fay tried to calculate how many gin and tonics would be required to make it up to her. Only one was offered, so she had to settle for that. The boys had cans of lemonade, and Rupert was too bloated to eat his meal. She packed the manageable bits into her bag—you never knew when a couple of crackers and a bit of cheddar would come in handy. She was about to sneak the same items off Oliver's tray, but he realised what she was doing and put them out of her reach.

The children slept for the last hour. Sod's law, she thought ruefully. At Gatwick, when I could have done with some time to myself, to read, or just to think, they were resolutely awake and wanting to be entertained. Now, when I'm beginning to worry about what's ahead and need the distraction of their conversation, they're both sending them home like Rip Van Winkle.

She sat with her fears, apprehension mounting until it made her feel slightly sick, and eventually they landed at Corfu.

'Shall we get a taxi, Mum? Or get on one of those buses?' Oliver, dancing with excitement, thrilled at being up after midnight in the warm darkness of the Greek night, was almost more than she could bear.

'I don't know, Oliver!' she snapped. Then came instant regret, as his face fell—too late, she remembered his youth. How much this trip meant to him. How he'd made a calendar, weeks ago, and had religiously crossed off the days.

She put down the bags and crouched beside him, arms going round his strong, stocky body. 'Sorry, Ol.' She nuzzled into his neck, smelling his Oliver smell.

'It's okay, Mum.' He returned her hug, too young, unlike Rupert, to be embarrassed by public displays of affection. '*I* understand.'

He did, too. She knew that.

'We can't go on any of the buses,' she said, forcing herself to be business-like, 'they're just to transport the people on package tours.'

'People who want the whole lot done for them,' Rupert added, slight superiority in his tone. She recognised her own words. '*We're* not going to be like all the other sheep,' she'd said, making it sound daring, as if they were doing something special. 'We're going flight-only, and we'll find ourselves somewhere really lovely, away from the hordes.'

It had been easy, in safe old England, to think of being daring. Everyone had said, oh, there are *heaps* of places, you won't have any trouble at all! It was a different matter now, standing forlorn outside the airport buildings at one in the morning with nowhere to go, surrounded by groups of happy confident people who all knew exactly where they were heading. English—hundreds of English—and Greeks. Clutches of men, eyeing the arrivals, picking out the ones they were detailed to meet. That red-faced, bull-like man, she thought, he's looking out for someone. Some lucky person, who's going to be whisked away to their accommodation without lifting a finger. Who's going to have old bull-face carry the bags and make them feel welcome.

I wish someone were doing that for us.

I've got to do something. Before the kids tumble to the fact that I'm scared silly.

17

'Rupert, put out your hand and hail us a cab,' she said grandly.

Rupert giggled. 'Call me a cab.'

'You're a cab,' Fay and Oliver chorussed.

The taxi driver got out and helped her put the cases in the boot. 'Where you go?' he asked.

Fay pushed the boys into the back seat and shut the door.

'Er—I'm not sure,' she said. 'We—'

'You want what hotel? Apartment?' He was looking concerned now, as if accepting her as a fare had placed a duty on him to share her problems.

'I don't know.'

'Where? You have address?'

'No. I—' She didn't know how to go on.

The taxi driver stood looking at her, frowning, resources at an end.

'You have a problem?' The voice spoke from behind her. A deep voice, slightly hoarse. But the English was good. She turned, and came face to face with the bull-like man.

'We haven't booked anywhere.' How ridiculous it sounded. How stupid he must think her, how irresponsible, to come out here with two young children and nowhere to lay their heads. 'I was hoping to arrange something when we got here.'

She'd said it. Let him laugh his scathing laugh. Damn it, wouldn't he do the same if he were desperate to take his kids away but didn't have the money to do it in style?

'We've just arrived,' she hurried on, 'the flight was delayed. And now we're so late, I—'

'No problem.' He wasn't laughing. Wasn't looking critical at all. And he spoke with such certainty that she was instantly convinced. She found herself smiling, and his ruddy, broad face smiled in response, making the small hot eyes almost disappear in the uplifted flesh of the cheeks. He really was a hideous man, she thought, then chided herself for being so unkind about someone who was trying to help her.

'Can you suggest somewhere, then?'

He studied her, large head on one side, thick neck settling into a deep crease. As he stared, she had the strange feeling that someone was charging around inside her head, trying to see into her mind. Instinctively she recoiled, and the sensation stopped.

His expression was friendly and relaxed. There was no threat from him. I'm being stupid, she thought. I must be over-tired.

He was speaking, saying something about a house. 'Sorry?'

'You like a house in Corfu town?'

She nodded vigorously. 'Yes! That's exactly where I want to stay. Not in any of those ghastly resorts, but somewhere nice. Really Greek.'

She wondered belatedly if it was tactless to refer to his island's prize holiday spots as 'ghastly'. But then perhaps he didn't know the meaning of the word.

'Corfu Town,' he repeated. 'I can take you to house, nice house for you.' He paused, apparently thinking. Fleetingly, she had the strange impression that he was listening. Then, 'Right house for you. Corfu Old Town. Is good?'

It sounded more than good. But it was probably too good. 'How much?'

'How long you want to stay?'

'One month.'

'One month?' He stared at her, eyes wide open for an instant in surprise. Then he nodded. And named a price.

'That's for the month?'

'Sure!'

She calculated rapidly. It was too much. 'I'm sorry. I can't afford that.'

Immediately he responded, 'How much you wanna pay?'

The question seemed absurd. She felt very odd, as if the world had changed its rules and no-one had told her. How much you wanna pay?

She offered a figure marginally less than she'd budgeted for their accommodation. Then she held her breath.

He shrugged, as if it really didn't matter. He said, 'Okay.'

Dazed, she got into the taxi beside the boys, shushing the inundation of their questions, saying briefly, 'It's all right. We've got somewhere,' and hoping they'd be quiet and let her concentrate. I'm all at sea, she thought wildly, I'm not sure what's going on. I feel . . .

She didn't know what she felt.

The bull-like man, talking to the taxi driver, presumably in Greek, got into the front with him and began giving him directions. And in no time, they were speeding away from the airport, ahead of them the lights of Corfu Town.

Leaning forward, she tapped the bull-like man on the shoulder.

'Where are we going?'

He turned. Under the orange street-lights, his little eyes looked even redder. Briefly they scanned her, then, grinning, he said, 'I take you to The Twins' House.'

*

The Twins' House.

In the flurry of impressions and the strangeness of last night, the peculiar name of the house had been just one more oddity. But now, lying in her wide and comfortable bed in the early morning light, she thought about it again.

What twins? Who are they? Is it their house really, or is The Twins' House a name, like Dunroamin' or The Chestnuts?

It's his house, I suppose, and he lets it. The Bull man. My saviour, so I really should start to be more polite about him. Not that I'd suggest he was bovine to his face. Wouldn't dare.

She smiled, stretching, luxuriating in the smooth cool sheets and the warmth of the sunbeams already creeping in through the shutters. Beyond them, the french windows giving on to the little balcony stood open, so that street sounds from below floated up to her. From closer at hand, perhaps up there on her own roof, she could hear the affectionate cooing of pigeons. The room, furnished simply but very tastefully, was the best in the house, and she'd had no hesitation in choosing it for herself last night, it being the only one with a double bed instead of the paired singles in the other three rooms.

She gazed around her: at the wardrobe and dressing table, golden wood beautifully carved; at the thick, sumptuous wallpaper, striped in white and gold against the white-painted woodwork; at the deep yellow carpet, the colour of sunshine; and up at the ceiling, which, surprisingly, was painted dark midnight blue and dotted in gold with the constellations.

The taxi had driven them through night-time streets still busy with sauntering people, and she'd been aware of the Bull man pointing out this and that place, names meaningless to her and instantly forgotten. Then, in a square at the top of a slight rise that led away from the centre of activity, they had come to a stop. Pointing towards a building painted in gentle fading yellow, its façade bisected by a staircase leading up to a surrounding balcony, the Bull man said, 'The Twins' House.'

21

He'd produced keys, helped with the luggage, even paid off the taxi. Ushering Fay and the sleepy, bemused children inside, he had thrown open doors and blazed on lights with the air of a man greeting long-awaited, welcome guests.

And Fay, too tired to think any more, had accepted everything and been thankful to her depths.

She wondered if the children were awake yet. She thought not—they'd surely have come to look for her if they were, eager for food, talk, a hug. She got out of bed and went over to the window, opening the shutters so that she could look out. The square below was busy, cars moving slowly in the streets, held up by meandering pedestrians. Not holiday people, she noticed, or they didn't look as if they were. No beach-mats beneath the arm, no revealing shorts and brilliant baggy t-shirts. Instead, women in black carrying baskets and bundles. Men pushing bicycles, the carriers loaded with fruit and vegetables. People, local Corfiot people, going about their day's work.

By amazing, wonderful chance, she'd ended up in exactly the sort of place she'd hoped for.

I'm going to look at the rest of the house, she thought. Right now, before the boys are up. Just by myself.

Quietly she crossed the room and opened the door. Down the steps to the next half-landing, she peered into the boys' room; their sleep-abandoned attitudes suggested she'd have a while before they joined her. Briefly she looked into the remaining bedrooms, but they were shuttered, the curtains drawn, and she could make out little but the humps of beds and furniture.

Downstairs. Down a curving flight with a delicate, white-painted wrought-iron rail. She thought, what does this place keep reminding me of?

She couldn't bring it to mind.

At the back of the house was a kitchen—functional, clean, stainless steel implements and pans, a dinner service in white china on the dresser—and a dark dining room with a long table and chairs for twelve. Twelve! she thought. I can give a dinner-party.

Back across the hall to the room at the front of the house. The one which opened on to the balcony, up at first-floor level and above the dust and noise of the street.

This, she realised, was the heart of the house. And last night's hurried glance hadn't begun to do it justice. For it was a beautiful room, its golden colours mellow and restful, its appointments and furnishings plain and good and quite obviously expensive. She walked over to the balcony doors, opening the long shutters to admit the sunlight.

Turning back into the room, she noticed the paintings.

They were on the opposite wall, and until this moment she'd had her back to them. She certainly hadn't seen them last night, and for an uneasy moment she wondered if she'd have taken this house if she had done.

They disturbed her.

Before her eyes could carry the message of their content to her alarmed brain, they had already upset her, made her shy away, want to hide her eyes.

She stood quite still at the centre of the room, raiding her resources in her search for control. Stop being stupid, she ordered. This place is wonderful, better than I'd ever thought I'd find. Far better, for God's sake—who would *dream* of getting a palace like this, at the rent I'm paying?

Palace. The word stuck in her brain, arresting the progress of her thoughts as a bone in the throat halts breathing.

That was what it was! What this house, with its

23

curves, its perfect proportions, its fittings of quiet understated luxury, called to her mind.

A palace. Only it wasn't called a palace, it was called a palazzo, because it had been in Italy. Near Venice. And to call it a palace had been an exaggeration—it hadn't really been one, merely a beautiful country house. She'd seen a programme about it on television when she was small—she'd expected to be bored then been amazed to find herself entranced, so much so that she'd gone into the grown-ups' section of the library and shyly asked the man behind the desk if there was a book about it. There was: she learned that the house had belonged to a Venetian, but its architect had been a Frenchman.

And it had looked—and felt—just like The Twins' House.

She'd been distracted, whisked away into the sanctuary of her memories. But now, flung back to the present, she was once more confronted by the paintings.

Braver now, she went nearer. Switched on the spotlights suspended over the frames.

And looked up to see what it was that was disturbing her.

There were two paintings, vast canvases which reached almost from the ceiling to the floor. Their subjects were mythological, she could see that at a glance, and she thought she recognised in the left-hand painting Ares, God of War, bronze helmet on his head, in his stupendous body a sense of potency so strong that it seemed to reach out for her and stroke against her flesh. Above him was the sun, a great fireball of white heat, and its earthbound rays led like stairs to the curly-fleeced back of a ram which lay at the feet of the god.

The creature was dead, and the small figure of a man was flaying the fleece from the body.

24

Turning away, for the detail was too vivid, she looked at the right-hand painting. And here, surely, was Aphrodite, a seductive, rosy body clad in clothing of such transparency that she need hardly have bothered. Fay stared at the rounded breasts, the nipples erect and pink against the white skin. At the wide hips, perfectly curved. And, raising her eyes, up into the face, whose expression was a mixture of mischief and blatant desire.

The object of her desire was not apparent. For beside her, in the foreground of the picture, was another woman, but this one was magisterial and stern, her robes clutched tight around her. In her hand was a set of scales, in one pan of which lay a white feather.

. Fay shook her head, trying to understand. She felt as if there was a message in the paintings, not for everyone but meant just for her. But why . . .?

No. It was absurd. They were good, the pair of paintings, too good. That was the trouble—their power of suggestion had found too willing an audience in her.

She thought, I can ignore them. Keep my back turned, if we use this room. *When* we use it, she amended, because it's too nice to waste, and after all we're paying for it. And maybe we'll prefer to sit out there on the balcony.

In which case I shan't need to look at them at all.

Feeling better—feeling once more completely happy—she left the room and closed the door behind her.

TWO

Castor and Pollux

The boys, predictably, wanted to go swimming. They also wanted to eat; a more thorough exploration of the kitchen revealed a jar of olives and one of jam, a bottle of kumquat liqueur and some dried figs, exotic fare which left them in no doubt that they were *abroad* but hardly suitable as breakfast for two hungry boys.

She gave them an aeroplane cracker and half each of the cheddar cheese, with glasses of water. Oliver said the water tasted like flat Alka Seltzer. She didn't let herself think about how he knew what flat Alka Seltzer tasted like. When they'd finished, she announced that before anyone went swimming, they had to find the shops and do some provisioning.

They went down the grand staircase leading from the front door and stood uncertain in the square.

'Which way?' she asked.

Rupert was looking along the narrow streets which led away behind the house. 'Not there,' he said. 'It's all tall houses and people's washing hung between the balconies.'

'A residential area,' Fay said. 'No good. Let's go back down there,' she pointed, 'to that street with the arcades we passed last night. It looked lively—there were cafés and tourist shops, so maybe there'll be food shops too.'

It was only a short walk, and almost immediately they were rewarded by the sight of an elderly woman carrying a stick of bread, so fresh that they could smell it as she passed. It was easy, after that, to find the baker's shop by following the trail of emerging customers. And, as they got nearer, their noses.

Provisioning shops, conveniently, were grouped together. After the baker's they went into a supermarket and a greengrocer's, then staggered back to The Twins' House with an arm-wrenching collection of bulging plastic bags. Unpacking the eclectic contents into the fridge and the bare kitchen cupboards, Fay realised happily that it would be some days before they'd need to shop again, other than for things like bread and milk. And, now that they knew where to go, the boys could fetch those.

'*Now* can we go swimming?' Oliver asked.

'Yes.'

The two of them threw themselves at the door. 'Hold on,' she said. Her heart sank: she should, she realised, have thought of this before the present moment. 'It'd be an idea to know where we're going.'

'The beach?' Oliver said hopefully.

'There isn't one in the town,' she said, trying not to make it sound disappointing. 'But there's a lido,' she hurried on, as his face fell. 'It says so in the guide book. We just have to look at the map, to find out where it is,'—she ran upstairs to her bedroom to fetch the book, the boys hot on her heels—'and then we'll go and find it.'

They breathed warm eager breath on her face as she flipped through the pages. 'There!' She pointed triumphantly. 'What does that say?'

'Lido!'

It appeared from the map that it was just across the road: its situation couldn't have been better. As she followed her sons down the stairs, more patient than they and able to think about things like packing sun tan oil, books, towels, into a bag, she said a quiet prayer of thankfulness.

The days fell very quickly into a pattern. The boys' priority was to swim: the lido proved to be perfect for them, for beyond its narrow strip of pebbly beach the sea bed shelved away steeply, forming a calm stretch of water out over which there jutted a ricketty pontoon. It was high enough above the surface for the first plunge off it into the water to be something of an ordeal; it took Oliver half the morning to pluck up the courage to follow where Rupert had led.

The lido was perfect for Fay, too. For the first few days she was content just to lie on a wooden bench (all that the lido had to offer in the way of sun loungers, but then, she reasoned, what could you expect for 120 drachmas a day?), reading, stirring herself once in a while for a slow leisurely swim, dozing. And, above all, lying in the sun in an attitude of worship and letting it do its healing work on her tired body.

The lido had a small bar, which sold drinks and simple snacks. Towards the middle of the day, she'd beckon the boys to come and eat, and they'd take up occupation of one of the tables set back in the shade. She worried a little about the amount of time they were spending in the sun, and it eased her mind to think that they were out of it at the height of the day. Not that they seemed to be taking any harm: she'd made them wear t-shirts in the water for part of the time to start with, increasing their exposure gradually, and, with the use of water-resistant sun cream, they'd avoided any sun burn. Already they were tanned, and their fair hair was bleaching so that they looked like Palominos.

In the late afternoon they would go back to The Twins' House, for cups of tea and cold drinks.

Sometimes she could persuade the boys to take a short rest, more often they'd be up and down the stairs at the front of the house, watching the passing pedestrians, trucks, taxis and horse-drawn carriages, or trying to attract the ever-present, wheeling clouds of swifts by lobbing pebbles in the air. You won't do it, she thought, watching them. Swifts are canny birds, quite well able to distinguish an appetising morsel of insect from a pebble.

The town was almost insect-free. She silently blessed the swifts.

Before going out for the evening, they'd all have showers. The bathroom was the one feature of the house which was Greek rather than Italian, which she thought was a pity, a Greek bathroom surely being fairly low down on most people's list of desirable things. The pipes, all too visible, emerged from the walls as if they'd only just that minute been stuck through, no-one having bothered to fill up the gaps and make a proper job of it. The basin's plug didn't fit, the lavatory seat had a crack in it, and the glass shelf was crooked, so that everything slid down to one end. And the shower, unless you crouched to about eighteen inches high, sprayed out profusely all over the room, soaking everything in reach. Fay, resignedly squeezing out the clean underwear she'd been about to put on, reflected that perhaps the Greeks designed their bathrooms that way deliberately, so as to provide a built-in self-washing facility. Self-regulating, too, in that the more often you showered, the cleaner was your bathroom.

She sat in her bedroom one evening, too damp after her shower to dress yet. The boys were outside waiting for her, but apparently quite happy for the moment. The thin curtains were drawn across the open windows, blowing gently in the breeze off the sea.

She stood naked in the middle of the room, enjoying

the feel of the air on her skin. Then, prompted by something she couldn't name, slowly she turned to look at herself in the full-length mirror on the cupboard door.

In the gentle, golden light, her tan looked darker than it did in the sunshine. The stripe of white across her loins and the two pale mounds of her breasts stood out starkly, as if it were her intention to draw attention to the erotic areas of her body. White breasts on a brown body, she thought vaguely. They look like Madeleines. Supposing Proust's memory had been for a pink-nipple-topped creamy-skinned breast, and not for a cherry coconut cake? Unlikely, given Proust's proclivities, but he could have been remembering his mother.

Perhaps it was a sexual thing after all, and he only said it was a Madeleine.

She controlled her thoughts, with an effort. Somehow it seemed slightly disrespectful to think of Proust in such terms.

She went on staring. I haven't done this for years. God, I can't think when the last time was that I looked at myself! *Really* looked, I mean. And at all of me.

She was slimmer than the image she'd been carrying of herself. She'd been aware of losing weight gradually, over the years, the hard work and the worry having exacted their price, but until that moment, she realised, her mental picture hadn't caught up with actuality. Much of the flesh had fallen off, although the heavy breasts and the wide hips that were a fundamental part of her were still evident.

There was, she thought, feeling guilty even as she did so, nothing to be ashamed of *there*.

The guilt increased, out of control. Days of youth raced into her head, of getting changed for games beneath a towel, of running so quickly through the shower to avoid being seen that the tepid water barely touched her; of the heavy serge uniform dress, bodice sewn into a pin-tucked double thickness to restrain burgeoning curves; of Sister Bernard, correcting her posture with a vicious hand in deportment class as if a jutting chest and a bottom that curved as round as a water melon were somehow Fay's own fault.

Galloping in, unstoppable, came the memory of Barry. Of how it had been, in the beginning. Admiration in his dark blue eyes, giving way to lust. His hands, his body . . .

NO!

Forbidden. It's forbidden, as taboo as a sexy young body was to Sister Bernard. I *do not allow* thoughts of Barry.

She was panting, sweat breaking out. Reaching for a towel, wrapping herself in it, securing it so that she was swathed, her flesh hidden.

Her back to the mirror, she sank down on to the bed.

From below, she became aware of the boys' raised voices. They seemed to be arguing. Wondering how long it had been going on, she got up and dressed.

*

The boys were making friends, with local boys, mainly, for the foreign tourists stayed in the resorts which Fay had so wanted to avoid, and came to Corfu Town to sightsee and to eat their evening meals rather than to swim; that, presumably, they did from the crowded beaches of their holiday villages.

The Greek boys all seemed to speak English. Not much, but enough. And she listened to her sons pick up, without noticing it seemed, words of Greek. Probably swear words which they'd have to un-learn if they were ever to be taught Greek in school, but it didn't seem to matter. She saw less and less of Rupert

31

and Oliver, and sometimes, although she fought against it, she missed them.

'Ma, we've been invited to play table-tennis!' Oliver, racing up to her as she began to pack up her bag at the end of another lido day.

'Who by?' she said, the instinctive wariness making her ungrammatical.

'We've met these boys—well, they're big boys, men, really,'—her wariness increased—'and they're twins! They thought *we* were twins too, me and Rupe!' His eyes were alight with joy and hero-worship. 'Wasn't that wicked, Ma?'

She wasn't surprised. Born so close—less than two years between them—her sons were often taken for twins. They were alike, and Oliver was big for his age. Wouldn't fate just do that, she thought before she could stop herself, make poor little Oliver arrive so soon on his brother's heels?

'Can we?' Oliver was asking urgently. 'It's only up there,' he gestured to the basketball court up behind the lido, 'there's a club thing up there, the twins say we can use it if we go with them. There's table tennis, pinball machines, there's somewhere you can get Cokes . . .'

His voice trailed off, as if he'd given up trying to get across to an unresponsive audience the sundry delights waiting for him.

It sounds innocent, Fay thought. Doesn't it?

She looked down at him. He was biting his lip in anxiety.

'Yes, of course you can go,' she said, reaching into her bag for her purse. 'I'll give you some money, you can buy these twins a drink since they're being kind enough to take you to their club and . . .'

She was interrupted by Oliver's arms round her neck in his stranglehold grip. 'Ma, you're great!' he said. 'When do you want us back?'

'Is Rupert wearing his watch?'

'No.'

'Are you?' She looked at his wrist. He shook his head. 'Then you'll have to ask someone. Come back at seven, then you can have your showers before we go out and find our supper.'

'Seven.' He was frowning. 'What's the time now?'

'Five.'

'Two hours! Thanks, Ma!' He kissed her, wetly and affectionately, and sped off, calling to Rupert as he ran. She watched him, thinking with amusement that it was always Oliver who got despatched to ask the favours when it was really important.

Am I that partisan? she wondered. Do they really think there's more chance of me saying yes if my younger son asks?

She hoped it wasn't true. But she was afraid it might be.

She first met the twins the next day. Rupert and Oliver had returned the previous evening full of them, what they did, what they thought, every other sentence prefaced with, 'The twins say . . .' She wondered if they were identical, if her sons were forced to refer to them generically because of an inability to tell which was which. She'd enthused, when she could get a word in, and said something to the effect that she'd like to meet them.

Rupert and Oliver brought them over to her just as she was emerging from her first swim of the morning.

'Mum, these are the twins,' Rupert said. He turned to the young men. 'This is our mother.'

She wished it had been any moment but this one. Standing before the twins, who had only just arrived and who were still wearing their jeans and t-shirts, she wished her bikini were not quite so small.

'Er—how do you do?' she said stupidly. Did they speak English? 'I'm pleased to meet you.'

The twins, in unison, tall strong bodies and golden-fair heads moving as one, spoke together. 'The pleasure,' they chorused, 'is ours.'

And, one after the other, they took her hand and kissed it.

She'd had enough. Couldn't bear to stand there in her confusion any longer.

'I won't keep you from the water,' she said hastily. 'You must be dying for a swim, it's so hot today! I'll be over there,' she said to Rupert, 'in my usual place.'

He smiled, face full of fun. 'I know you will. I helped you move your bench, remember?'

Flustered, embarrassed, she turned her back on them all and hurried away.

She christened them Castor and Pollux. Her sons went on calling them the twins, so in the absence of an update, she stuck to Castor and Pollux.

They were glorious. Lying on her stomach on her wooden bench, she would please herself just watching them. Wearing her dark glasses, head turned as if she were looking in another direction, she studied the twins for hours.

They moved with the grace of animals. Arab horses, she decided, or perhaps big cats. Their bodies were perfection, wide at the shoulder, pectorals and biceps clearly defined but not too big—nothing approaching the exaggeration and vulgarity of iron-pumpers. They wore tiny swimming trunks, one pair purple, one pair scarlet. She didn't let herself look for long at their swimming trunks. And their legs, long, muscular, strong—she could, she thought, write a sonnet to their legs.

They were fair, their hair the ripe-corn colour of the ancient gods. And their eyes were bright Ionian blue.

When she could turn her mind away from their physical appearance—difficult, considering the impact

34

it was having on her—she spared a few thoughts for them as people. Very quickly they had taken to coming to the lido each morning, to join Rupert, Oliver and all the other boys and young men in a free-for-all of the ages, swimming, diving, disappearing to the basketball court or the club up above to play football or whatever other sports boys and young men played on a hot summer day.

But the twins always found time, at some point during the long hours, to come across to Fay. To sit, perching on the end of her bench or joining her at her table, and spend a few moments in courteous conversation.

Once it had suddenly occurred to her that she was being buttered-up, but instantly she dismissed the thought as unworthy and unkind.

They knew she was staying in The Twins' House— the boys had no doubt told them. They asked politely if she were happy there, and she said, oh, yes, it's lovely.

There had been a pause. As if Castor and Pollux were waiting for her to add something else.

'You must come to visit us there,' she found herself saying. 'Come any evening—have a drink with us, before dinner.'

They said, thank you. We will.

And, starting that very evening, that was what they did.

The twins in The Twins' House. It seemed too much of a coincidence, and she wondered if the house belonged to them. No, surely not—this was a rich man's house, and the twins, for all their good looks, did not dress with much style, didn't wear expensive watches. It was the Bull man's house, she'd decided that.

And to find a pair of twins was just coincidence after all.

THREE

Breaking the Pattern

Time, Fay decided, obeyed a different set of rules when you were on holiday. A fortnight of idling the days at the lido stretched until it felt like a month. Six months. As if she'd been doing it for ever. She knew the rest had done her good: she was eating well, and her skin and her hair shone with health in a way she hadn't known in a long time. And at night she slept in peace, untroubled by the repetitive dreams whose ability to disturb was not lessened by the fact that she'd seen it all before.

But a fortnight of idling was quite enough.

'Let's *do* something today,' she said to the boys over breakfast.

'We are,' Rupert said, his face already hardening into the expression he wore when he was called on to do battle with her.

'What?'

'We're meeting the twins. At the lido. We're in a match today—there's a whole lot of us, some other English boys and their sisters are coming as well. The twins have each picked a side and Ol and me are playing.'

She didn't even bother to ask what they were playing; there didn't seem any point. She said, 'Okay.'

The abrupt cessation of hostilities, before a skirmish had even broken out, seemed to take the wind out of Rupert's sails. He said, 'What did you want us to do, Mum?'

She noticed his use of the past tense. She smiled, despite herself. 'I don't know,' she admitted. 'I suppose I just thought it'd be an idea if we did something else. Hired a car for the day, or something.' Anything, except spend another fourteen days at the lido, she added silently.

The boys looked at each other. She saw that her vague suggestions hadn't exactly set them on fire.

Oliver said, 'Why don't you go, Ma? We'd be okay, we'd be with the twins and the others.'

The thought hadn't occurred to her. Old habits died hard, and she'd spent so many years being solely responsible for them. They were, after all, precious. But they're older, now, she thought. Getting sensible. I think. Hope. And they know the routine here, know their way about.

And I'm sure the twins would look after them.

'Well—' she began.

'Yes! Go for it!' Rupert shouted.

'I haven't said anything yet! You don't know what I'm going for!'

'Whatever. I think you should. Don't we, Ol?'

Oliver, mouth full of bread and jam, nodded vigorously.

And she couldn't really think of any reason why not.

'I'll come and find you,' she said decisively. 'At the lido. Some time late this morning. In time for lunch, so you needn't worry that my break-out will inconvenience you.' She glanced at Oliver, who had the grace to blush.

They were up and running before she could change her mind. She sat at the table, listening to the fading echoes of the front door banging behind them.

It was so nice getting dressed in something pretty instead of the usual bikini and t-shirt that for a while she didn't think about what she was going to do. She put on some make-up, and brushed her hair, and went down the front steps feeling like minor royalty.

She had her guide book in her hand, turned to the page with the map. The Old Town, she thought. I'll wander off down one of these intriguing little lanes, and I'll just walk. That'll be enough—it's so nice not to be dashing to the shops, or hurrying to the restaurant because Oliver's starving, or being dragged to look in some window at the latest thing one or other of them wants to buy.

Rupert had bought a ferocious knife the previous evening. She was still wondering how they were going to get it home without coming under suspicion as potential terrorists.

Wandering off down the narrow, shadowy lane was like setting out into another world. Like going through the wardrobe into Narnia, she thought, and being aware that it had been there all the time, had one only known. The Corfu of today was left behind, along with its traffic and hurrying people; here, it was quiet, peaceful and cool, and there was little to indicate which century she was in.

The Old Town had a character. No, a personality, she amended. It's quite happy with itself—it has turned its back on the fast pace of the modern world. Has judged it, decided it wants none of it. And continues as it's always been.

She walked on unhurriedly between the tall, shuttered, shabby-faced houses. They still displayed the remnants of their flamboyant past, proudly, like an old and worthy regiment holding out tattered battle-honours. She stopped to admire, here a brightly-decorated doorway, there a blue-painted oil-drum full of brilliant geraniums in front of a wall covered with spreading bougainvillea. Paused to stroke a young ginger cat, lazing in a sunny patch. Found, in the total absence of people, a rare peace.

I'm walking in a place out of time, she thought. A refuge, perhaps, for people like me who have come to grief in the mad rush and the crazy values of the world outside. And it's always here. Waiting quietly to offer its solace to the wounded.

She emerged suddenly from a silent lane into a busy square. Jumping out of the way of a youth on a Vespa, she was disorientated. And, when she looked about her in an attempt to see which road she'd just come from, was unable to tell.

Perhaps it really was like Narnia. And you only got in when someone else summoned you.

She crossed the square and set off down a paved street, its traffic mainly consisting of pedestrians and its flags foot-shiny with their passage through the ages. And it wasn't that busy, after all; it had only seemed so, in contrast to the suspended animation of the Old Town.

On her left, down another lane, she came upon the church of St Spiridon, and she knew then exactly where she was. They'd passed it before, lots of times, she and the boys, but the time had never been right for going in.

It was right now; she thought it was quite likely she wouldn't get another chance.

The heavy doors were ajar, and the incense-fragrant gloom seemed to settle itself around her, like a kindly relative putting a shawl over her shoulders. I feel welcome, she thought. As if they—whoever they are— have been expecting me.

She stood still, looking all around. The church, she decided, felt more Roman than Greek Orthodox, with a high rood screen reaching to the roof and, somehow, giving the effect of a Roman temple. Perhaps that's why it suggests the church of Rome, she thought, confused. Rome is in my mind because it looks like a pagan temple, and somehow I've jumped the points.

She shook her head, unable to work it out. She felt for an instant as if she were on the brink of understanding. Then it was gone.

She walked towards the back of the church, pausing to light a candle and add it to the many others whose soft light shone gently into the darkness. Then she went up into the area which housed the saint. I can't see you today, she said silently to him, it's not one of your days for being displayed and you're hidden away deep inside this rather wonderful coffin. She put out her hand, stroking the ornately-decorated silver. But I know you're in there, and I'd like you to know that I've come to pay my respects.

A party of elderly women came to join her, and she stood back to let them approach the coffin. It really was enormous, and she wondered if the men who carried their beloved saint around the town on feast days were obliged to carry the catafalque as well. She hoped not.

The women were gathered around the coffin. After some muttered prayers, they resumed their conversation in their normal everyday voices, and Fay thought how nice it was that they popped in to pass the time of day with their saint and then picked up just where they'd left off. That's a good sort of faith to have, she thought. One for every day, not just high days and holidays. And this is a happy church to drop into, for a rest, a prayer, or just a few moments' quiet contemplation in the middle of a busy day.

When she went back out into the lane, she felt as restored as any Corfiot grandmother.

On the way back to The Twins' House, her eye was caught by the bright posters in the window of a tourist office. Trips were advertised in glowing terms: see the Citadel by moonlight, visit the beach at Sidári, learn to windsurf at one of the island's best schools! I don't want to windsurf, she thought. Nor do I want to go to the beach at Sidári. Although I suppose I should, really.

In the corner was another poster. Retaining the feeling that she should do *something*, she gave it her full attention.

'CORFIOT CULTURAL EXPERIENCE!' it proclaimed. 'Enjoy the delights of dinner at a typical restaurant, followed by the famous *son-et-lumiere* at the Citadel.' Moonlight thrown in? she wondered. 'Relax in the company of a small select group, all your needs met by our professional guides.'

The advertisement said the next Corfiot Cultural Experience was tonight.

She thought, piercingly and disloyally, how very nice it would be to go out to dinner without the boys. To sit in the company of adults, enjoy conversations about sensible, serious things. To relax, and not have to watch that Oliver didn't stuff himself silly or to tell Rupert not to pick his nose.

And she thought, why not? Why don't I go?

She had the door of the office open, about to go in, commit herself. Then she stepped back. She thought, and it felt as if she were chickening out, I really should talk it over with the boys first.

Then she thought, I can't. It's not possible. Because I can't leave them on their own. And it was only then, when she knew she couldn't go, that she appreciated how very much she'd wanted to.

She trailed back to The Twins' House to change, then went on to the lido to find the boys. They were sitting with Castor and Pollux at a table in the shade, all four of them drinking lemonade.

'We won!' Oliver greeted her. He nodded triumphantly towards Rupert. 'Stuffed that lot out of sight!'

Rupert didn't look pleased at the reminder, and she wished her younger son would learn diplomacy. The twin next to Rupert said something quietly to him, and his anger subsided. Fay thought, now why can't I do that?

The other twin said, 'Did you have a pleasant morning, Mrs Leary?'

'Lovely.' She'd tried to make them call her Fay, but they stuck to the formal title. It made her feel old. As if she were being excluded, a grown-up left on the outside of the charmed circle of youth. 'I went walking in the Old Town,' she said brightly, trying to stop the self-pity before it went any further, 'then had a look in St Spiridon's church. It's very interesting, isn't it? And the coffin is magnificent.'

She thought they might have reacted with pleasure to her compliments about their precious saint. But the beautiful faces were impassive.

The boys were claiming back the twins' attention. Minimal notice having been taken of their mother and her doings, they wanted to return to more interesting topics. So I sit here like a dummy and listen, she thought. I hurry to get here so they can be fed, I curtail thoughts of what *I* want to do for their sake, I . . .

She remembered the Corfiot Cultural Evening. How much she'd wanted to go.

'I saw an evening outing advertised, in one of the tourist places,' she announced loudly. Four pairs of eyes turned to look at her. Surprise, surprise, she thought. The woman has interrupted. 'Dinner at a typical restaurant, then on to the *son-et-lumiere* at the Citadel.' She looked at the twins. 'Do you think it'd be any good?'

The twins turned to each other. They spoke quietly,

42

in their own language. One of them nodded. The other said, 'Yes. It will be a pleasant evening.'

In for a penny, she thought. 'I'd rather like to go. But, of course, there's the question of the boys.'

Oliver began to say something, but the twins held up their hands and he stopped. As if responding to the silent order, let us take care of this. More quiet talk. Then the same twin spoke to her again. 'We were going to ask your permission to bring the boys here this evening. There are matches, for table tennis—a—what is it?' He turned to his brother.

'A tournament.'

'Ah! Yes. A tournament. Many players, playing against each other until one person has beaten every other person.'

It was a charming definition of 'tournament'.

But that was beside the point. 'What time will it finish?'

The twin shrugged. 'Ten o'clock? Eleven?'

'But—'

'If you will entrust to us your door key,' the twin continued, 'we shall take the boys back to the house when all is finished. There we shall await until your return.'

He seemed so earnest. As if it was really important to him—to both of them—that she go. Again, and more strongly, she felt she was being buttered-up. Manipulated.

'I don't know,' she began. 'I—'

A pair of bright blue eyes locked on to hers. Held them. She couldn't look away. He seemed to grow before her, standing up straight and tall, the amazing body clad in a long white robe and a purple mantle, and in the depths of his eyes she saw a force against which she was nothing.

Then the illusion was gone. He was once more a handsome young man sitting at a café table, offering his help, making it possible for her to do something she very much wanted to do.

'Thank you,' she said graciously. 'If you're quite sure it's no trouble, then I accept.'

She sat in front of her dressing-table wondering what to wear. She'd just spent half an hour in the shower, washing the last of the salt out of her hair and spending ages rubbing in conditioner. She felt good.

The ticket was in front of her. It hadn't been cheap, but then dinner was included. She'd raced back to buy it as soon as the decision had been made, desperate in case she should get to the tourist office to find a 'SOLD OUT' sticker plastered across the poster.

She hadn't. It was all right.

The twins had called to collect the boys earlier. She'd shown them the ticket, asked them for directions to the restaurant.

One twin took the ticket in his hand. It seemed to take him a long time to read it. Then he spoke at length to his brother. Quietly.

He looked up at Fay. 'I shall draw you a picture,' he said.

'A what? Oh, a map. Diagram. Thank you.'

The blonde heads bent together over the ticket, on the back of which one twin drew streets, squares. And a big black cross to indicate where she had to go.

'Now, you understand?' He came to stand beside her. She could feel the warmth of his body. Could pick up, animal-like, the scent of him. 'Here is The Twins' House,' he pointed, a long, fine forefinger with a perfect nail, 'and here is the Listón.' She nodded. The Listón, she knew, was the street with the arcades. Where all the night life congregated. 'Now you must go in the other direction,'—so much for the Listón—'past the Old Town, to the Old Port. Restaurant where you must go is here.'

44

It looked simple. And the girl in the tourist office had said she'd easily spot the rest of the party, lots of them were Swiss. Fay wasn't sure why that made it easy— would they all be in leather shorts and dirndls? No doubt she'd find out.

She looked now at the twin's map. Picked up the ticket. Put her fingers where his had been.

Stop it.

She got up and went across to the wardrobe to choose a dress.

Carefully, with many stops to read almost illegible street names, she made her way to the restaurant. This is it, she told herself. This is definitely it. And I'm *not* about to make a fool of myself by going in, a lone woman, and finding there's no sign of the party I'm meant to be joining.

It had been so long since she'd been out to dinner. On her own or not. Even longer since some presentable man had come to her door to collect her, treated her as if she were precious, valuable, as if it were an honour to him to have her on his arm.

So long since Barry.

Don't think of Barry. Not *now*, for God's sake.

She strode into the restaurant.

There were a great many tables, and most of them were occupied. By couples, quartets. It can't be any of these tables, she thought anxiously, they're too small. It'll be a big group. All those Swiss people.

She walked on between the tables. Beyond, in an outdoor section covered with a vine-clad trellis, were bigger tables. Two of them, long, rows of chairs down either side. She sighed in relief. This must be it.

She approached the first table. Two elderly men sat at one end, and she heard them speak in Greek. They didn't look at all like Swiss tourists. As she stood there, a gaggle of people—women, more old men, several

45

children—came in behind her, pushing past her and taking their places at the old men's table. It had all the hallmarks of a large family gathering.

The other table, then.

She went and stood behind a chair halfway down one side. Opposite to her was a woman, attractive in a brittle sort of way, with a lot of make-up and a big jangly gold bracelet. Her smooth dark hair was elegantly twisted on top of her head. Her dark eyes, holding mischief, looked up into Fay's.

'I—er, I'm joining a party,' Fay said. 'Meeting some Swiss people.'

The woman said, 'We are Swiss.' She glanced to the tawny-haired man on her right. 'N'est-ce pas?' He grinned.

'Wine! I shall order the wine!' A man at the end of the table was standing up, calling a waiter. Wondering aloud how many bottles they'd want. A dignified woman sat at his side—his wife?—and her calm eyes held a hint of sorrow. Next to her, a younger man whistled to Fay to gain her attention, and when she looked at him, he blew her a kiss.

Confused, she didn't know whether or not to sit down.

Someone dug her in the ribs with a sharp elbow. A crabby voice said, 'Who are you?' An elderly woman, face set in a permanent frown of discontent.

'I'm Fay. Fay Leary.' Was there the faintest hope that they'd know the name? Would have been told by the tourist place to look out for her?

The crabby woman was shaking her head. Pushing at Fay's legs with her stick. 'That's *my* seat. I go there,' she snapped.

Fay moved hurriedly out of the way, pulling out the chair so the old woman could settle into it. 'I'm sorry. I'll sit somewhere else.'

'Sit?' The dark-haired woman again, her tone

teasing. 'You are going to join us? Give us the pleasure of your company?'

'Yes.' Oh, God. 'If you're the Swiss people, then I'm meant to be here. I've paid.' How feeble it sounded. Where was the bloody guide? The professional who was going to meet all her needs?

'You have a problem?'

I know that voice! She spun round, face to face with the Bull man.

'Oh! I don't know—I'm meant to be meeting a group for the Corfiot Cultural Evening, and I'm not sure if this is it or not. I can't find anyone to ask, they're all—' She broke off. The Bull man might well be of this party, so it would be tactless to say, they're all being singularly unhelpful.

'No cultural evening.' He sounded as if the idea was quite disgusting. 'This is a party. Private party.' He put his face up close to hers, and she could see into the small red eyes. It was not a nice sight.

'Yes, I can see that. I'm sorry, I—' She felt an inch high. Mortified. Wished she could be swept up by a typhoon and deposited somewhere else.

'You may stay,' the dark woman said, as if conferring a great honour. 'If you want.'

I don't want, Fay thought desperately. I just want to go. The evening's a disaster, I should never have come. Wasted all that money, and the budgeting's tight as it is.

To her horror, she felt tears prick in her eyes.

'No, thank you,' she said, forcing a smile, 'I really should...'

But the dark woman wasn't listening. None of them were. They had turned, as one, to the head of the table, where a newcomer was taking up his place.

Fay turned too. Stared at him.

He was dark haired, brown eyed. His face, smiling in welcome, creased into warmth. He was of medium

47

height, clean-shaven, broad in the shoulder. And, for all that his cream sweater and cord jeans were informal, he radiated a sense of wealth.

And, overwhelmingly, of power.

Suddenly everyone spoke at once, clamouring for his attention, telling him what they wanted him to hear like a crew of disruptive children when their father returns.

He tolerated it for a few moments. Then, over all the heads, he looked directly at Fay.

It was as if she'd come home.

The relief was indescribable, and she knew he must see it. She didn't care—in that first instant she recognised him. Felt she had met him before, that already she knew him to be good. Dependable.

Knew him to be someone who was crucially important to her, and whose absence she'd suffered for far too long.

He was moving round the table now. Coming towards her.

'Aaron, I must tell you!' the dark woman was saying.

'Wine, Aaron? Should I order more than six bottles?' The man at the end with the sad-looking companion.

'She's not one of us!' The crabby woman. 'She took my place!'

On and on they went. And he ignored them all. Came up to her, put his hand on hers.

He said, 'I am Aaron. It appears that you have come to the wrong place.'

And the smile in his eyes, just for her, made her realise it didn't matter at all.

FOUR

Aaron

'I'm so sorry I gatecrashed your party,' she said as he steered her out of the restaurant. For a moment she'd been afraid he'd suggest they stay, sit down and calmly eat dinner with the others. But he seemed to divine her unease; taking her arm, he bore her away.

She heard them protesting. 'Aaron! Where are you going?' 'Come back!' 'Aaron, you promised to spend the evening talking just to me!' She was quite sure that was the dark-haired woman. His wife? She looked as if she might be. If so, Fay could sympathise with the plaintive tone.

Even while the major part of her mind was singing in triumph.

'You did not gatecrash,' he said as they walked off along the road. 'You made a mistake, I think. An understandable mistake. And my people, instead of behaving as they should to a stranger, were impolite to you.' He glanced at her. 'I apologise for them. Sometimes they do not act like . . .' He broke off. 'Sometimes they forget who they are,' he finished enigmatically.

'It's all right.' The memory of her extreme discomfort was fading to nothing. She felt inexplicably happy. 'I'm Fay,' she said. 'Fay Leary.'

And, smiling, he said, 'I know.'

With no idea how to answer that, she fell silent.

After a few minutes' walking, he stopped beside a Range Rover with Greek number plates, unlocked the passenger door and handed her inside. Getting behind the wheel, he started the engine and they moved smoothly away from the kerb.

She wondered, without caring very much, where he was taking her.

'What about those people?' she asked suddenly. Not a whole foot, but perhaps one toe was back on the ground. 'The Swiss people.' No. They weren't the Swiss people, she'd gone to the wrong restaurant. Despite the twins' careful directions, she hadn't managed to find the Corfiot Cultural Experience. 'Your wife, and everyone?'

'She is not my wife.' He paused, as if deciding whether to go on. 'I have no wife. And we are not Swiss.'

'I ought to go home!' she burst out. Leaving her children with near-strangers to go out for a cultural experience was one thing, but it wasn't justifiable simply in order to to go joy-riding round the island with a man who'd just picked her up. If that was what he'd done. 'My boys—I left my sons with Castor and Pollux.' *Damn*. She could have bitten out her tongue. *Stupid*, to have blurted out her private names for them! 'I mean, with the twins. They met them at the lido, and they're taking them to a table tennis tournament tonight, but it'll be over soon, and they—I mean, they said they'd take them home, but I . . .'

She trailed to a stop, confusing even herself with all the 'theys', so heaven only knew what he was making of it all.

But he said calmly, 'Everything is all right. Your boys will be perfectly safe with the twins.' How could he be so sure? Did he know them? It wouldn't be unreasonable, in a small place. 'Castor and Pollux will not let any harm come to them.'

He'd used the names now! She didn't know what to make of it. Had he picked them up from her, thought them appropriate? Or was that really what the twins were called?

Surely not!

He said, after a moment, 'You have not had any dinner. Nor have I. Would you like to rectify that?'

Absurdly, she felt a sense of anti-climax. As if, having been rescued, swept away, driven off, something more exciting should follow than merely going out to dinner. 'I don't know, I—'

He laughed. A quiet, warm sound, which seemed to say an awful lot. 'I shall take you somewhere very special,' he said. 'It will not be a disappointment.'

They were nearly out of the town. She saw a sign for the airport, and the runway lights were fleetingly visible out to the left. Then they were past, accelerating, speeding away into the darkness.

She sat back and waited to see what would happen next.

They turned away from the sea, climbing inland, passing through small villages where people sat at cafés under lights strung in the trees. Then they left the main road, and, putting the car into first gear, he set it at a steep, potholed track which wound away between fir trees. She could smell resin, as the tyres crunched over pine needles. They came to a pair of gates, green-painted, closed and padlocked. He sounded the horn, and from nowhere a boy appeared, leaping at the gates to unlock and open them. Aaron acknowledged him with a lift of one hand.

She turned round, to see the boy locking the gates behind them.

Anxious now, the questions were loud in her head.

But she didn't speak. Then, emerging from the trees, he swung the car in a circle and parked it, facing back the way they'd just come, in front of a house.

He came round to help her out. 'Go round the house on to the terrace,' he said. 'Up those steps.' He pointed. 'You must excuse me for a little while—I shall go and order our dinner.'

Was it a club? A damned exclusive one, she thought, if they kept the gates locked. And, although a man had come out to welcome them—was even now going up with Aaron to the open front door, where two other men waited to greet him—there didn't seem to be too many other members.

She went where she'd been directed, towards the steps at the side of the house. What a place, she thought. Italian influence again, long thin shutters, small balconies at each of the ground-floor windows, and built in warm, glowing terracotta-coloured stone. Tiled roof, too. You could be in Verona. Or Venice.

The steps emerged on to a path, which proceeded in a series of bends around the house, at each bend a statue on a plinth. Scents rose, from flowers, from the trees. The air was still and heavy.

Around the last bend now, and, laid out in front of her like some enormous chess board, a black-and-white flagged terrace, bordered on two sides by the lighted windows of the house, on the third side by a balustraded retaining wall, and on the fourth by what appeared to be a broad flight of steps leading downwards.

She glanced towards the house. A row of nine statues stood in the spaces between the windows, and she thought she'd go over for a closer look—the Muses, would they be? It seemed likely. Then she changed her mind—supposing someone looked out through the French windows and saw her nosing about?

Instead she went across to the balustrade, stepping

up so that she could lean on its smooth top. She was momentarily surprised to see how high they were, having forgotten the long climb in first gear—the ground fell away, steeply, and the thick woods below concealed what lay down there at the distant end of the escarpment.

She walked slowly on, trailing the fingers of her right hand along the warm stonework, looking out for a break in the trees which might afford a view. And, gradually, the pines and the undergrowth thinned, disappeared.

And below her, spread out in perfect panorama, lay the pointed-foot-shaped peninsula of Corfu Town.

At first she merely stood and drank it in.

It was breathtaking. And fascinating—when the initial impact had worn off, she began identifying places. The Citadel, that great dark double-mound out to the right. The airport, just down there. A jet taking off. The heart of the town, where the lights were brightest. Inland, the hills. And, to the east, the protective sea.

She heard a faint sound. Turning, she saw Aaron moving cat-quiet towards her across the marble flags. He held out his hand and she jumped down beside him.

'You have discovered the view,' he said.

'Yes.' Almost she wished she hadn't. That she'd given him the pleasure of revealing it to her.

'It is even better, from down there at the lower level.' He indicated the flight of steps on the fourth side of the terrace. 'We shall have a look, after dinner. For now, a drink, I think.'

He had released her hand, and now she walked, by his side but separate from him, to a round stone table which stood on a circular balcony projecting from the terrace. They sat down on the bench—someone had put cushions on the cool marble—and Aaron beckoned towards the house. A waiter, apparently prepared for this moment, came out, carrying a tray of bottles and glasses.

She chose gin and tonic, he had a beer. The waiter, nodding to Aaron's instructions, went back into the house. In the silence, she couldn't think of a thing to say.

'You like islands?'

The abrupt question was unexpected. Had she heard right? Or did he mean, did she like this particular island? No. His English was too good to make such an elementary mistake, and he might be insulted if her response implied otherwise.

'I hadn't thought about it,' she said honestly. 'But yes, I suppose I do. I like Greek islands.'

Memory came, treacherously. Barry, in torn and shrunken shorts, his hand on her bare sun-hot stomach as they lay by the sea on Kea.

He didn't speak immediately. She had the absurd notion that he was waiting till the memory faded back to wherever it had come from.

'This is not a Greek island,' he said. 'It has, nominally, been the island of many peoples. Phaeacians, Illyrians, Romans, Byzantines, Vandals, Normans, Sicilians, Angevins, Venetians, Ottomans, French, British.' He reeled them off, too fast for her to take them all in. 'And it has belonged to none of them.'

In a flash she recalled her fanciful thoughts in the Old Town. That it had a personality, was unaffected by what went on in the world around it. Was he saying something similar about the whole island?

'So many races,' she said. 'So many influences. And yet—' She couldn't express the thought—it was incomplete. Wouldn't come into focus.

She realised he was looking at her, dark eyes intent. She felt somehow she was failing him. That he was

54

expecting some wise comment from her which she was unable to produce.

'I'm sorry.' She looked down into her lap.

His hand briefly covered hers. 'You have no need to be sorry.'

The French windows were opening again, the same waiter coming out with another, bigger, tray, a second waiter, similarly burdened, behind him. With a feeling that she'd been let off the hook, Fay looked up eagerly to see what they were going to eat.

When they had finished, rounding off the meal of lamb, vegetables, bread and salad with a huge bowl of fruit, Aaron took her down to the lower terrace. The view, she knew, was the object, but as they went down the steps, the view wasn't what struck her.

Directly ahead, appearing as they descended the steps, was an enormous statue. Plumed helmet, its cheek panels concealing much of the hard, noble face. Armour, curve of the breastplate emphasising the strong pectorals. Kilted skirt, made of squares of bronze. Shield on one arm, sword in the other. Long legs, clad in greaves, sandals on the feet.

When all of him was visible, she stopped. And said, almost without being aware she did so, 'Ares.'

Beside her, she was aware of his nod of satisfaction.

He took her back. Drove her down the potholed track and through the gates—she wondered if the poor boy could at last turn in for the night now—through the villages, still full of life, and so to Corfu Town.

'I'm staying in The Twins' House,' she said as they drove past the Listón. He nodded.

'They seem so at home in the house!' she exclaimed suddenly. 'The twins, I mean. They come to collect the boys, you see, and often we sit round all together having a drink, or something to eat.' She wondered

55

why she was blurting out all this, when for the rest of the journey she'd been content to sit quiet. 'And there's the name,' she went on. 'The Twins' House. I thought it must be their house, it seemed too much of a coincidence, but then I realised it belonged to the B... to the red-faced man who let it to me.' She remembered. The Bull man had been there in the restaurant, earlier. He knew Aaron, and Aaron knew him. 'Well, that was what I decided,' she finished lamely.

He didn't answer at first, and she wondered if he'd switched off and hadn't heard her. But, as he pulled up in front of the house, he said quietly, 'No, it does not belong to the twins. Nor to the other man.' He turned to look at her, dark eyes in shadow and unreadable.

'It is my house.'

Why am I in his house? What is all this about? she asked herself frantically. I feel I'm in the middle of a play, and someone else wrote the script. I'm moving to their direction, without control over what's happening.

She was in bed, at last, and the whirlwind of her thoughts could be allowed to break out. She had come in to find the twins in the kitchen, sitting either side of the table in total silence. She'd wondered distractedly why—did they commune by telepathy? Anything seemed believable, tonight. They stood up at her entrance, told her solemnly that they had all spent a happy evening and hoped that she had, too. The boys were asleep in bed, they said. Would she care to look?

'No, no!' she said, knowing full well she'd tiptoe in as soon as the twins had gone. But to do so *now* seemed to imply a lack of faith in them. As if she suspected the children might have come to some harm. Might no longer be there. Whisked away, by a great golden ram or a god disguised as a thundercloud.

WHAT?

She went with the twins to the door, over-effusive in her thanks and her goodnights, trying to make up for the treachery—the hysteria—of her thoughts. And the boys, when at last she could go and look, were fine. Of course they were.

There had been nothing else to do but go to bed.

But she was awake, wide awake, sleep a total impossibility.

Aaron's house. The Twins' House belongs to him, and I'm staying in it, brought here by the Bull man, who knows Aaron. Well enough, it appears, to be included in the party who were to have enjoyed a special dinner with him tonight. Till I blundered in and broke it up! Did they proceed without him? Cursing me, no doubt? I bet the dark-haired woman cursed me, within an inch of my life.

What am I to make of all this?

Her mind couldn't grapple with the problem. She didn't know why—it wasn't that she was sleepy, but the effect was the same. As if, slipping into unconsciousness, her thoughts were leaving her control.

She could see Barry. Standing in front of her at the Christmas Hop, asking her to dance. The first time ever that he spoke to her.

Saw herself. Dressed in a suede mini-skirt and a flowery blouse with a big frilled collar. Suede boots, up to the knee. Biba pink. The height of late Sixties fashion, or so she'd thought.

Standing up, moving towards him. Going with him into the ballroom, strobe lights flashing, some local band thumping out their own version of 'This Old Heart of Mine' quite well enough for drunken undergraduates to bounce about to. Dancing four fast ones on the trot before the pace slowed and Barry took her in his arms. Gasped, as for the first time her breasts hidden under the froth of frills were pressed up against his chest.

'Can I see you home?' he said, somewhat breathlessly, at slinging-out time.

She remembered how she'd laughed. 'Home' was what the university administration referred to as a 'study-bedroom'. Hers was homely—though he couldn't know that yet—but many were not. Especially those of the young men, whose rooms tended to smell of dirty socks and stale milk. One boy had a petrol pump in the corner of his room, but he was reputed to be eccentric. Daft, Fay thought, was more like it.

It was a wonderful moment, walking back to her room with Barry. Barry Leary, an Irishman abroad, more charm and good looks than any other fresher—than any other student, she considered—and the finest stand-off the university had fielded in years. She'd fancied him from the first moment she'd set eyes on him. Waited, with decreasing optimism, for him to set eyes on her.

Now he had. Had asked her to dance, had kept hold of her hand for the rest of the evening.

Was walking into her room with her. Putting his arms round her, beginning to kiss her . . .

'Coffee.' She broke away. 'I'll put the kettle on.'

He flung himself down on her bed, on top of the thick knitted patchwork blanket her grandmother had given her. Much softer, much warmer, than a University bedspread.

She was sure he didn't want coffee. But, under the strange rules which operated in that isolated campus, you always had coffee *first*.

When at last he kissed her, pulling her down on the narrow bed beside him, she knew she was lost. And when, a very short time later, he had her blouse open and her bra undone, he gazed down at her breasts and she thought that his eyes filled with tears.

'Fay, oh, Fay,' he whispered, delicate fingertips playing over her curves, touching, light as a snowflake, 'I don't believe you.' He bent to kiss the cream flesh, and when he raised his head and she could see his face, wore an expression such as Perceval might have had when the Holy Grail floated within reach. 'I've found me a woman,' he said, 'a real woman, after all this time.' He bent to kiss her again, taking longer about it this time, his tongue flicking over her nipple and sending waves of shuddering desire through her. 'They're no use to me, these stick-like girls,'—his mouth once more free, he was whispering again—'what use has a red-blooded man for something that looks like a thin boy? Oh, Fay!' And he was down, sucking, drawing on her as if he could never get enough.

She'd expected him to go on. Expected his hands to explore, down, down, removing her clothes piece by piece until she was naked and ready for the taking. She was ready, more than ready, would have gone along with him. Encouraged him.

But he was content with her breasts. Seemed to want nothing more than to touch, kiss, suck, suckle. And, eventually, to fall asleep, head buried in her flesh as if she were a living, breathing pillow.

Fay, alone in a wide and empty bed in Corfu, turned into her own pillow and wept.

FIVE

The Bringer of War

She awoke, just after five, from a piercing nightmare in which she'd slept with a rock star only to have him tell her she'd better have a blood test if she ever wanted to be a blood donor.

She was horrified. Felt guilty. And why the dream, anyway, when she'd never slept with a rock star, never had the least desire to be a groupie of any sort, even in the heady university days? And her modest amount of promiscuity—a boy at home, two or three lovers before Barry—had been in the safe days, when all you risked was pox if you were unlucky, pregnancy if you were really unlucky; AIDS, then, was still a disease of African primates.

How had it jumped the quantum leap to human beings? she wondered, trying to occupy her mind with an intellectual problem and take it away from the dream. Perhaps it was Carruthers. As in the old joke. 'Carruthers has run off with a gorilla.' 'Male or female?' 'Female, of course! Nothing funny about Carruthers.'

Now look what Carruthers had done.

But the memory of the dream persisted. The nasty thing had been that, even in the dream, she'd been frantically telling herself, this isn't really happening. It's only a dream.

She hadn't believed it then, and was finding it difficult to believe it now.

I shan't sleep again, she thought. And I don't want to lie here wondering what on earth has been stirred-up in my unconscious mind to produce such a nightmare.

She reached for her book. She read, until the boys woke up and the day could begin.

Rupert asked her if she'd had a good time. She was at a loss to know how to answer—should she lie, and say the Corfiot Cultural Experience had been terrific? Should she confess she'd done something else?

No. For if she did that, he'd ask, what? And she was *certainly* at a loss on that one. I went off with a man I've never met before, but who seemed as familiar to me as you do. He drove me away to this wonderful place up in the hills, where a smiling waiter served us nectar in golden cups. He owns this house we're staying in, isn't it funny? And I can't get rid of the thought that he meant us to be here. Sent his Bull man out to find us, bring us here.

Sent his twins, even, to look after you for the evening.

And to direct me to him.

She couldn't possibly say all that to Rupert. It was quite worrying enough for her. She didn't like to think what a twelve-year-old would make of it.

He was spreading butter on his bread, humming to himself. Apparently unconcerned at her failure to respond. So she said, casually, 'Thanks for asking, Rupe. Yes, I had a very nice evening.' And, varying the attack-as-the-best-form-of-defence strategy, went on quickly, 'What about you two?'

Oliver, pulling on his t-shirt, hair a sun-bleached haystack, came into the kitchen. 'I played doubles with Castor,' he said proudly. 'We got through to the semis.' Castor must be good, she thought disloyally. 'Rupe had to pull out 'cos his twin had a groin strain. What's a groin strain, Ma?'

'Pulled muscle. Here,' she pointed to the inside of her thigh. 'Footballers get it a lot.' She was aware of explaining badly; her mind was reeling with the surprising fact that her own boys, too, referred to the twins by the whimsical names she'd given them.

'Castor,' Oliver said, sitting down at the table and reaching out across Rupert for the juice carton. 'Like castor sugar.'

'Mm.'

Oliver was whispering to his brother, and there was quite a lot of giggling. She thought she heard one of them say 'Pollux.' Or, more probably, 'Bollocks.' She had to agree, it was an unfortunate name. She turned to the sink to hide her smile. One could only hope that Pollux was blissfully unaware of English slang. Hope, too, that the boys would have the sense not to put it in their 'My Holidays' essays at school. 'We went to Corfu and I met a man called Bollocks.'

Rupert came to put his dirty plate in the sink. She was quite surprised, and paused in her washing-up to give him a hug. 'Thanks, son.'

He returned her hug. 'Mum, we said we'd go to the lido again today. But if you really want us to go out in a car with you, we can do that instead.'

She looked down at him, into the heavy-lashed blue eyes so like Barry's. At the table, Oliver was protesting, quietly but vehemently. '*I* don't want to go out in a car. I'll have to sit in the back.'

'Shut up, Ol.' Rupert's body went tense in her arms, as if he were gathering the energy to thump his brother. She held him more tightly, just in case, and felt him relax again. 'It's Mum's holiday too.'

'You're lovely,' she said softly. 'I appreciate the

62

offer. But the lido's fine—I quite fancy a day doing nothing.'

His relief was palpable. Grinning, he disentangled himself. 'I'll go and get my mask and flippers, then.'

Watching him go, she thought, I'm not sure I should break away any more. It looks as if it might be dangerous.

Late in the afternoon, when she was coming to from a doze and thinking how much she fancied a cup of tea, she heard a car pull up outside the gates of the lido. Idly she turned to look: not many cars ventured down the track, which was more suitable for the whining motor-bikes of the local youths.

It was a Range Rover. His.

He'll have come to see the twins, she thought. And, simultaneously, I don't want him to see me. In my little bikini.

Not stopping to reason out what she was doing, she got to her feet. Back turned to the gate, she sauntered off towards the water as if she hadn't noticed him. As if, with nothing better to do, she'd decided to go for a swim.

Nobody called out after her. She walked on. Climbed down the steps, launched herself into the warm water. In blinkers, staring straight ahead. Not letting herself look to find out if the twins had seen him, were going to greet him. What her boys were making of him.

She swam out under the pontoon. Turned to the right, into the deep water beneath the towering walls of the Venetian bastions, where the carving of the Winged Lion reigned in proud splendour.

And wondered, when she'd swum as far as she usually did and was ready to return, what the hell do I do now?

She swam slowly back. Got out of the water, had a shower. Finally, walked back to her bench.

Where Aaron, sitting waiting for her, handed her a towel.

'Oh, hello!'

He smiled, and she knew he hadn't been fooled for a moment. 'Hello.' He watched her as she towelled herself. His eyes on her both thrilled and upset her. She wrapped the towel round her, sari-fashion. He said, 'I was pleased when you turned right. I thought you might be heading for Albania.'

The anxious, worried mood evaporated as she laughed with him.

He had bought drinks—bottles of beer and lemonade—and two glasses. He mixed them both shandies. 'I have met your sons,' he said. 'The twins introduced us.'

'Where are they?'

'Up above.' He jerked his head in the direcion of the unmistakable sounds of youthful merriment. 'They are polite children.'

'Yes.' She was relieved he should think so. But not surprised: the boys didn't often let her down when it came to good manners towards strangers. And there's something awesome about Aaron, she thought—they'd have been *intimidated* into remembering to behave, if nothing else.

She wondered why he had come. To see the twins, of course. And he's stayed to say hello, that's all.

It was as if she were telling herself that deliberately. To make sure her hopes didn't build up, only to be crushed.

But he said, eyes gazing out over the water and not looking at her, 'There is a concert, this evening. On the Esplanade.' She held her breath. 'Given by a visiting Italian symphony orchestra, on their way to Athens from Brindisi. They are staying here tonight, and will play for us on the bandstand.' He frowned. 'Or possibly in front of the bandstand. I think they

64

would impede one another, a symphony orchestra on the bandstand. Do you not agree?'

Now he was looking at her, his face full of warmth, inviting her to share his amused pleasure at the prospect ahead. She felt as if she were being soothed. Groomed, like a horse, and revelling in the luxurious touch. His eyes, dark, impenetrable, held a mystery; she was powerless, quite unable to turn away.

'Yes,' she said. Yes, yes, yes. 'What—what will they play?'

He shrugged. 'Light classics. Probably something loud, to compete with the traffic. And the noise of the children.' He turned away again. As if, their work having been done, his remarkable eyes could once more enjoy the view out to sea. 'Will you come?'

'I'd love to.'

*

Barry left her a note the morning after the Christmas Hop. She'd dashed across to the Students' Union for a coffee between her 9 and 10.30am lectures, almost certain he'd be waiting for her, excited, heart racing at the prospect of seeing him again.

He wasn't there.

She waited for as long as she dared. Longer—her next lecture was with a professor who had a habit of closing the doors dead on ten-thirty and then leaning on them, physically barring late-comers and turning them away with a barrage of rude remarks about their abysmal failure as time-keepers. Leaping down the stairs, she took a late and risky diversion to the mail pigeon-holes, rummaged rapidly through the 'M's. Found a folded page torn from a note pad. Addressed, in an unknown hand, to Fay Morrison.

She knew. Could wait, now, until she was in the lecture theatre, flopped down, panting, in the back row, the lecturer beginning on his opening remarks from just behind her where he leant against the doors. As soon as he had gone, making his stately progression down to his rightful place on the platform, she unfolded her note.

'What about the cinema tonight? The Graduate's on in town. Meet me in the Union, 6.30pm, and we'll go for a drink first.
                                Love, Barry.'

She thought, love Barry. Perhaps I already do.

They went into town on the bus, holding hands. The film didn't start till 7.45pm, and she wondered why they'd met so early—could it really be that he'd been eager to be with her again? The thought gave her a glow inside. They went into the spit-and-sawdust bar of a pub—nothing special, he said, but the beer was cheap—and he got her a half of shandy. He had a pint of Guinness, two bottles in a straight glass. When he'd finished that, he went back for two more bottles. Being only halfway down her glass, she said she didn't want another.

At the cinema, she offered to pay for herself, and he accepted her offer.

They sat in the back row, and he put his arm round her. When he kissed her—gently, on the cheek—he smelt of Guinness. Simon and Garfunkel sang, the lyrics and the melodies sinking deep in her heart, linking themselves irredeemably with Barry so that, hearing them afterwards, she would feel his warm lips on her face. Smell the peaty, bitter Guinness smell.

When the film was over, they went back to the pub. For more Guinness, and a glass of whiskey. She wondered what he would do for money for the rest of the week. He was thin, she'd noticed—when he'd lain in her arms last night, she could feel his ribs. When the landlord finally threw them out, the last bus had gone and it was raining.

'We'd better hitch,' she said, turning up her coat collar.

'My lady fair shall not battle with this downpour, this howling gale!' he declared dramatically. She'd have called it a light drizzle. And a friendly westerly wind. 'I shall transport her home in luxury.' And he called a taxi.

Outside her hall, he put his arms round her, hugging her close.

'Come up for a coffee?' she asked, already moving towards the door.

But, 'No,' he said.

Her eyes shot to his face. Desperate in her disappointment, she said, 'Why not? What's wrong?'

He pulled her head down against his chest, so that she could no longer look at him. 'This is special,' he said quietly. 'You and me, Fay. I want—I want us to appreciate it. *Properly*.' I do, I do! she protested silently. 'It's only a week till we go down for Christmas,' he went on.

'So?' She couldn't help herself. Going down! Three weeks away from him! Wasn't that all the more reason to be together now?

'If I make love to you tonight,' he whispered, ' I don't think I'd be able to bear being apart from you.'

Sweet words. So winning, so captivating. She said she understood. Said, goodnight, and thank you for the evening. Could do nothing else.

Upstairs, alone, she was torn almost equally between joy that she mattered so much to him and anguish that he'd gone, left her to her cold bed when she was churning with desire.

And, insidiously, creeping into her mind came the memory of the drinks. All those drinks. And how he'd *leaned* on her, coming out of the pub. Tripped, almost fallen, on the step.

Before she could banish it, the thought flashed out, perhaps he was drunk. Too drunk to make love. And all that about not being able to bear being apart was bullshit.

'No!' she cried aloud. Don't think that, don't spoil this wonderful thing we've got with thoughts like that!

Right from the start, the taint had been there.

*

The boys went down to the Esplanade with her. They were meeting some lido friends; the English children and their parents. Someone was bringing a football and they were having a free-for-all. She remembered Aaron's remark that the orchestra would have to play up, to be heard above the children.

He was waiting for her just where he'd said he'd be, in the end café under the arcades of the Listón. He stood up to greet her, and asked what she would have.

'What are you drinking?'

'Beer.'

'I'll have the same.' It was easy, to say that. Easier than asking to see the tariff, keeping him waiting while she wondered what she felt like.

He smiled briefly. 'Do you like beer?'

'Yes! Of course!'

His smile deepened. He said, 'I'm sorry.' And, catching the waiter's eye, ordered her drink.

'This is very cosmopolitan,' she said, indicating the arcade. 'I love the hanging lanterns.'

He watched her, his head on one side. 'It was built by the French,' he said. 'Possibly the architect was homesick for the Rue de Rivoli.'

'The Twins' House—your house—feels the same,'

68

she said. 'French influence, I mean. It's the staircase, I think. And—oh, I don't know. I'm pretty ignorant about architecture.'

He seemed to be digesting her words. 'You may be ignorant of many facts,' he said eventually, 'but your instincts are sound. My house was designed by a French architect. The staircase was his masterpiece— he had to argue quite hard to persuade his client to permit him to include it. But, like you, his instincts also were sound.'

He must love his house, she reflected, to have gone to the trouble to find out all about its history. 'When was it built?' she asked.

'At the beginning of the nineteenth century. When Venice had fallen to Napoleon, and the French took over from the Venetians as rulers of Corfu.'

The French. Had he included them, in his list last night of the successive interlopers on Corfu? She couldn't remember. 'Why was it called The Twins' House?' That, she thought, was more important.

But he was calling the waiter, settling the bill. He didn't answer, and she assumed he hadn't heard.

They walked across the road, on to the Esplanade. The wide paths that wound between the grassed areas and the flower beds were thick with people. Families, mostly, parents and grandparents doting love on to little children, shouting orders at the older ones who played further afield. Everyone dressed in their best.

'Is it always like this?' she asked. 'I mean,—'

'Yes,' he replied, before she'd had a chance to elaborate. 'On Sundays, saints' days and special days, yes. And in the summer, that means most days.' He took her arm as a gaggle of children, screaming in excitement, sped by on small bicycles. 'The people of Corfu are very sociable. They like to see their friends, be seen in their good clothing. They like, above all, to gossip.' He smiled indulgently, as if he were speaking about his own wayward family. 'But then, who does not?'

They had reached the bandstand. Rows of chairs fanned out in front of it, many of which were already occupied. He led the way to a pair of seats in the sixth row, more or less in the middle.

'We shall sit here,' he said, waiting until she had settled before seating himself. Lowering his voice, his mouth close to her ear, he added, 'We shall enjoy the spectacle of the orchestra arranging themselves.'

Looking towards the bandstand, she saw immediately what he meant. It had always sounded like a tall order, to fit a symphony orchestra on to something built for the town band, and the Italians clearly hadn't been willing to settle for the obvious option of fielding only a token number of players. It looked as if they'd all insisted on turning out, and now they were jostling for position like thoroughbreds lining up for the National. They were using the bandstand as a sort of rear tier, for percussion—rather a lot of it, Fay noticed—and for just the back rows of the various sections. Even so, the players were having to fight for space; she watched some violas arranging their chairs on the slant, and thought they were probably being grateful none of then was left-handed.

In the foreground, on a makeshift wooden dais, sat the bulk of the orchestra. And they didn't look very confident.

Aaron had bought a programme. Passing it to her, silently he indicated the first item.

Gustav Holst. Selections from *The Planets Suite*.

Wondering whatever sort of a fist they would make of that, she joined in the enthusiastic applause that was greeting the arrival of the conductor and sat back to enjoy it.

As the conductor stepped on to his podium, an

70

ominous growl of thunder muttered from the hills behind the town. He glanced over his shoulder, in the direction of the sound, then looked up into the clear starry sky. Immediately, as if he were thinking, if it's going to rain I'd better get on with it, he lifted his baton and the orchestra edged into the imperative five-beat rhythm of the first bars of 'Mars, the Bringer of War.'

She was hit—hard—with the thought, but they're brilliant!

The ludicrous position of the orchestra was forgotten, the sight of them pushing, shoving and complaining quite obliterated in her mind. For her skin was crawling, her heart was racing and her mouth was dry—this wasn't some third-rate Italian symphony orchestra playing 'Mars', this *was* Mars, the god himself, and he was gathering himself, plunging the world into war. Chaos. Death, disease, misery and mourning.

And he was revelling in it.

Thunder came again, nearer now. And a great bolt of lightning split the sky. Fay felt the hairs on the back of her neck stand on end.

The orchestra played louder, thundering now in competition with the elements. Drawn out, elevated by something they didn't understand. She studied their faces. Tense. Even afraid.

And playing as if the god were driving them on.

The music had her in its grasp. She seemed to feel it in every cell of her mind and her body, each new note, each crashing chord directed like an arrow straight at her. Directly overhead the thunder banged again, right on cue as the music reached its first overwhelming climax and a sound like the end of the world reverberated over the terrified crowd.

I can't bear it! she wanted to shout. I've got to go, get away!

But her limbs wouldn't obey her.

The tension was building again. Creeping onwards, upwards, to some ghastly catastrophe. Then it came again, that awful, death-knell rhythm, and the thunder boomed out of the sky to greet it as it blasted upwards. She tried to cover her ears, and Aaron's hand shot out, imprisoning her wrists and holding them on her lap.

She stared at him in horror. He was in profile, stern, unreachable. And from him, blazing out like an earth-bound response to the unleashed cacophony in the heavens, emanated a sense of power so strong that, her flesh cold and shuddering into goose-bumps, she cowered away.

The end was close. End of everything, end of them all. Disjointed chords burst in the air, crackles of thunder sounded out over the water. As the world around her came to its final apocalypse and the dread sounds faded to nothing, she closed her eyes and waited to die.

Silence.

Release, as Aaron let go of her wrists.

She opened her eyes. Risked a look at him.

Incredibly, he was smiling.

Shaking, she turned to see what everyone else had made of it. Whether they'd been as scared as she was.

They had been. One brief scan of their faces confirmed that.

She looked up to the conductor, who was slowly turning to face the different sections of the orchestra. Taking a handkerchief out of his pocket and mopping his face. Looking at his players ruefully and, as if they were fellow-conspirators, breathing, 'Phew!'

He made some remark to the orchestra leader in his own language. Quite a lot of people, overhearing, laughed uneasily, and quite a lot crossed themselves. And Aaron laughed too, only he didn't sound uneasy at all.

Fay whispered, 'What did he say?'

Aaron turned to her. His dark eyes catching the orange street-lamps took on a reddish tinge, and the thought flew into her head, red planet.

He laughed again. And translated for her.

'The conductor suggests that Ares came a little too near, that time.'

Ares. The Greek name for Mars.

Again, she had the feeling that something was trying to break through in her mind. That, so nearly now, she almost understood.

Then, the sounds caressing her like a calm and soothing hand, the orchestra began to play 'Venus, the Bringer of Peace'.

SIX

Earthly Paradise

The Sunday after she and Barry went to the cinema, he borrowed a friend's van and they went to North Wales.

She'd set the day aside to struggle through 'Piers Plowman', but Barry was very persuasive. As a sort of sap to her conscience, she put the book in her bag—there might well be a moment to read some during the day. Barry threw it out of the car window. She made him turn back—she couldn't abide waste, and anyway knew she wouldn't be able to afford to replace it—but when she ran back to the car and settled into her seat, he snatched the book from her hand and put it in his pocket.

'Today is for fun,' he said. 'All of it.' And would not listen to her protests.

A whole day of fun. She couldn't imagine wilfully ignoring the nudgings of her conscience to get this done, see to that, finish off all that came under 'work' before she embarked on 'play'. Yet Barry had phoned her so early, arrived at such an unlikely hour on her doorstep, that she'd gone out without making even the least attempt to tidy up.

And, listening to him singing some lively Irish folk song in a surprisingly musical tenor voice, trying to join in because it was so lovely, she didn't care a bit.

The van produced an ominous volume of black smoke and made a noise like a death rattle every time they asked it to climb a hill. And there were lots of those, in North Wales. When progress upwards came almost to a standstill, Barry would put it into first and rev the engine till it screamed.

'Be careful!' She couldn't stand the car's pain any longer.

'Fay, I know what I'm doing,' he said, smiling. 'Don't worry, we'll make it.'

'But the car! It's making such a noise, and . . .'

'I shall get you to the seaside, just as I said I would.' He started humming again, breaking off to add, 'No more hills after Lake Bala, we follow the river valley from then on.'

She felt sorry for the friend. She wondered guiltily if he'd given Barry permission to borrow the car—she wouldn't have put it past Barry to have tiptoed into his room and taken the keys without asking.

'We must make sure we fill it up with petrol, before we get home,' she shouted over the engine's last gasp.

'What?' He turned to her, frowning slightly.

'Petrol!' she repeated. 'The least we can do, to thank your friend.'

He shook his head. 'No need. He owes me a favour.'

And there didn't seem to be any more she could say.

The sun came out as they left the shores of Bala behind and headed south-west for Dolgellau and the sea. The car ran sweetly enough now, and Barry reached out and took her hand. To the left the great guardian mountains rose formidable and stern, harshness unalleviated by the purple-red vegetation clinging to the rocks. There was snow on the peaks. It was good, then, to be safe in the car, warm in the sunshine and with Barry's strong fingers twined in hers.

He taught her all the words to a sad song about a soldier leaving his pregnant love. Then, because it made her feel emotional—and foolish for feeling so— he stopped at a village shop and bought her a bar of chocolate.

'Nearly there,' he said soon after that.

'Nearly where?'

'The seaside!' The way he said it—seaside, not just sea, or coast—made her think of a small child with a bucket and spade. And something in his excited eyes made the impression all the truer.

And suddenly they were there. He drove the van right down on to the sand, and it was hard, and black, and he raced for half a mile and wheeled round in a ferocious, sand-flying handbrake turn.

Black Rock Sands. Nobody there, and an endless canvas on which to inscribe with sticks. Hearts. A huge rose. Artistic Barry, able to draw in sand with a chunk of driftwood. Her own name, FAY, in ten-foot letters twined with fishes, mermaids and dolphins. And, trotting down to where he was writing in quick, tiny letters, a glimpse of 'Barry loves Fay' before an incoming wave swept it away.

'Shall we eat?' he asked when the sun went in and a cold wind off the sea made her shiver.

She nodded. 'Mm. Now, please.'

Back in the van to Barmouth, to park beside a ladies' lavatory where she went to have a wee and tried to remove tangles and sand from her wild hair. Emerging, she found Barry staring down into the sordid harbour.

'Look,' he said, holding out his hand. She wondered, since he hadn't turned round, how he knew it was her.

'What?' She went to stand beside him, and he wrapped her in his arms, pressing his cold cheek against hers.

'Someone's had enough of sewing fine seams.' He pointed to where an ancient Singer sewing machine lay tiredly on its side, half buried in silt and dirt.

For the second time that day, she felt an irrational sympathy for an inanimate object that couldn't possibly be hurt by its harsh treatment at the hands of human beings. She wondered at herself, that, sensible and not over-imaginative, she should be so affected.

'Never mind,' Barry said. For a moment he stared down into her eyes, and, staring back, she noticed that his deep-blue irises were flecked with navy. Then he put his hand to her jaw and, turning her face up to his, kissed her lips.

The kiss accelerated all by itself. His warm mouth tasted slightly salty, his tongue sliding against hers invaded her and she opened in welcome. Standing behind the Ladies, they were out of sight of the few people about, but she wouldn't have cared if they'd been in Oxford Street on the first day of the sales. He undid the buttons of their coats, hastily, and pulled her body against his. Through two sweaters she felt her breasts crush against his chest, through two pairs of jeans she felt him rise for her, push rhythmically against her as if already they were making love.

He broke away. Bereft, she opened her eyes to see why he had stopped.

He was looking down at her. Right into her soul.

'Fay, oh, Fay,' he whispered.

Then, as if he could no longer bear her eyes on him, buried his face into her neck.

She stood, fingers gently stroking into the long soft hair on the nape of his neck, until eventually he stood up straight and said it was time for lunch.

When they counted their money, they only had enough between them—after putting some aside at

Fay's insistence for petrol—for two bags of chips. They salted and vinegared them, warming their hands on the hot newspaper, and went to sit on the sea wall to eat them.

'Fay, me darling, I know the best places for lunch. Finest foods,'—he held a chip up in the air and sucked at one end, as if it were the fattest Dublin Bay prawn—'loveliest views.'

She agreed. Despite the fact that it was nearly four—far too late for lunch by the most liberal timetable—that the chips were soggy and unappetising, that the foreshore revealed by the retreating tide was black, slimy and foul-smelling, at that moment she wouldn't have swapped *here* with Barry for the best restaurant in the world with anyone else.

They set off for home, slowly, dreamily, stopping frequently to look back as if both were reluctant to leave. The short day was over, and December's eager darkness fell. The lights on the van were dim—she had an idea the nearside one didn't work at all on dipped beam—and with the night came a cold that would not yield to the halfhearted efforts of the heater.

There were no more protests now from the engine when they came to the hills. Perhaps, she thought distantly, he's tamed it. Let it know who's boss. Entranced it, put a spell on it, like he has on me, so that we do his bidding and have forgotten self.

Or on the other hand, perhaps it was just because he wasn't hurrying, on the homeward journey.

'We'll stop for a jar in a while,' he said, breaking a silence that had lasted for half an hour. 'We'll stop at every ale house,' he sang, almost to himself, 'and drink when we are dry, be true to one another . . .' He broke off.

The thought of a warm cosy pub was nice. But, thinking of going up to the bar, buying drinks, suddenly she said, 'We can't. We've no money.'

He laughed softly. 'Have we not?'

'That's petrol money! We can't drink that!'

He was looking ahead, at a pub sign swinging in the wind. She thought she heard him mutter, 'Just watch me.'

He had stopped the van, was out and running for the pub. She was thinking, well, we can give his friend the money instead, I'll cash a cheque tomorrow, make sure he gets it, when she saw that Barry was turning away from the public bar. Throwing himself at the saloon bar. Rattling the door, before turning away, an expression of disgust and extreme disappointment on his face.

'What's wrong?'

'Sunday. Sunday, that's what's wrong. This is Wales, and this is a fucking dry county.'

For a moment she failed to understand, either his words or his anger. Then she remembered. In North Wales, they didn't drink on Sundays, and, by keeping their pubs shut, they made sure no-one passing through did either.

'It doesn't matter, does it?' She reached out, trying to take his hand as he threw himself back into the van and slammed the door, so hard that tinkling bits of rusty metal fell off on to the floor. 'Does it?'

She couldn't bear for her lovely day to disintegrate with his fury.

He turned to her, eyes black. He opened his mouth, about to speak.

But stopped. And, instead, put his arms round her. Kissed the top of her head.

'Fay,' he murmured. 'Fay.'

He started the engine and drove them home.

They found other pubs, English pubs on the wet side of the border, pubs with friendly welcoming lights and lots of cars parked outside. Pubs probably full of jovial people playing darts and cribbage and buying each other pints of beer and pickled eggs.

They passed them all.

Barry drove straight to the University, parked the van in the Health Centre car park just beyond her Hall of Residence. Came up with her, lay back silent on her bed while she made a pot of tea.

And the tea, poured into two red mugs, went cold as he took her in his arms, removed her clothes and his own, and made love to her.

*

Setting the table for breakfast while the boys were out getting bread, Fay ranged wildly through her mind to find some sort of policy for the day—the days—ahead. Lying awake half the night had left her out of sorts, head aching and eyes itching. And she wished for a calm voice—an *adult* voice—to tell her what to do.

After the concert, Aaron had suggested dinner. But she said, no, I must take the boys home.

'Bring the boys out to dinner.' He fixed his eyes on to hers, and instinctively—protectively?—she looked away.

'How kind,' she said, voice sounding nervous in her ears, 'but, really, they'll be worn out by now, they're up so early and on the go all day, and I think . . .'

He put up his hand, silencing her. 'I understand,' he said calmly. 'In that case, I will wish you good night.'

And he was gone. Just like that. Leaving her alone on the hectic Esplanade, solitary where everyone else seemed to *belong*, to laughing, happy, hand-holding, loving groups.

The boys, rushing up and throwing themselves on her, had saved her. Made her part of a group, too.

Thank God for my boys. She'd hugged them, very tight, one arm round each all the way home. Said to herself, bugger Aaron.

But the long restless night had indicated that it wasn't as simple as that.

'When is anything ever simple?' she muttered, banging cups and saucers down on the table. 'Why the hell can't we say what we think? Put things down in black and white? Why, *why*, does it all have to be so mysterious?'

I've forgotten, she thought sadly. I've forgotten what it's like to meet someone, find them attractive, enjoy their company and look forward to the next time you'll be together. I can't remember if it's normal to live on a sort of higher plane of existence when you're with them, so that quite ordinary things like thunder over an orchestral concert take on worrying shades of the supernatural.

It all seemed so silly, in the daylight—without Aaron by her side—that she was ashamed of her terror.

I *was* afraid, though, she admitted honestly to herself. When I think of him now, I'm still afraid.

Suddenly she abandoned her table-laying, throwing the cutlery in a clattering heap on to the draining board. Striding upstairs, she ran into her bedroom, slammed the door behind her and flung herself face-down on her bed.

I'm afraid. And it has nothing to do with Aaron, and whatever mysteries I'm weaving so romantically around him. I'm afraid because I'm interested in him—even in the privacy of her own thoughts she balked at a more emotive term—and I thought I was finished with being interested in anyone.

She pressed her face into her pillow, hands clenched into fists thumping again and again on the bed. Oh, I don't want this! Don't want the turmoil and the pain of liking someone! Especially not *him*, a man I've met in this heady holiday atmosphere where all my sense and all my values seem to have been left at home! I was okay! Doing all right, before. Not happy, but then not unhappy, either.

And now, because I'm—because I like him, my peace is threatened. Because whatever does or doesn't happen, I shall be going home at the end of my month here and probably shall never see him again.

Great, Fay. Really brilliant.

She rolled over, staring up at the stars on the navy-blue ceiling. Anger was giving way to distress, and she couldn't cope with that.

Decision time, she thought. Make a plan. Even a lousy one'll be better than this aimlessness. We'll go out today, me and the boys, get on a bus, go and have a look at one of the resorts. Take our swimming things, and some money so they can buy a souvenir.

Right! She jumped off the bed. If they don't like it, that's too bad. The twins and the lido will just have to manage without them for once.

The boys were in the kitchen, Rupert cutting bread with a huge knife which she'd have leaped to wrest from him if she hadn't known it was as blunt as a bit of two-by-four.

'Hi, Ma!' Oliver looked up from his careful setting-out of knives and spoons. 'I'm finishing the table for you.'

'So you are. Thank you.' She went to give him a kiss. He smelt of vanilla; the baker's wife must, as usual, have been persuaded by his blue eyes and his hungry-dog, 'please feed' expression into giving him a cake.

'Sorry we were so long,' Rupert said. Were you? she thought. I didn't notice. She put her arm round him, careful not to jog his cutting hand. 'We met the twins.'

'Right! And they . . .'

'Oliver, *I'M* telling her!'

'But you . . .'

Internecine strife loomed. '*BOYS!*' she yelled. Then, more quietly, 'Rupert, carry on.'

'The twins are outside with Aaron's car. It's great, it's a Fiat jeep, and . . .'

'With the top down!' Oliver, hopping with excitement, couldn't contain himself. She gave him a look.

'They say he says we can use it. Go driving round the island. They said could you drive, and we said yes, you were quite good, and they said if we liked they'd come with us today and show us some really nice beaches. Quiet, you know. Where people don't go, well, only Corfu people and you wouldn't mind those, would you, Mum?'

Running out of breath, he stood staring at her. She could feel the great intensity of his wish that she should agree. To have such power! she thought wonderingly. To stand here, and in my hands the making or breaking of this beloved child's day.

'Rupert, it sounds marvellous,' she said enthusiastically, biting down her reservations about spending all day with Castor and Pollux. Damn it, they may well prove a delight. What am I worrying about? 'Thank you—both of you—for coming up with such a good plan.'

The boys were either side of her, hugging her in gratitude. And it occurred to her to wonder why Aaron should be so generous. The thought took the shine off the happiness—she felt wary, then cross with herself for her ingratitude. He's Greek, they're like that. Hospitable in the extreme. 'Be not forgetful to entertain strangers, for thereby some have entertained angels unawares.' Why, that might have been written for the Greeks. Engraved on their hearts, at birth.

The boys, peace reigning now that they had a common adventure to anticipate, were getting down to breakfast. Not hungry, she poured herself a cup of tea and leant against the sink.

Suddenly she thought, *is* he Greek? He didn't say so. Only that he wasn't Swiss. 'We are not Swiss.' And, come to think of it, Aaron's an odd name for a Greek. It's Biblical, isn't it? But Old Testament, whereas the involvement of the Greeks began with the New.

'Oliver, who was Aaron?' she asked. 'The original one, I mean. Was he in the Bible?' Oliver had been doing the Life of Moses—his class had even performed an assembly piece on it, and Oliver had learned a bit of Exodus by heart.

'He was the first High Priest of the Israelites,' Oliver said, swallowing a huge mouthful of bread and jam. 'He was Moses's brother,' he added helpfully, 'Nicholas Davies was him.'

'Now we've met an Aaron,' Rupert said.

'Is he an Israelite, Ma?' Oliver broke off his *sotto voce* recitation from Exodus.

'I've no idea,' she said absently. Was he?

'He wears a medal thing round his neck, on a gold chain,' Rupert said. 'I saw it when he came to the lido. His shirt was open.'

'What did it look like?' She was surprised she hadn't noticed. Perhaps Aaron had buttoned himself up when she arrived out of the water.

Rupert frowned. 'Can't remember, really. It had a sort of design.'

She fetched the pad of paper she used for shopping lists. 'Pencil?' Oliver gave her one. 'These are some of the things people wear round their necks.' She drew a crucifix, then an outline of the Virgin and Child. Then a Star of David, enclosed in a circle.

Rupert, intent, shook his head. 'It wasn't like any of them.'

'Those,' she corrected automatically. Poor kids, she

84

thought, having a grammatical perfectionist for a mother. She'd once made herself laugh driving with Rupert—he'd said on the motorway, 'Cor! There's one of them poxy bangers in the fast lane!' and she'd left the 'poxy' and pulled him up on the 'them'.

'What, then?'

He took the pencil from her hand. Drew a careful circle, and inside it two curving lines above an animal head. 'Oh—I can't get it right. But it looked something like that.'

'Zodiac sign?' she said. 'Could be. Not that it matters.' She scrunched up the paper, throwing it in the bin.

Rupert was drawing shapes with his knife on the table cloth. She realised he was still absorbed in what they'd been talking about. 'Mum, how can they all be right?' he asked. '*And* all the rest?'

'Who, darling?' She went to sit beside him.

'Oh—Jews, people who believe in Christ, Hindus, Buddhists. Mormons.' He grinned suddenly, and she did too; near them at home was a church of Jesus Christ and the Latter-Day Saints, who, ever since the boys had been old enough to understand the pun, had been referred to as the Saturday Saints.

'The old Saturday Saints,' she said.

'Yes. I mean, all the...'

'Sects?' she supplied.

'Yes. They all have followers, don't they? Believers? And they all think they're right. But if every sect thinks they're right, that's not possible. I mean,' she watched as his face furrowed in his efforts to understand the problem which had, since mankind began, baffled far more mature minds than his, 'it's just not possible. So which one's right?'

She put her hand to his forehead, smoothing out the frown. 'I don't know, Rupert. I don't think anyone does, for certain. People tend to grow up in the religion of their parents,'—she saw he hadn't got that, and hastily paraphrased—'believing what they're taught as chidren. And I suppose that's enough for most—they accept. They don't think about the other alternatives.'

He nodded sagely. 'What do we believe, Mum?'

She'd hoped he wasn't going to ask that. Her own honest answer would have to be, I don't know *what* I believe. But she didn't think now was a time for strict honesty.

'We're C. of E.,' she said, getting up. 'Like most of Britain. Now I must do the washing-up.'

SEVEN

Awakening

Castor and Pollux were sitting side by side in the back of the jeep, eyes forward, not speaking. She wondered if they'd been there since the boys rushed home with the bread. Surely not—that had been a good forty-five minutes ago. And what would they have done, she thought, if I'd said, 'no thanks, I don't want to borrow Aaron's jeep'? Would they be cross at having wasted the best part of an hour for nothing?

Somehow, watching the impassive profiles, she couldn't imagine them being cross.

'Here we are!' she said brightly. 'This is a great idea—I hope you'll convey our thanks to Aaron. And I'm grateful to you both, too, for your kind offer to come with us.'

One twin inclined his head. 'Gratitude is not—appropriate,' he said. 'We are pleased to be with you.' He gave her a dazzling smile whose impact at close quarters was almost too much to take. 'We know of a beach. Very quiet. Maybe just us, né?'

'How lovely!' She tried to make it sound sincere, while thinking that she'd really prefer to have a few other people around. Nice normal ordinary-looking people. Families, with fat chuckling grandmothers and lots of mischievous children. But she couldn't possibly say so.

The other twin was moving over, making room for Oliver to sit between him and his brother on the back seat. Rupert, apparently, had drawn the short straw and was to be allowed in the front with her.

'Won't one of you drive?' She looked from one to the other. It was slightly nerve-racking, to think of getting in, driving off through the meandering, undisciplined town traffic, with these two demi-gods observing every crashed gear change and every near-miss on Aaron's paintwork.

But, 'We do not drive,' a twin said.

Good grief! she thought, settling in the driver's seat. Surely they're not too young? No! Those bodies belong to men, not boys. They must be in their early twenties, at least, unless they've filled out spectacularly early.

The image leapt before her eyes of the pair of them in their swimming trunks. She was glad they were in the back and couldn't see her blush.

Why else would two handsome and sociable young men not drive? She wrestled the jeep into first, trying to rid her thoughts of erotica. It must cramp their style, not to be able to take their girlfriends out somewhere quiet in the car for . . .

She picked up her mind and put it firmly to the myriad problems of an unfamiliar controls lay-out and a gear-lever on the wrong side. Wanton thoughts, she told herself firmly, shall not be allowed all their own way. And I've got the rest of the day to dwell on the twins' swimming trunks.

As she was edging, at a twin's direction, into the right-hand lane at the traffic lights, she suddenly thought, if they don't drive, who delivered the jeep to my door?

Cars behind began a barrage of beeps the instant the

lights changed. At quite the wrong moment for her, as she'd just realised it must have been Aaron.

They went north-west out of Corfu town, at first following signs to Palaeocastritsa but then, turning off on to smaller roads, to towns and villages apparently too insignificant to have their names written up in Roman letters. And Fay wasn't quick enough at deciphering Greek ones to read the words as they flashed by.

The road became a track, and a twin leaned forward to direct her.

'A little road, on the left.' His warm breath in her ear set her shivering slightly. 'You must watch for an old olive tree...ah! Here, please.'

'Here?' Even in a jeep, she was doubtful. 'You're sure?'

'Yes. *Endáxi, endáxi*—it is okay. Aaron comes here. Brings this jeep. You will do no harm.' She flashed him a quick glance. He was bestowing on her a benign look, as if he read her concern for Aaron's car and was awarding her a house point for it.

She turned her full attention to getting the jeep down the steep narrow slope without grounding it on any of the big boulders that stuck up out of the sand, apparently intent on ripping out the sump of any vehicle foolhardy enough to try to pass.

But not mine, she thought triumphantly as, after five anxious minutes, she emerged on to the flat beach at the bottom. Not Aaron's, rather.

Then she looked out at the scene before them. And let out a cry of pleasure.

'You like our beach?' a twin said. She could hear that he was smiling.

'Oh, yes! Who wouldn't?'

It was glorious. A small bay, a perfect semi-circle, clean sand like soft brown sugar in a narrow band from the low cliffs at the back of the beach to the shallows at the water's edge. And the sea was the colour of aquamarines, deepening to sapphires as the sea bed fell away.

There wasn't a soul in sight.

'Hurry up, Ma, we want to get out!' Oliver said from behind her, knees pressing into the back of her seat.

'Yes, of course.' She stepped out on to the sand, taking off her sandals and throwing them back into the jeep. Then she walked slowly down to the sea. She stopped a yard or so clear of the water, and stood waiting, toes curling up in expectation, for the first little ripple to wash over her feet.

I'm in heaven, she thought as the cool water lapped round her. Thank you, Aaron.

Whoops and shrieks echoed from the beach behind her, and in a sudden great rush, the twins and the boys raced past her and into the sea, leaping quickly at first through the shallows then, as the deeper water began to impede their progress, flopping down and starting to swim. She watched them, smiling, glad and proud at the same time that her boys could swim, that they'd become strong swimmers, and that she didn't have to watch them every second to make sure they were okay.

She wandered back to the jeep, picking up her bag and a beach mat, then looked around for the very best place to lie down. I'll be able to get on with my book, she realised, and the thought gave her a surge of pleasure.

She sat down on her mat to take off her skirt and t-shirt, making sure they were within reach in case she should want to put them on again. In case I start to feel the sun, she told herself. Then she lay down on her back, head propped up against her bag, and got out her book. She read a page. But the content hadn't gone in, so she read it again. Her mind was distracted by the sounds of merriment from the sea. The boys, shrill treble voices shouting, high-pitched laughter so infectious that she found herself joining in. The twins' deep voices. And their laughter, which wasn't boyish at all but which carried an equally compelling sense of delight.

What happiness they bring, she thought drowsily, abandoning her book and shading her eyes with her hand so that she could study the pair of them. How blessed they are, to give pleasure just by *being*. She watched as one twin—in the red trunks, so that was Castor, wasn't it?—swam back into the shallows and slowly, gracefully, stood up. He was looking out to where the other three were still cavorting, a smile on his beautiful mouth and every line of his body carrying the unconscious perfection of classical statuary.

As if he felt her eyes on him, he turned. Looked at her for a long moment, his face falling into gravity. Before, very slowly, nodding.

Instinctively she threw her arm across her face, hiding herself from him. Holding the sight of him from her eyes. Her body felt on fire, as if his intent look had swept along the length of her flesh like a burning torch. She lay, counting her pounding heartbeats, until the heat died and she knew he'd gone.

She stared down at herself from under her sheltering forearm, trying to see what he had seen. This bloody bikini, she thought, I *knew* it was too small when I bought it. I can't think what possessed me. It doesn't cover nearly enough of me. Impatiently she sat up, pulling her t-shirt from her bag and dragging it on over her head. There! That'll show them! They needn't go on staring at me, measuring me against the sort of model girls they go out with and finding me lacking! She giggled suddenly—'lacking' didn't seem appropriate, under the circumstances, when she was worried because there was too much of her.

91

They'd be perfect, the twins' girlfriends. They'd have to be. It's just unimaginable, to contemplate that glorious masculinity paired with a femininity that's not equally unflawed. Which, of course, cuts out 99 per cent of the human race. Poor old twins!

She'd had enough. Turning on her stomach, she made another, more determined effort to get back into her book.

'You have not been into the water yet.' The quiet voice at her ear made her jump: she'd read four chapters and then gone into a pleasant sort of waking doze.

'Oh! No, I haven't.' It was the purple-trunked twin. Pollux.

'Will you come with us, now?' The voice came from behind her, and, twisting round, she saw that Castor was there too.

'Where are the boys?' She couldn't see them.

'They are up there.' Castor nodded. 'On the hillside, with some other boys who have found a tortoise.'

She followed his pointing arm, and saw Oliver and Rupert's fair heads among several dark ones, bending over something in the olive grove beside the track they'd driven down.

'They are quite happy,' Pollux said gently. 'So, please will you swim with us?'

She sat up, looking from one to the other. Perfect faces, perfectly alike, not a curve or a line out of place to mar the flawlessness or the similarity. Across the short distance that separated her from them, she thought she could feel the radiance of their bodies' warmth. Such beauty, she thought distractedly, what a lot of heat it produces.

'No, really, I . . . I can't.' I'll have to strip off, can't possibly go swimming in my t-shirt.

'We think you can.'

Which had spoken? She didn't know. Couldn't stop

to work it out, because each had taken hold of one of her hands, and they were pulling her, gently but firmly, to her feet. Letting go, at the precise same instant, and, one each side of her, grasping the hem of her t-shirt, peeling it off her so that she stood, naked and vulnerable as if she'd been skinned, in her tiny insubstantial bikini.

'Come,' they said. And, again, took hold of her hands. Walked with her to the sea. Into the shallows, wading, deeper, deeper, the water seeming cold on her sun-heated skin, climbing over her knees to the soft flesh of her thighs, up, up, over her hips now and chilly, chilly into the warm dark heart of her, taking her breath away, making her gasp so that her two guardians, understanding, laughed softly.

And, as one, squeezed her hands in a gesture that said, we know.

They broke free, leaping into the water dolphin-like, bodies curving in arcs above the rippling waves. She threw herself forward too, wanting to be with them, and, aware, they turned and waited for her. She was with them, moving between them through the brilliant blue as if they'd lent her some of their confidence and their grace. She *felt* beautiful, elegant, as delighted with herself as she was with them. They didn't speak, but from time to time she would catch the eyes of one of them on her, and again there would be that grave expression and that accepting, approving nod.

Time went away, and she had no conception of how long they'd been in the sea. But she became aware of feeling tired. Picking it up, they turned back, swam either side of her, somehow supporting her although she felt no touch, until the three of them grounded on the soft sand of the shore and came to rest.

As one, they rolled over on to their backs. Resting on her elbows, one twin took hold of each of her

93

hands. Their grip was strong, too strong for her to have broken away. Even if she'd wanted to.

An image burst fully-formed into her mind. Aaron, last night, his hand imprisoning her wrists as she'd instinctively tried to raise her own hands to cover her ears. Aaron's grip had felt like this: undeniable. She saw his hand, long-fingered, perfect, strong; holding her like manacles. Fingers curving round the edge of her palm, pressing down into her lap, touching her flesh. So near, his fingers, to her secret hidden place, so extraordinary, that he should do that, touch her in that way, and that she shouldn't mind. Shouldn't even have registered, until this moment, that he'd done it.

The twins' hands, the memory of Aaron's hand, combined in her mind like the vast thundering climax of a storm bursting overhead. Her body, obeying a command she had no knowlededge of sending, went tense, then instantly relaxed into waves of pleasure that surged along her like the ripples of the friendly sea. She closed her eyes, head lolling back, spent and unable even to think.

She became aware that they'd gone. Quietly got up, detached themselves from her, inched away. She was alone.

Silently thanking them for their tact—how on earth was one to face two extremely attractive young men after something as weird and unexpected as that had invaded one's brain!—she withdrew from the water and walked up the beach to lie down on her mat.

The day had taken on a dream quality. The twins had gone off somewhere to buy lunch, and, returning, had collected the boys and persuaded them to leave the tortoise alone and come to eat.

They sat in the shade of the cliffs, and with an appetite greater than she'd known in ages, she had torn at hunks of fresh bread, breaking bits off a cube of moist salty feta cheese with her fingers, picking black olives out of their twist of paper and spitting the pits into the sand. The meal was an orgy, a yielding to hunger that bordered on the gluttonous, and she laughed with the twins and the boys and revelled in—copied—their masculine disregard of good manners.

The twins had brought cans of soft drink for the boys. She was thirsty, would have liked a cool Coke too. But, 'This is for us,' Pollux said. And produced a bottle of retsina, cold, moisture frosting its outside and dripping in icy drops on to her stomach as she took it from him.

He had drawn the cork, was offering her first draught.

Obedient to his will, she put the bottle to her lips. And, passing it on, watched as the twins put their lips to the same place. Then passed it back to her, so that her mouth kissed the impression of their lips on the glass neck.

In that way, they finished the bottle.

She slept, after lunch. Satiated, her body seemed to float slightly above the firm sand as her mind wandered off into the freedom of unconsciousness. In her dreams she saw bottles of wine on dirty kitchen tables, knew herself to be at university, at some party thrown with more optimism than organisation, where too few people brought drink and too many scroungers turned up to consume other people's. Then Barry was there, French kissing her in a corner with a mouth tasting of wine while the Stones said 'You'd better move on.'

She could still taste him when she awoke. Lying on her side, she stretched, pushing out her bottom as she always did into the curve formed by his belly and his groin as he curled round behind her.

Encountering not a warm body but emptiness.

Before she could be annihilated, she sat up. Reached

for her bag, dizzy, pulled out her brush and dragged it through her hair. Found her watch, saw that it was nearly five. Became the efficient mother, packing up the picnic detritus, looking round for the boys.

Who, predictably, moaned that they didn't want to go, they were just about to have another swim and why did she have to *spoil* everything?

The twins, studying her, must somehow have perceived. For one of them, putting on his jeans as if declaring that there would be no more arguing, said quietly that it was time to leave.

In Aaron's jeep—Aaron, who by lending his car to her, his twins to her, had made the day possible—she settled into her seat and prepared herself for the long drive home.

EIGHT

Mortal Sin

The Christmas vacation after her first term at university had been a time of puzzlement and barely-suppressed irritation. Her parents and her sister seemed determined to keep her in her place—her mother had actually used the words—meaning, Fay assumed, that they intended to go all-out to show her *they* weren't going to be impressed by a girl doing a degree in English and psychology and neither was anyone else in Sidcup.

Fay wasn't trying to impress them. It wasn't that which made her tell her sister she had to get on with her reading and couldn't go shopping with her. It wasn't for that she told them eagerly about the lectures she'd enjoyed, the interesting friends she'd made, the late-night discussions over coffee that set her brain reeling with the huge potential of the world. About the lively, wonderful atmosphere of the Students' Union, no matter if you went in at nine in the morning or eleven-thirty at night.

She wanted to share it with them. To make them appreciate, if she could, how good it was. How grateful, even, she was that they were scrimping and saving to make it possible for her to be there.

Her gratitude faded a little, the day her father told

her categorically he didn't want to hear about a load of long-haired layabouts who wouldn't recognise a hard day's work if it jumped out and hit them. She began to protest—'Dad, they're not like that! Not all of them, anyway! They—' She wanted to tell him about the fervent socialists, the earnest ones who genuinely felt for the working man, did their best to spread the message of the dignity of labour, the right of every man to a decent wage and fair working conditions.

He railroaded her into silence. Then picked up his *Daily Express* in a scrunching, furious fist and threw himself out of the room, slamming the door in her face.

Her sister had put up a poster of Barry Ryan in their communal bedroom; she played 'Eloise' constantly on the Dansette record player. But when Fay, seeing an opening, suggested they listen to her 'Songs From a Room' or one of the Dubliners' albums she'd borrowed, Julie flatly refused. 'I *hate* that folk rubbish!' she said belligerently. 'All those people, they think they're so clever!'

Another door slammed in Fay's face. Hurt, stung to reaction at last, she put on 'All Along the Watchtower' and turned up the volume till the walls of the semi-detached shook.

She'd been going to tell her mother about Barry. Not everything about him, just a brief mention. For the pleasure of talking about him. Of saying his name aloud. But her mother, seeking her out one morning when her father had gone to work and her sister to school, took the tender impulse away.

'I know all about these colleges,' she said flatly, looming towards Fay, duster aggressively in her hand as if she wanted to clean up her daughter as well as the already immaculate house. It's a *university*, Fay wanted to protest. Aren't you the least bit pleased, that your child has won a place at a university? 'I'm well aware what they get up to,' her mother was saying, nodding knowingly as if she'd read every line of the latest Vice Chancellor's report. 'Behaving like married couples, going on the Pill, I shouldn't wonder!'

Fay felt the hot embarrassed blood rise in her face. She looked away, guilty, as if in the place of her one union with Barry she'd slept with half the University, started taking the Pill on her first day and instantly gone out hunting for men.

The guilt was out of all proportion to her offence, if it was an offence. And it was more than enough to stop her defending herself against her mother's implications.

'What are you saying?' she asked quietly, when her mother's continued presence in the room indicated she hadn't finished.

'I'm saying, don't you go getting any ideas!' her mother hissed, dropping her voice as if the neighbours were crowding against the party wall with glasses pressed to their ears. 'I'm not having you come home with any little bundles of joy!' Fay forebore to say that if the entire female student body were on the Pill, as her mother seemed to think, then little bundles of joy were unlikely.

Her mother was drawing breath. Squaring her shoulders for the final clincher. Fay, knowing what it would be, dropped her head so that she could mouth the words as her mother said them out loud.

'You a convent girl, too!'

They were not Catholics, Fay's parents. Not even regular churchgoers. But in the intensity of their desire for *respectability*, for themselves, for the two curvaceous and handsome daughters who were the improbable product of their loins, an education at the stern and repressive hands of the convent must have seemed like the answer to their inarticulate prayers. So first Fay and then Julie had been removed from the local state primary school to the rarefied, regimented, beeswax-smelling world of enclosed womanhood.

Fay had been seven, the day she set foot behind the Convent walls. Had gone into morning assembly and immediately been herded off as a goat, made to stand at the back of the hall in the section set aside for Protestant girls while the blessed sheep, expressions of beatitude on their upturned, eyes-closed faces, apparently worked on perfecting the angle at which their hands were held out in prayer.

She had noticed, appalled, the painting of Jesus. Holes in his palms, pale skin torn back so that the red flesh underneath seemed to pulsate towards her. What was the matter with him? Turning away, trying to look somewhere—anywhere—else, her eyes fell on the crucifix. The tortured, twisted figure. And she'd suddenly understood. Hung on the Cross! Oh, oh, it didn't mean what she'd thought it did, that they'd nailed him up by his garments and left him there to starve to death.

It meant they'd put nails through his hands. Through his feet. Made those awful, terrible wounds.

The hot sweat broke out on her body, the room seemed to go black and Mother Superior's voice sounded as if it came from the end of a long tunnel. Think about something else! Think about the other girls—*they're* not upset! Some of them look really happy! Perhaps they're used to it, perhaps being a Catholic all your life makes you immune.

Listen to the words of the prayers.

She lowered her eyes, and, with a monumental effort, turned her mind away from Jesus and on to the pretty blue bow tying the plait of the red-headed girl in front of her.

The bow on the plait had helped her to cope for eight days. On the ninth day of the term, the red-haired girl was away. And Fay fainted.

Lying on the glossy wood floor, she returned muzzily to consciousness. Felt black serge flap against her face, smelt briefly a body smell waft out from beneath the engulfing undergarment. Wanted to be sick, and suffered the firm claw-hands of Sister Bernard as she half-pulled, half-marched her out of the hall.

Sister Bernard, not one to let a heaven-sent opportunity pass by, cashed in on the moment.

'Yes, Our Lord suffered!' she said in response to Fay's mumbled explanation, pale eyes intent on her, face as furious in her outraged indignation as if Fay herself had driven in the nails. 'And He goes on suffering, every time a little girl sins! Oh, yes!' Fay had not protested, had not dared open her mouth. 'He sees, poor Jesus, He sees and He weeps! For you, because you will not obey His commandments and foresake your sinfulness, and for Himself, because He must suffer the agony of crucifixion all over again, feel anew the . . .'

But Fay didn't hear any more. It was either stay and listen and be sick all over the stiff black habit, or run. She ran. Vomited into the low, pee-smelling lavatory until her convulsed stomach knotted into cramp and she couldn't bring up any more.

The day she went back to university, no-one came to see her off at the station. And in contrast to home and the people in it, Barry seemed all the more wonderful. Nobody's perfect, she told herself as the Intercity pulled out of Euston on the long journey north. *They* aren't. I'm glad Christmas is over, I shan't go home for as long next vacation. A week at the most. She didn't stop to think where she'd go for the rest of the time. I know Barry's not perfect, either. Don't want him to be. Love him as he is.

Determined that life at university with Barry should be much better than life with her parents and Julie in

Sidcup, she sat staring out of the window and turned her mind to the happy prospect ahead.

'We've got to do something about it, Fay,' Barry said.

He was lying on her, between her open legs on her bed. They still had on their jeans, although above the waist they were bare. His hands were on her breasts.

She knew, lamenting, that he wasn't going to make love to her. That he was afraid of the consequences. And, aware she was full of desire and therefore vulnerable, that he'd renew his arguments that they be sensible.

'You mean, I've got to do something,' she said. Got to nerve myself to go to the Clinic. And, for I won't go on the Pill, ask what alternatives there are.

'Fay, me darling, we've been through this.' His voice was soft, and his fingers on her nipples were sending such feelings through her that she wasn't able to argue. 'It's no good, if we leave it up to me. Like taking a shower with your raincoat on.' She didn't know, had only his word for that. 'It's got to be you. And it's much more reliable, if you do it.' He put his lips down to her skin, nibbling, sucking. 'Better for both of us,' he whispered winningly.

She tried again to analyse her reluctance. It wasn't just the natural horror of having strangers examine and probe her, she could deal with that. Everyone else could, presumably, so why should she be the exception? And she knew he was right—it was stupid to make love unprotected. It was the sensible thing to do, to take precautions. The only thing, if he were ever to be inside her again—he was making that quite clear.

So why won't I do it?

The answer was there, if she had the courage to face it. It was Jesus, wasn't it, poor loving Jesus, suffering the agony all over again for every girl who sinned. And while she could tell herself it wasn't much of a sin to get carried away once in a while—a very *human* sin, and one which her idea of a loving Jesus would be likely to understand—to get herself fixed up at the clinic deliberately, so that lust could overtake her any time she felt like it with no worrying results, was quite a different matter.

She said, as she'd said before, 'I'll think about it.' And, twisting out from beneath him, reached for her clothes.

She thought about it. Agonised over it. Alone—Barry had made it quite clear what *he* thought, and there wasn't anyone else to ask. She had made friends with girls in her Hall—was quite close to two of them—but what would they say if she dropped in for coffee one evening, or joined them down in the utility room while they were all doing their laundry, and said casually, 'By the way, Barry's pressing me to go and see the family planning people, do you think I should?'

Quite a lot of the girls had boyfriends. Fay had met some of them, seen them in the corridor, sometimes very late. Not that there was any particular significance to the time—it was just being naïve, she told herself, to assume that the likelihood of sexual intercourse increased with the lateness of the hour. Maybe I'm being silly, she thought anxiously. Maybe everyone's doing it but me, and if I did mention it, they'd say, good for you!

She didn't. Eventually took the decision all by herself. Made the appointment, went into town on the bus, took another bus up to the clinic. Sat till it was her turn. 'Miss Morrison?' Was it her imagination, or was a slight emphasis laid on the 'Miss'?

Into the doctor's room. Where on a high, narrow couch on a sheet of plastic which let out a noise like a pistol-shot every time she moved, the middle-aged woman doctor spent what seemed several eternities fitting her up with a diaphragm.

'Nurse'll tell you how to look after it,' the doctor said, back to Fay as she washed her hands at the basin. Fay jumped down off the couch and into her knickers and jeans before she turned round.

The doctor returned to her desk. Am I dismissed? Fay wondered. I think I am.

'Thank you,' she said. Was that right? And thank you for what? For kitting me out so I can sleep with my boyfriend? 'Goodbye.'

Embarrassed, guilty, she hurried out of the room. The doctor neither looked up from whatever it was she was writing nor responded to Fay's farewell. Annoyed, Fay thought, that's a fine way to treat someone when you've just been rummaging around in their insides.

She endured ten minutes' lecture from the loud-voiced nurse, whose instructions were far too full of words like 'front passage', 'sperm' and 'INTERCOURSE' for someone speaking not five yards from a waiting-room full of people. As soon as the nurse had finished, Fay hurried out of the room. Ran down the corridor, and leapt down the steps into the street.

I should feel elated, she thought, as the bus took her back to the middle of town. I should feel full of the joyful anticipation of telling Barry that it's all systems go. That we can now make love as hard and as often as we like, until the spermicide cream runs out or we punch a hole in my cap.

She felt neither joyful nor elated. Felt depressed, touched with a sense of foreboding.

I'll treat myself to something pretty, she thought desperately. I know! A new nightie! Something sexy. And perhaps some perfume. Eau de toilette, anyway. She made her way into a department store, and for what seemed a disproportionately large amount of money, bought a black frilly garment with lace shoulder straps whose hem barely covered her bottom. It was transparent, and showed her bra and pants. She imagined how it would look over bare skin. On the way out, she bought a small bottle of cologne.

Then she went to wait for the bus back to campus and wondered how she was going to break the news to Barry.

She caught him coming out of his Hall. He was wearing a track suit, and had his rugby bag in his hand.

'Oh, are you playing?' She'd forgotten Wednesday was rugby afternoon.

'No, I'm just taking my kit for a walk.' He grinned, putting his arm round her and giving her a hug. 'I am indeed. Liverpool University. Where have you been? I came round to your room earlier so that we could go and have lunch together, but you weren't there.'

She stared up at him. Into the handsome face, tanned and healthy-looking. Into the blue, blue eyes. Her heart lurched.

'I went into town,' she said quietly. Would that be enough? Would he guess, from her tone? From the way she was looking at him?

'Oh? What for?'

Appparently not.

'I went to the clinic,' she whispered. She was glad the nightie was hidden away in its bag, so that he wouldn't see what she'd bought and think how silly she'd been, buying it specially.

He didn't speak. Just stood, staring at her. Then he put down his kit and wrapped her in his arms.

'Fay. Oh, Fay.' He found her mouth, kissing her lips, gently forcing them apart, moving his tongue against hers. After a moment, breaking away, he said, 'Tonight?'

And, overflowing with love, she said, 'Yes.'

She thought of going over to the Students' Union in the evening. It tended to be lively in the bar, after a rugby game—the visiting side usually stayed for a few beers, and she'd spent some happy times with Barry and his mates. They seemed to hold him in as high esteem as she did, though for very different reasons. Once when he'd scored three tries, including the last-minute one which had won them the game, he'd spent most of the evening standing on the table.

I won't go tonight, she thought. Barry won't stay long. And if I go with him, I'd have to leave before him anyway, to come and . . . To get ready.

She packed all her books away in her desk and tidied her room. Borrowed the Hoover from the cleaners' cupboard and put it over her piece of carpet. Plumped up the pillows, smoothed the patchwork blanket on the bed. Found a couple of candles, put them ready with a box of matches beside them.

Then she had a bath. Sat on the edge when she'd dried herself and took the diaphragm out of its box. Poked its rubber dome with her finger, and watched it go plop! back into shape.

It was a ghastly thing. And it smelt like... like... She couldn't remember. Then she did—it smelt like teats on babies' bottles.

Yuk.

She laid the tube of spermicide cream on the side of the basin. They'd given her a giant economy size. As the nurse had taught her, she squeezed a great dollop inside the cap, outside the cap, inside herself. It was thick, white, and quite revolting.

She sat with the cap in her hand.

Tears stung in her eyes. She blinked them away.

Stop being stupid! This is great, it means we can make love and not worry! It's only a matter of getting used to it.

She looked again at the cap, oozing white cream.

Thought of Barry, his hands, his mouth, all over her body. Touching this stuff, this alien stuff which she was sure had a life of its own and would be bound to get everywhere.

Barry.

Resolutely, she pushed the flexible circular rim of the cap into a narrow oval and, standing up, one foot on the bath, pushed it inside her.

She lay on the bed, dressing gown tied tightly over the new nightie, waiting for Barry. It was nearly eleven. I wish we'd said a time, she thought. Wish I knew when he was coming.

She'd got ready far too soon. Could have done an hour and a half's work. Which, apart from being a good thing in itself, would have stopped her thinking—worrying—about Barry.

She sniffed at her wrists. The eau de toilette had been cheap—too cheap to last long. She reached for the bottle and sprayed on a little more.

She shivered slightly. The heating would be going off soon—she hoped he'd arrive before it did. She wanted—or thought she wanted—to be able to parade before him in her finery without looking perished with cold.

She heard voices from outside. Laughter. Singing. 'The Irish Rover', as only Barry could sing it. Then someone began on a chant of 'Fifty—nil, fifty—nil, Liverpool, Liverpool, fuck off home!' We must have won, she thought abstractedly. Someone shouted, 'Goodnight, Barry!', and he broke off from singing to respond.

She heard the outer door bang shut, and hastily put a match to the candles and switched out the light. Heard footsteps on the uncarpeted stairs. Heard the door on to her corridor creak open and shut. Heard him come closer, closer. Pause outside her door. And, at last, watched as he came in.

He stood in the open doorway, hands against the sides. He was smiling, and in the dim light she could see he looked very happy. Oh, Barry, she thought joyfully, it's as important to you as . . .

He gave a great burp. Said, 'Fifty—nil, Fay! We stuffed the bastards out of sight!' Then he lurched into the room, leaving the door wide open, and fell across the bed.

She could smell beer. And the potent aroma of whiskey.

She didn't know what to do with her disappointment.

She sank down into the chair, just staring at him. Wet flannel, to revive him? Black coffee? No. Nothing could compete with this.

His breathing was already deepening. He gave a small snore, then, as if he'd woken himself up, muttered, 'Said I'd be here. Special, tonight.'

He raised his head, and hope flared in her. But his eyes, bleary, the whites red-veined, were looking in slightly different directions. And his mouth was wet, loose, and all but inarticulate.

'Fay,' he said. 'Two Fays. Double your money.'

'I—'

The random eyes filled with tears. He said, 'Sorry, Fay.' Then, as if his neck had abruptly given up the struggle, his face fell down into the pillows.

She was crying, too. His maudlin tears had unmanned her, taken away her hot savage impulse to tip him off her bed, kick him out into the corridor, leave him there to be found like a sack of rubbish in the morning.

She knelt on the floor by his side, face close to his, and with gentle fingers stroked the sticky black hair away from his brow.

NINE

Evening Eternal

On the way home from the beach, the twins proposed stopping for a meal.

'Oh—we were going to eat back at home,' she said. She wasn't sure if she had enough money with her for eating out.

'Let's stop!' Oliver said. 'We *always* eat at home, let's go to a taverna!'

'We don't always eat at home!' she protested. 'And I've got things ready for this evening.' It was a downright lie, and she was sure he knew it. He began to say something, but one of the twins broke in.

'If you wish to return, then of course that is what you shall do,' he said. 'However, my brother and I should be most glad if you would consent to be our guests at a restaurant we know. It is good, and it is in the next town.'

Asked so charmingly, she didn't think she could do anything else but agree.

The twins directed her into the town, and suggested a place to park. It was one of the new resorts—in a corner of her mind, she wondered that they should know the place at all, never mind patronise a restaurant there. Oliver—it was his turn in the front—

leapt down as soon as she'd stopped, and the twins and Rupert clambered out from the back.

'Could you give me a minute?' she asked, reaching on to the floor for her bag. 'I'd like to comb my hair.'

'Of course,' a twin said smoothly. 'We shall walk with the boys over there, to look down at the boats in the bay.'

As soon as they'd moved away she got out her make-up bag. In the small mirror, her face looked much as she'd expected it to look after a long day on the beach and in the water. She put on some eye make-up, then smoothed some cream into her skin and gave it a light dusting with the pad from her compact, which effectively took off the worst of the shine. Then she undid her hair from its slide and brushed out most of the salt and the sand.

There was nothing she could do about her rumpled clothes. She got out of the jeep and went after the others.

The twins turned as she approached. Together, as if their mouths were operated by a single brain, they smiled their appreciation.

'We think you look very beautiful,' one said.

Beautiful! She bit back the exclamation of disbelief. 'Thank you,' she said gravely.

And, one either side of her as they'd been in the water, they each took one of her hands and led her off towards the town.

The streets were heaving with people, most of them holiday-makers and most of them British. Young men in hunting packs, young girls wanting to be caught but preferably not by the sort of British lout they'd presumably come out here to get away from. Heads turned—especially the female ones—to watch the progress down the pavement of the stately twins. Fay, hand in hand with them both, felt a surge of pure delight at the unmistakable envy on other women's faces. She heard a girl say, 'Two of them! She can't have two of them!', and said under her breath, 'Oh, can't I?'

The twins went past all the crowded tavernas on the main street, and eventually stopped outside a quieter, less shrieking establishment on a side road leading down to the beach. Here were local families, the mix of generations typical of the Greeks on a night out. The twins greeted several people, and a waiter appeared to show them to a table.

They ordered a simple meal, but it took a pleasantly long time both in the arriving and the consuming. She was quite content to sit there, making easy conversation, watching the boys tucking in, watching the twins, whatever they were doing. The twins filled her glass for her as soon as it was nearing empty, until, head feeling swimmy, she told them to stop.

'It is not far to go to Corfu Town,' one twin said, touching her arm with his hand. 'And we know you will drive safely.'

Not if I have any more retsina, I won't, she thought. His hand was still on her arm, the fingers moving over her skin like a blind man reading. Not if you go on doing that, either.

In time, the bill was called for and settled. The boys, sleepy now, trailed behind her back to the jeep. The twins, as before, took up their stations either side of her. How shall I manage tomorrow, she wondered, when I'm called upon to walk on my own again?

She was, she realised, slightly drunk.

The traffic had eased now, and she drove slowly and carefully. They had the road almost to themselves, for which she was grateful. Approaching the town, a twin, unasked, gave her directions, and without even one wrong lane or turning, she pulled up outside the house.

Oliver had fallen asleep, and from the look of Rupert,

111

she guessed he'd just woken up. 'Bed,' she said softly to them.

'We will help,' the twins said. They each took hold of a boy, gently, a supporting arm round the shoulders, and guided them up the steps. One twin carried the remains of the picnic. Fay looked round the jeep, not wanting to leave any of their litter in it for Aaron to find. One of Oliver's shoes was on the floor, and she picked it up, then followed the rest of them into the house.

They'd gone upstairs. She could hear the tap running in the bathroom, heard the lavatory flush. There was a chorus of goodnights, then the twins came down again.

'Your sons are ready for your valediction,' one said. She resisted the urge to smile.

'Thanks. I'll go up, then.' She wondered if that sounded dismissive, which would be ungrateful in the extreme, after all their kindness. And I don't want to be rid of them, she thought. Do I?

She wasn't sure.

'Help yourselves to a drink,' she said. 'Do! It'd be nice, wouldn't it, to have a last one, just the three of us?'

Solemnly, in unison, they nodded.

'I'll just have a quick shower,'—she was warming to the idea, rapidly—'then I'll join you. Why don't you take a tray of drinks out on to the balcony?'

'We shall,' they said. 'Please, take your time.'

And they smiled.

She raced upstairs, into the boys' room for a brief but intense hug and kiss, then into her own room and the shower leading off it. The water felt wonderful, and as it flowed over her dirty, dusty body, she stretched her limbs with pleasure. The sweet scent of shampoo filled the air, and with a last long rinse, she was done.

What do I wear? Doesn't matter, really. It's pretty dark out on the terrace. She put on underwear, then a short t-shirt dress. Then, on an inexplicable whim, removed her bra.

She brushed her hair, staring at herself in the mirror. Her skin seemed to glow, and there was a sparkle in her eyes which she ascribed to the retsina.

'I don't care,' she whispered to her reflection. 'Don't give a toss!'

And, elated, expectant, went barefoot down the stairs.

No sound of voices greeted her from outside as she hurried across the living room. But then, they never did seem to *talk* when it was just the two of them. But there were no other sounds, either. No chink of ice in a glass. No slight scrape as someone moved his chair.

Nothing.

Alarmed, disappointment flooding through her, she was sure they must have gone. She rushed across the last few yards of the living room, leapt out through the open doors.

To find, sitting at the end of the balcony, a full tumbler in his hand and totally at home, as well he might be, Aaron.

She said, stupidly, 'I thought you'd be the twins!'

'The twins have gone.' His voice was dark-brown in the soft night. 'But, not wanting you to be alone, I have taken their place. I trust you do not mind.'

She sank down into the chair pulled up by his side. He reached out to the table behind him and passed her a drink. She tasted it; gin and tonic. Exactly what she wanted.

She couldn't find the words to say what was in her mind. That she was pleased, much more than pleased, he was here. That his presence was *right*, in some unfathomable way. The perfect end to a perfect day.

113

'Thank you for your jeep. And for arranging that the twins take us to that lovely beach.'

'You enjoyed it?' She nodded. 'I am glad.'

'The twins...' She stopped. How to put into words, the twins have made me feel good? He'd never understand, in a million years, what she wanted to say.

'They did? I am glad of that, too. It was what you needed.'

Did I say what I was thinking? She felt confused, the strong drink rushing to her head bringing back the muzziness she'd felt earlier. I suppose I did.

No, you didn't. He was speaking—he must be, his words were in her brain. But she wasn't aware of hearing him.

Then, breaking the enchanted mood, he laughed. And she thought he said, 'I am sorry.' But before she could puzzle over whether or not he'd spoken aloud, she had something far more imperative to think about, because he'd reached over and taken hold of her hand.

'Don't jump like that,' came the chocolate voice out of the darkness. 'You did not mind when the Dioscuri held your hands.'

'I didn't . . . how did you know? *Who?*'

He laughed again, a rich warm sound in his throat. 'The Dioscuri,' he repeated. 'Castor and Pollux. The young sons of Zeus.'

She wasn't following. Didn't care, really. Drained her glass, and was aware of him refilling it. Putting it back in her hand, guiding it to her lips. This must be the last, she thought, and even as she thought, seemed to see the words written up in front of her eyes against the starry sky, at first bold and clear, then fainter, then nothing.

So she said them aloud. 'This must be the last.'

And he said, 'It will be.'

She frowned, trying to remember what she'd

wanted to say. 'What's all that about sons of Zeus?' she asked.

'You do not know the legend?'

'No. We weren't encouraged to read Greek myths. Myths of any kind.' She wished there were another word instead of myths. It was proving difficult to pronounce. 'Myths,' she said carefully.

'Everyone should learn the myths of the ancient peoples,' he said. 'They are far more than stories. They are the heart of our early humanity. They express our fears, our joys. They are for all time.'

It sounded so right. 'Yes. I wish I had been allowed to learn them. But the nuns said they were pagan. Anything pre-Christian was pagan, and therefore not allowed.'

His hand was warm around hers. She put down her empty glass and slid her other hand under his on her lap. He squeezed her fingers together, as if he'd been doing it for years.

'That is a remarkably narrow attitude. They must be very afraid, your nuns. They must feel threatened, if they will not even permit their children to read of other credos.'

Afraid? Sister Bernard? Mother Superior? Ha!

But it wasn't funny. He was dead right.

'Good grief,' she said slowly. 'I'd never looked at it like that. You . . .'

The thought had been there, clear as crystal. Then it was gone. Quite, quite gone. She looked at him, greatly surprised, and saw that he was laughing again.

And inside her head she heard him say, I do not want to talk of such things tonight. I want to laugh with you.

'Oh, I want that too!' she said fervently. So long, so long, since I laughed with a man. Relaxed in the dark with him, felt at ease, able to say exactly what popped into my head without first working out whether or not it's going to go down well. So long since anyone said they wanted to be with me.

He was nodding, as if he knew what she was saying. Had known already, and that what she was saying—*thinking*—now was merely serving as confirmation.

She said, wonder in her voice, 'Why do I feel I know you? Why, when you appeared at that dreadful restaurant where I was so embarrassed, did I think, here he is! As if we'd already met? Were already dear to each other?'

He leaned forward, putting his hand to her chin so that he could hold her face still. He stared into her eyes, and she felt as she'd done in the sea. As if a great unstoppable tide were flowing through her.

It felt marvellous. Instinctively, she smiled.

'You do know me,' he said. 'As I know you.'

'But . . .'

He put his finger against her lips. Before she could think what she was doing, she kissed it. And it was his turn to smile.

'Not in the way you understand,' he said. 'We had never met, before that night.'

'Then how . . .?'

His hand once more around her jaw, he lifted her face towards him. Bent his head and kissed her gently on the lips. The briefest of touches, as if he were saying, this, just this, for now.

'I shall explain, but not tonight.'

Her curiosity was being soothed from her. The questions could wait.

She lay back against the cushions, tired suddenly, the evening—the whole day—catching up with her. She yawned, hugely, and wondered why she didn't feel awkward at not having put her hand over her mouth.

I'm not even sure I can locate my hand, let alone lift it.

Beside her, she heard him get to his feet. Then his hands were on her, and he had picked her up out of her chair, carrying her with one arm under her shoulders and the other under her knees. Pressed to his chest, she fancied she could feel his heartbeat.

She closed her eyes, head falling back. I wonder where he's taking me?

Up the stairs. Up, up, one step after another, with no apparent effort. No increase in that thump, thump of his heart.

He's taking me to bed!

The cool sheet was under her, the top covers folded back while he laid her gently down. Before she could protest, he had slipped off her dress, and for a moment stood looking at her. Then, eyes on her face, he did just what the twins had done. Smiled, and nodded.

But he, unlike them, spoke. Only he said something in a language she didn't understand. Then, when she was beginning to wonder what he had in mind to do next and whether or not she was going to agree, he reached out for the bedclothes and covered her up.

'You will sleep, now,' he said. It sounded as if he were putting a spell on her. Her eyes began to close.

There came the small sound of the door handle rattling. She made an enormous effort and opened her eyes one last time, and saw him in the doorway, closing the door behind him.

TEN

Aphrodite Rising

Waking to the cooing of the doves and sunshine intruding through the shutters, her slight headache was an indication that she'd had too much to drink last night. She took a long draught from the glass of water beside her bed, analysing it as the sort of headache which would respond to a good breakfast and wouldn't need aspirin to send it packing.

Serves me right, she thought. How irresponsible, to knock back the retsina and then drive home. I won't do that again.

Suddenly she remembered the two large gins which Aaron had poured for her. Remembering a lot of other things as well, she peeled back the bedclothes and looked down at her almost-naked body.

One confirming glance was enough. The hot blood rushing to her face, she hastily covered herself up again.

He stood there—*right there!*—just staring at me! And all I had on were my panties! He did it on purpose, the rotten sod, got me drunk and carried me upstairs to bed so that he could take advantage of me! He'll have forgotten all about it, this morning, they always do, they get what they want and then...

She made herself stop. Realised, as the affronted

reaction abated, that it hadn't been like that at all. That he'd behaved towards her with perfect courtesy, laid her gently on her bed and, for all that he'd taken off her dress, had done no more than look at her.

But I *hate* being looked at! There's always some comment, some joke about stomachs or thighs or big women being a handful. Even if they don't say it, you can see it in their faces. In their eyes.

She saw Aaron's expression again.

And for the life of her, she couldn't convince herself that there had been anything in it but approval.

She was on her second cup of tea when the boys came back with the bread, and already her headache had cleared. She felt she'd got off lightly.

'What are we going to do today?' she asked. 'Lido?'

They both nodded.

'Okay. Maybe we should treat the Twins to lunch, since they took us out last night. Or ask them here. What do you think?'

Rupert was reaching in the pocket of his shorts, pulling out a crumpled envelope. 'Forgot to give you this,' he said. 'Sorry.'

Her name was on the envelope, printed in capitals. The 'e' of 'Leary' was a Greek Epsilon, ε. As if the writer had momentarily forgotten he was writing in English.

'When did he give you this?'

'Who?'

'Oh—I mean, who gave you this?'

'Nobody. It was tucked in the door downstairs. Who's it from?' He was leaning on her shoulder, trying to see as she opened the envelope.

'Never you mind!' That was the trouble with sharing almost everything with your kids, she thought, you have to fight for your privacy when you *do* want it.

She got up from the table and went to lean against the sink. She pulled out the single sheet of paper.

'I hope you slept soundly and are feeling well and happy this morning. I understand that the Dioscuri intend to organise some swimming event at the lido, at which the presence of anybody over the age of twenty-five will be superfluous. I suggest that, instead, you come out with me. I have something I wish you to see.

'I shall call to collect you at ten o'clock. You will be back with your sons in time for lunch.

Sincerely,
Aaron'

Her first reaction was sheer delight, that he wanted to see her again. Then, reading through his brief note a second time, but this time more carefully, she thought how considerate he must be. He's provided me with a good reason for not going with the boys. He's also managed to convey that I needn't worry about being away from them too long.

Finally it occurred to her to wonder where he was going to take her.

She heard the Range Rover pull up outside a couple of minutes after ten, and ran down to greet him. He leaned over and opened the car door for her, and the look in his eyes made her glad she'd decided to wear her best dress. She'd wondered if it'd be too posh; he didn't seem to think so.

He drove out of the square and into the thick of the morning traffic. She asked, 'Where are we going?'

'Somewhere cool and sophisticated, where you will be the perfect English lady in your garden party frock.'

She laughed, although a part of her mind detached to cope with her surprise that, again, he had read her thoughts with such total accuracy.

She didn't know what to say, so kept quiet and let him concentrate on driving. Considering the number of vehicles and wayward pedestrians clogging the road, it seemed a wise decision. He was a patient driver, she noticed, apparently not minding being held up while all manner of traffic sorted itself out in his path.

They cleared the town and headed off around Garitsa Bay, but before they'd gone a couple of hundred yards, he turned off to the right. Pulling up in what seemed to be a fairly expensive residential area, he said, 'Here we are.'

Where? Were they going visiting?

'Are we going to one of these houses?' She tried to sound as if she did this sort of thing all the time.

He laughed, reaching out to touch her hand. 'No. We're going to the Archaeological Museum.'

They walked side by side through the porch, and even after the short distance from the car, the deep shade was welcome. Cool and sophisticated, he'd said. She looked around at the statues. He was right.

He was buying tickets at the desk. She was relieved to see that there weren't very many other visitors: presumably the sun and the sea were too strong a rival attraction. He came back to her, pocketing his change.

'I did not buy you a guide book,' he said. 'You have me, so you have no need of one.' He glanced at her, and she saw amusement in his dark eyes. 'Do not look so alarmed. I shall know when you have heard enough.'

Sometimes, she thought in the midst of her laughter, having someone read your mind isn't a bad thing at all.

They went upstairs to the long galleries on the first floor. For some time he let her wander where she would, materialising at her side now and again to tell her briefly what she was looking at and filling in a few details. Then he said, 'You must see the main attraction.'

She had been staring, entranced, at a small marble head of Aphrodite. Noticing, his eyes widened for an instant and he gave her an assessing sort of a look. He muttered something, but she didn't understand. He took her arm and guided her towards the large open space at the end of the gallery, and she came face to face with the Gorgon Pediment.

She stared up at it. The original pieces of sculpture had been placed in a representation of their original setting, with incised lines to show where the now missing bits would have been. The pediment was triangular, reaching its apex above the figure of the Gorgon, her tongue out in a grimace, snakes twisting in her hair and in a twining, living girdle at her waist. On either side of her were the figures of a man and a winged horse, and they were flanked by two mythical beasts that looked like a cross between a lion and a panther.

Aaron said quietly in her ear, 'The winged horse is Pegasus, and the man is Chrysaor. They were Medusa's children from her union with Poseidon. See, she is framed by animals, as if, like Artemis, she too were a deity of the wild things.'

Fay tried to take it in. She wished she knew what he was talking about. She could think of no sensible reply, and she felt it was rude not to respond.

He said, as she'd feared he would, 'What do you think of it?'

She debated with herself. It's no good, she thought, even if I do say what I ought to, he'll know it isn't the truth.

She turned to him, looking him straight in the eye, and said, 'I think it's atrocious.'

His laughter echoed round the gallery, and a small

party of visitors at the far end stared at him. She wished he wouldn't draw attention to them, but then she thought, what the hell?

'Sorry,' she said. 'I should have been polite and said, it's lovely. But it isn't. Is it? It's ugly, and it's frightening.'

'I agree. It is not a lovely thing at all.' He said under his breath, 'Atrocious.' Then he reached out his hand and gently squeezed her arm.

She'd turned back for another look at the Gorgon. At his touch, which made her jump, her eyes flew back to his.

'What?'

He squeezed her again. 'I am just making sure. But it is all right, you are still stubbornly flesh and blood.' He waited, smiling. She shook her head.

'Sorry,' she said again. 'I don't know what you're talking about.' He looked disbelieving. 'I don't!'

'The Gorgon turns people to stone,' he explained patiently. 'When Perseus slew her, Athene lent him a highly-polished shield so that he only had to look at the Gorgon's reflection. She was a fearsome creature, and Perseus was wise to take care. But, since you are still you, we must conclude that her power has waned, after two and a half millenia.'

He let go of her arm and walked away. He looked at her over his shoulder. 'Come!' She followed him. She could hear him talking to himself.

He stopped in front of a life-sized statue of a woman. She was made of marble, but so realistic that Fay could almost see the rise and fall of the chest as she breathed.

'Oh, yes!' She turned to him. 'That's better! Now *she's* lovely!'

'She is indeed. She is Aphrodite.'

'That little head I was looking at—that was Aphrodite, too.'

'Yes. There was a cult of the goddess, here.'

He fell silent. The words she'd been about to speak died in her throat, as if he were commanding her, too, to silence. She felt him move closer. Felt the warmth of his body as he stood right at her side.

She became aware that there was no noise at all. The gallery was empty: the two of them, and Aphrodite, were quite alone.

He put his hand up to the statue's face, his long fingers touching Aphrodite's chin in exactly the same place as, the previous night, he had touched hers.

She watched, transfixed. And on her jaw, the skin awoke as if he were touching her again.

His hand moved to the marble neck, smoothing, the fingertips going up into the hollow behind her ear. Fay felt a shiver of pleasure down her spine. His hand moved to the dip above the statue's delicate collarbone, and he traced its outlines with his thumb. He said, so softly that she barely heard, 'See. See how beautiful she is.'

She could not reply.

Her blood was racing, nerves alight as if it were she and not the cold dead marble who was the object of his admiration. Eyes on his hand, quite powerless to look away, she watched as his fingers moved down across the white chest.

Her breath seemed to stop in her throat, for she knew what he was going to do next. Was answering deep within her body, responding, even as he did it.

His hand moved slowly into a cupping shape and enclosed the statue's breast. His fingers played with the small, sweet nipple, then, as if he could no longer contain his power, pressed hard against the stone flesh so that she almost believed she saw it yield. She, too, was being squeezed; from her sensitive, vulnerable neck right down to her trembling thighs, she felt as if a mighty hand were closing around her, tightening on her, and was not going to stop.

124

She wanted to run away. Escape. But yet she stood still. And, his hand moving from the marble breast downwards across the curving stomach, he turned to look at her.

The dark eyes stared into hers. Into her mind. Her soul.

And silently she pleaded, Too much! *Please!*

His hand fell from the statue. Like a tap being turned off, the wild, tremulous, thrilling flow of feelings through her subjugate body ceased.

And the moment was gone.

She tore her eyes from his. Out of his gaze, out of his power. Running, half-stumbling, she made for the stairs. Out through the entrance hall, to collapse on a stone bench in the shade of the museum's tall smooth walls.

Where, in due course, he found her.

She closed her eyes. Felt him sit down by her side.

'Do you know why I took you there?'

Flustered, she said quickly, 'The Pediment, I suppose. It's on lots of postcards, isn't it? It must be famous.'

He sighed. 'Don't fight me,' he said softly. 'Let me come through.'

What does he mean? I'm not fighting, why does he say I am?

Even as the thought raced through her head, she realised. She'd filled her mind with trivia. Facile answers, to occupy herself. To keep him out?

Yes.

Gathering her courage, she cleared her mind. Sat, relaxing, and thought of nothing at all.

And his voice said, I brought you to show you Aphrodite. She is here, she is also on my wall in The Twins' House. Where I think you saw her, and were disturbed.

'Yes,' she said aloud.

Do not fear her. Accept her. She is woman. Her shape, her nature. Her sexuality. Accept her.

Sexuality! She gasped, simultaneously dragging out from the corners of her mind a protective screen of distractions. Don't think about that! It's wrong. Pagan. *Sinful!* Think about something else. The trees, the sun, the great blue sky . . .

He said, 'Enough.'

And stood up. Took his keys out of his pocket, and led the way back across the road to the car.

*

Fay was looking for Barry. He wasn't in the big common room downstairs, where the music was. She'd looked into several of the rooms in the block— the ones whose doors stood open—and he wasn't in any of those either. She didn't want to look behind any of the closed doors. Not that he'd be likely to be there—at this sort of party, doors were only shut if the occupant was away or if a couple had crept in for some private lovemaking.

And Barry, she was learning, didn't put that very high on his list. Not even with her, never mind some strange woman he'd just picked up.

She went upstairs, pushing through a solid press of people, aiming for the second-floor kitchen where the drink was. Barry was far more likely to be there than anywhere else.

It was nearly the end of the summer term, and the windows of the common room were wide open so that the music belted out, reverberated off the other residential blocks, and came in again through the windows on the upper floors. Wherever you went, you couldn't escape it. Someone had done a party special, fifty or sixty tracks on each side of a reel-to-reel tape, and the music was, literally, non-stop.

The someone liked it loud and fast, she thought. 'I Heard it Through the Grapevine'. 'Pinball Wizard'. 'Get Back'. A Led Zeppelin track. Floor thumping stuff. 'Excuse me,' she said to a threesome on the stairs, the two men's heads resting on the outstretched girl's stomach. None of them opened their eyes, so she stepped over them, treading on someone's arm. She thought they might be stoned.

She made it to the kitchen. The door was closed, and she had to lean against it to open it.

'Close the door!' several people said at once. One voice added, 'We're trying to keep the noise out—this is a talking area!'

She did so, and the man who had presumably been leaning against the door prior to her entrance took up his position again. The window was closed, too—they were serious about keeping the music out—which she thought was a pity as the kitchen stank of booze. Wine bottles, most of them empty, stood thick on the draining board, and four-pint cans of beer were piled up on the floor. In front of the cooker, their legs and feet getting in everyone's way, sat a couple, one hand of each around a bottle of whisky. The girl's face was pale, and her eyes were almost closed. The boy was at the noisy stage of inebriation—Fay recognised it, recognised all the stages, now—and his voice, loud, argumentative, challenged anything anyone said.

'Hi, Fay me love.'

Barry's voice came from behind her. She spun round, to see him sitting on top of a worktop. He had a glass in his hand, a third full of beer. It was a half-pint glass.

Her heart filled with love. He meant it, she thought, wildly happy. He *meant* it! She grasped the hand he held out for her and clambered up to sit beside him. He put his arm round her, snuggling up to her, and offered her some of his beer. 'Share it with me,' he whispered, just for her ear. 'Then I'll drink even less.'

Loving him, already filling with desire for him, she did as he said.

'God is dead!' the boy on the floor shouted, apparently continuing the discussion her arrival had interrupted. 'Haven't you read Nietzsche?'

'Not all of him,' someone said.

'This is serious!' The boy lifted his face, desperately earnest, to the speaker. 'We live in a new world, we've pushed the frontiers of science back so far that there's no room for heaven any more! Men have been to the moon, telescopes can make out the edges of the universe, so where the fuck's heaven? Tell me that!' He sat back, smiling grimly, and pulled the whisky bottle from his girlfriend's hand to put it to his mouth. She emitted a groan.

'You surely don't expect that we should see heaven at the other end of a telescope!' a serious-faced girl said scathingly. 'How feeble-minded can you get!'

'Why not?'

'Harps, and angels? Nice pink clouds? Albert Schweitzer and Francis of Assisi having a chat?'

'Well, if no-one can see it, it doesn't exist,' the boy insisted. 'Haven't any of you lot ever heard of the empirical method?'

'So how are you going to prove God's existence in the laboratory?' the man leaning on the door broke in. 'Ask him if he'd kindly co-operate in a little experiment? How's omnipresence going these days, God? Getting a bit of a tall order, is it, now that your children have populated every bloody corner of the globe and there aren't any more empty bits where you don't have to go?'

'Over-populated, you mean,' someone said. 'And that's another thing—why doesn't the Pope give the Third World the go-ahead to use contraception?

I was reading something the other day, God it was awful, about this woman who lived on a rubbish-dump outside Rio and she had to make herself throw up to see if there was anything in it she could . . .'

Right on cue—or maybe, Fay thought, because of auto-suggestion—the pale-faced girl vomited. Over herself, her boyfriend, and the best part of the floor. The smell of half-digested whisky mixed with the sharp-sour smell of sick, and people looked down at their shoes, making various noises of disgust. Fay was thankful she and Barry were sitting up high.

The room cleared in seconds. The girl, crying now as well as moaning, was clinging to her boyfriend, who looked as pale as she did.

'Let's go,' Fay heard Barry whisper. 'Quick, before they realise we're still here and we get roped in to helping.'

'I don't imagine they were going to clear it up,' she said when they were safely outside and making their way downstairs.

He turned, taking hold of her hand, and she saw he was laughing. 'I wasn't thinking that,' he said. 'I meant, roped in to carrying them home.'

As they passed the common room, the music changed. The slow lead-in to 'Something in the Air', introducing a new mood, had people moving into each other's arms as if it were the last chance they were ever going to get. Without breaking step, Barry changed direction and led her inside. Put his arms tightly round her waist, dropped his face into her neck and sang softly along.

Leaning against him, moving with him, she was totally happy. His hands dropping to her bottom, she wasn't aware that he'd somehow managed to hitch up her skirt. Until she heard the remark.

'Barry likes them statuesque, with plenty of bum.

129

Reminds him of pushing up against the back of the scrum!'

She didn't know who'd said it. She didn't want to know—she wanted just to get out. Pulling at Barry's arm, she said, 'Come *on!*' with such urgency that he went with her.

She cried, as they hastened back to her room. And wasn't even consoled by Barry, who, after a couple of fairly unenthusiastic attempts to talk her out of whatever was upsetting her and come and give him a kiss, turned over and went to sleep.

Leaving her, wide awake, all the more convinced of her worthlessness.

ELEVEN

The Sleeper Awakes

Fay had known all along that Barry, reading German and philosophy, would have to spend a year in Germany. Her Finals year wouldn't be the year he took his degree: that would come the following year.

She found she could look quite dispassionately on the prospect of a year without him. Sometimes, indeed, she quite looked forward to it. Meeting him so early on in her university career—the first term, for goodness' sake!—had, she felt, cramped her style a bit. Once in a while, during one of their periodic break-ups, she got a taste of what life on campus would be like without him. While the possibilities always seemed at the outset to be endless, too soon she'd come down to earth. Realise that there weren't going to be crowds of men queuing up to go out with her. Either because most people looked on her as belonging to Barry, or—and she thought this was more likely—because they didn't fancy her. He was right, my Barry, that first night, she thought. Quite right, to say I was different from the sort of girl who is currently all the rage. He might like me the way I am, but his is a lone voice crying in the wilderness.

The break-ups never lasted long. She got lonely, and Barry found out that life without her was even less secure than life with her. Always the reconciliations were sweet. Always he'd promise: 'I'll try harder to be what you want. I love you so much, Fay, I can't live without you.'

You're going to have to, my love, she thought as the summer vacation passed and the time approached, faster and faster, for his departure to Berlin. They'd spent most of the holiday together, staying with Barry's aunt in Liverpool and both of them working in a biscuit factory to earn some extra cash. Fay only went home to Sidcup for one week. It was sufficient— for one thing she refused to take Barry with her and a week was long enough to be apart; for another, she had so little in common now with her family that they might have been beings from Mars.

'Who's this Barry?' her mother asked. She'd answered the phone to him.

'A friend.'

'Boyfriend, more like!'

'*Of course* he's a boyfriend,' Fay said wearily. She faced her mother, outstaring her. 'What did you expect?'

And, leaving the room, closing the door quietly behind her, refused to discuss him any more.

Her sister, at nineteen, was engaged to be married. In something of a hurry, before the bump should show beneath her white wedding gown. Fay felt a stab of sympathy for her parents.

'Why won't you take me to meet them? Barry asked when they were together again and he'd bought her two gin and tonics in an attempt to take the look of depressed hopelessness off her face.

'I don't know.' She didn't—it was instinctive, this resolve to keep them apart. But she suspected it had something to do with not letting her family put their disapproving death-kiss on him. On her love for him.

He didn't press her. Instead, put his arm round her,

anxious that she should cheer up, be his strong Fay again. For his sake she tried, and found, soon, that she'd convinced herself as well as him.

They went to Ireland for the last week before he went away. They stayed with his brother Liam, taller, stronger, a lot older than Barry, clearly devoted to his younger brother and intensely proud of his intelligence. 'My brother at the University,' he'd manage to drop into every conversation. 'Philosopher, he is. And linguist—he's going to Berlin for a year.'

She went to watch them at a pre-season training session, and, on the Saturday afternoon, saw them play in a friendly against another Dublin club fifteen. Big Liam played at No. 8, and when an opposing flanker did a high tackle on Barry, had to be dragged away from the offender by three of his own pack.

'I'll miss him,' he said to Fay in the bar afterwards while Barry was in the lavatory. 'God, girl, I'll miss him as much as you will!' Fay thought he'd probably miss him more. Or the *thought* of him, at least, for surely the brothers didn't see all that much of each other anyway. 'You'll come and see me, while he's off in Germany?' He looked intently at her, his face handsome like Barry's—they were quite obviously brothers—yet somehow coarser.

'I will, Liam.' She wasn't at all sure that she would. But it seemed simpler to agree, and with any luck he wouldn't remember the conversation afterwards.

She began her final year fitter—and slimmer—than she'd ever been. Working in a biscuit factory had had the unexpected bonus of taking away her sweet tooth: it must, she worked out, have been something to do with the constant sickly smell. Or repletion—the management, wisely, allowed employees to help themselves, knowing quite well the greedy-guts hands would falter and fall before a week was out.

Settling back into her little room, she re-arranged the furniture. Rolled up the old patchwork blanket and hid it away for the really cold weather. Put a new poster on the wall. Made it *my* room, not *ours*.

She missed him fiercely. She wrote him long letters, and was overjoyed when he replied in kind. Not having the happy distraction of his company, she worked harder than she'd done to date. She found a joy in it, a satisfaction she didn't know could be derived from something as groan-making as having to write a dissertation on 'Symbolism in the Modern Novel'.

She took to working after dark. Her days contained fewer lectures now, and she was able to arrange a sort of night-shift for half the week, settling down at her desk after a quick session in the bar and working right through the peaceful silent hours, sometimes till dawn. Then she'd have an early breakfast and go to bed. The cleaners, bursting in with fresh linen and finding her sound asleep at ten-thirty in the morning, would sniff loudly and disapprovingly. Fay took one of them aside to explain, but it didn't seem to do any good: in a cleaner's book, anyone still in bed in the middle of the morning was a layabout drug-crazed hippy.

Shades of Dad, Fay thought. And, reminded of home, was prompted to go out and buy her sister a wedding present, which with any luck would arrive before the day.

One Saturday night she went with some friends to see a jazz band play in the Union. She caught the eye of the trumpeter, a ginger-haired man with a broad Lancashire accent who made extremely rude asides between numbers. Hearing her laughing at a subtle remark which no-one else apparently had picked up, he winked at her and said, 'Glad someone's awake down there.'

When the band were having a break, he came up to her in the bar.

'I'll buy you a drink, bright-eyes,' he said.

'No, I'll buy you one.' She was confident in bars. Knew how to behave. 'To thank you for giving me the best laugh I've had in ages.'

'Good lass. I'll have a pint. I'm as dry as a nun's . . .'

He didn't go on. Imagination soaring, she wondered what highly appropriate noun would have completed the simile.

'Cheers,' she said, handing him his pint.

'Cheers.' He tipped his head back and downed it in one. Good God, she thought, even Barry couldn't do it as fast as that. But then Barry didn't play the trumpet.

From the ballroom 'Maggie May' ripped out—someone was playing records during the break.

'Come and have a dance,' said the trumpeter.

'Haven't you had enough of the ballroom?'

'No.' He grabbed her hand. Turned round to her, and winked again. 'I can never have enough.'

'Maggie May' gave way to an ear-bashing of Stones, and he danced her ragged. She loved it. Then, as if calming things down before the band's second set, the disc jockey played, 'You've Got a Friend'.

And the trumpeter said in her ear, 'I'm Steph. You're not dashing off afterwards, are you?'

She'd been going to. She'd told herself she was going to have an all-night session writing up her psychology experiment on creativity.

'No,' she said.

'We'll be going to eat, when we're finished. Come with us?'

'Okay.'

He ruffled her hair. 'What's your name?'

'Fay.'

'See you later, Fay.'

Steph slid into the vacant place in her life which she hadn't even been aware existed. When she thought

135

about it afterwards, it struck her as significant, somehow, that in the absence of Barry, in many ways more like a husband than a university boyfriend, she should now have Steph, a good fifteen years older than herself and even less like the sort of man everyone else had.

He wasn't there all the time, which seemed to be a good thing. Her new-found love of her work grew, and she felt that, were Steph always about, she'd have had to tell him firmly that she had to be alone sometimes. She was glad she didn't have to do that. He and his band played all over the North-West and the Midlands, and whenever they went up or down the M6, he'd give her a call or drop her a card to announce his impending arrival. Sometimes he'd just turn up, and she'd lift her head from her books at three in the morning to see him standing in the doorway.

She wondered what the other members of the band did while he was with her. Did they sleep in the van? Visit girlfriends? Did they *have* girlfriends here? Perhaps musicians were like sailors. A girl at every gig.

Sometimes he turned up when she wasn't on the night shift. Diplomatically, he wouldn't wake her, but instead would leave her a note to say he'd called by. Once, she'd opened her eyes in the morning to find him fast asleep in her armchair.

When he was broke and hungry, he shared with him whatever she had in her cupboard—bread and cheese, tins of soup, pork pies. When he was in funds, he'd roll up in a borrowed car, dressed in a suit, and take her out to dinner. She felt she was getting the better of the bargain.

He had friends all over the place. He took her to meet a sharp-faced, kind-hearted woman who ran a riding stables and who gave them free rides, taking the horses over to the farrier. Once she shouted at them, as they galloped off down a moorland track, 'Slow to a walk if you pass a pedestrian!' Fay—laughing, screaming—raced after Steph, copying his breakneck speed whether she liked it or not, and knowing full well she couldn't stop till he did even if a whole phalanx of pedestrians appeared in their path.

On the way home they stopped at a café for bacon and cheese on toast. And, on the bus back, sang together: 'You're not Sick, You're Just in Love', Steph being Ethel Merman and herself Donald O'Connor.

I'm not in love, she thought. Not with Steph. I'm in love with Barry, and it hurts, sometimes. Being with Steph is pure fun, and doesn't hurt at all.

She told Steph all about Barry. But she didn't tell Barry about Steph.

Christmas came and went, and, apart from four days at home for the feast itself, Fay stayed at university, taking advantage of the option offered to final year students to rent their rooms over the vacation at a reduced rate. Barry, without funds, couldn't afford to come home, and she certainly wasn't going to go out to Berlin. She imagined he'd drunk his way through his grant. Germans drank a lot of beer, didn't they? Barry should be right at home.

But then a present arrived for her. A gold chain, and on it a little figure dressed like a monk, in a hooded robe. He said in the accompanying card that he'd bought it for her when he went to Munich (for the Beer Festival?) and had saved it to give her for Christmas.

Feeling repentant—at least some of his grant hadn't gone on beer—she bought him a Marks and Spencer pullover and sent with it a longer-than-usual letter.

And then it was January, and the start of her penultimate term. She worked harder, caught up in the accelerating pace as the days till finals ticked steadily away. She embarked on her major English project, a discussion of the forces in man which make him terrified of himself. She terrified herself, too, in the dark hours, as she delved into the depths of other people's imaginations.

Steph kept her on a level. Almost, anyway. He noticed when she was getting fraught, and would think of something divertingly silly to do. He took her to the annual dinner of the university's Welsh Society—heaven knew how he'd got tickets, being neither at the university nor a Welshman—and provided her with one of the cheeriest evenings she'd ever spent. Three choirs came up from the Valleys, decked out in dinner jackets, and ate and drank as if they never saw food and booze in South Wales. Then, at the signal, they metamorphosed into sober-faced upright citizens and poured their hearts and their souls into their nation's great heritage of song.

Standing with Steph, tears rolling down her face, she felt him put his arm round her and give her his handkerchief. Then, as the echoes of the music and the applause died down, the leader of one of the choirs stood forward.

'Now we'd like to move across the sea to Ireland,' he announced. 'We're going to sing, "Danny Boy".'

Piercingly, she thought of Barry. In her emotional state, it was too much. But, saving her, unwittingly doing exactly the right thing, beside her Steph said in a voice of quiet disgust, 'Oh, Christ!'

It was a spring of dissatisfaction in the country. Head down, she didn't take much notice, except to moan about the power-cuts which made a bleak March on the windswept campus even bleaker. Steph lent her his army greatcoat, and with that on top of her grandmother's blanket, she slept warmly, even if she did wake up stiff from the weight of bedding.

Barry asked her to go out to see him at Easter. He sent her a cheque, to help towards the fare. She debated. Decided to go, then, cowardly, backed off. Only to have him phone her, down a crackly line with music playing in the background. 'American Pie'.

'Why won't you come, Fay?'

She didn't know. Felt only that she'd be lost, if she did.

'It'd be such a distraction,' she said feebly. 'The work's going so well, and I've only got a bit more to do. I . . .'

'I shouldn't have asked you,' he said quietly. 'Fay, me love, I'm sorry. I just wanted to see you. I wasn't thinking.'

If he'd argued, tried to persuade her, she didn't think she'd ever have forgiven him. But to have him change sides, *apologise*, even, for what had been really a very nice suggestion, that was something else.

She almost changed her mind. Thought of the cheque. Of him saving his money to send it to her. Being responsible.

'I miss you, Barry,' she said.

'Oh, Fay, I miss you, too.'

Finals came. Ten three-hour papers in a fortnight, and she'd never been so exhausted in her life. Steph waited for her outside the examination hall on the Saturday lunchtime after her very last paper and, in the company of a dozen other finalists, took her off to the pub, where for the only time ever she got uproariously, gloriously smashed. She vaguely remembered him taking her back to her room and going to sleep on her floor while, up on her bed, she tried to close her eyes without the room reeling.

When she woke up, sick, head thumping, he gave her a Prairie Oyster, considerately not telling her what was in it till she'd drunk it.

Results Day approached. Steph held her hand while she looked down the list and saw she'd got a IIii—'A

People's Degree,' someone beside her said—and they went into town for lunch.

'I'm going to Spain,' he said over coffee and brandy.

She looked at him. Smiled, for she'd known he'd be off. Knew he'd have gone already, except that he was fond of her and wanted to stay till she didn't need him any more. 'You'll have a great time,' she said.

'It'd be great if you were coming too,' he said abruptly.

It would, for a while, she thought. Not for ever. Not even for long. But she was grateful to him for expressing the sentiment.

He took her back to her room, and kissed her goodbye. He left her his greatcoat, and she knew he didn't have another possession, other than his trumpet, whose donation would be more meaningful.

'I'll take care of it, Steph,' she said.

And, winking, managing a smile, he said, 'I know you will.'

The Graduation Ceremony. Her parents weren't coming—her father said he couldn't afford the fare from Sidcup, let alone the night's accommodation on campus.

She didn't mind. Lots of graduates would be receiving their degrees with no-one of their own in the audience to applaud especially loudly.

The moment came. She walked smoothly in her stately black gown and mortar board on to the platform. Pot plants, huge and green; bespectacled faces of university top brass; the Chancellor, a small woman with bright blue eyes. Fay dropped a curtsey, and the rolled-up degree certificate, prize for four years' work, four years of her life, was put into her hand.

She turned, walked back down the steps. Through the aisle between the two great ranks of parents and friends. Smiled, at some familiar faces.

She lifted her chin and, at the insistence of some impulse outside herself, looked down to the back of the vast hall.

She saw Barry. His face was beaming, his eyes were full of love and proud tears.

She walked faster. Ran towards him. Into his arms.

Pressed against him, hearts racing together, she knew she wouldn't, couldn't, let him go.

And that she was lost.

TWELVE

The Horns of the Bull

She was aware of feeling happier with herself. More confident. Walking through the hectic streets with the boys, she was aware that people—well, all right, she amended, *men*—looked at her with appreciation. It's because they're Greeks, of course, she thought. They like the fair-skinned types. And they seem to admire the height and the breadth of northern European women—maybe it's the contrast we offer to their own girls.

Or perhaps—probably—it's because Englishwomen on holiday in the sun have an appalling track record of promiscuity, and most Greek men are looking for an easy lay.

She wondered, catching the eye and the smile of a tall light-eyed man who couldn't possibly have been born anywhere south of Calais, why she should have limited the accusation to Greek men.

She lay in the sun at the lido, her mind fizzy with thoughts, unable to concentrate on her book. Over half way through our month. The boys are loving it, I was right to bring us out here. *And* for so long. It was worth the effort, worth three months' data-processing and subjecting myself to an office routine five days a week. Three months' slog, one month's holiday. Not bad!

She deflected her thoughts from home. September would come soon enough, and she'd cope with it when it did. She had learned, over the years, to live for the moment. Not to let the depressing thought of what she had to do next week, tomorrow, in an hour's time, even, spoil the happiness of *right now*. Since Barry—during Barry—happy right nows had been few and far between, and she'd discovered that by concentrating on them extremely hard, really appreciating them while they were happening, she could make a perfect mental record of them. And, later, get them out of the box of her memories like precious gems and enjoy them all over again.

This, now, this is perfect ecstacy. I'm comfortable—as comfortable as anyone is, lying on a wooden bench—I'm well-fed, I have a cold bottle of lemonade by my side for when I get thirsty. I've been for a swim, and all my muscles feel smooth and in good shape. I had a shower, and my skin feels clean and fresh. The sun is caressing my body like a warm and loving hand. My children, through my own efforts, are in seventh heaven. And so am I.

One by one she concentrated on the input of her senses. When the picture was complete, she imagined she was pressing the 'enter' button on a word processor. Saving the memory for ever.

She was drowsy. She'd started waking early—four, five—unable to get back to sleep. Hadn't minded, because her thoughts were full of exciting possibilities. And those precious hours when the rest of the world was still asleep were perfect for contemplation.

Why do I feel so good? she wondered. The place, the relaxed holiday atmosphere, my physical well-being? The twins, bless them, looking after the boys so well for me and giving them such a great time! Never mind giving *me* a great time. She saw again the twins' approving smiles. Recalled the feel of their strong, smooth-skinned hands as they held hers. Remembered the girl in the resort. 'She can't have two of them!'

Crashing into her mind came Aaron.

No! Don't think about Aaron! I'm so happy, I don't want to think about him! About how my heart beats faster when I see him, about this strange feeling that I've known him before, about how kind he is, how he has an ability to get through to me down subtle pathways which I thought I'd blocked off for ever more.

Don't think about Aaron!

She sat up, flinging her feet to the ground, scrabbling in her bag to find her watch. With any luck it'd be nearly lunch time, and she could busy herself with rounding-up the boys and embarking with them on the pleasurable, lengthy process of deciding what to have to eat.

Later, when she had read all she wanted and was beginning to think about going back to The Twins' House for a cup of tea, the boys came to ask if they could stay out a bit longer today.

'Why?'

'There's a cricket match on the Esplanade,' Oliver said. 'The twins and everyone's going.'

'You can't play cricket.'

'I can!' Rupert said. 'But we're not playing, we're watching. If you don't mind.'

'Don't you want to come home and shower?' Of course they don't, she thought. Aren't I stupid?

'We'll shower later,' Oliver said.

'All right.' She could have a slow meander on the way home. Needn't hurry, for once. Could stand looking in jewellers' shop windows and drooling as long as she liked. 'When will you be back?'

'Don't know.' The boys, she'd noticed, had picked

up the Corfiot attitude to time—an interesting phenomenon but one quite irrelevant to everyday life—as if they'd been born to it. 'Why don't you come and join us down there?' Rupert suggested.

And, willingly, she agreed.

The town was pleasantly full of people, but it was too early in the evening for it to be really crowded. She sauntered along with everyone else, enjoying the slap of hundreds of sandalled feet on the smooth stones of the streets. Nobody was in a rush, people had the time and the inclination to stop for a chat. To exchange a friendly smile. From somewhere above, sounds of music floated out on to the still air—the town band, its members practising for the next concert. The discordant brass notes sounded awful, but then perhaps this was an early rehearsal of a new work.

She lingered in front of several jewellers' windows. The gold work was lovely. She was tempted, but it seemed wiser to wait for the end of the holiday and see how much money she had left. I won't have much, she thought. There's something about being on the go all day long, it's giving the boys monumental appetites.

Turning from the last shop, about to go home, she found the Bull man standing right in her path.

'Good afternoon,' he said formally. 'You are alone?'

'Yes.'

'You buy gold?'

'I'd like to,' she said, smiling. 'But I don't think I can afford it.'

'You have no money?'

'I've got *some* money,'—she wondered why she wasn't taking offence—'but other expenditure takes priority.' She thought she might have lost him, but he was nodding wisely.

'Children,' he said. 'You put the children first, né?'

How nice, that he should understand so instantly! 'Yes, that's right,' she said warmly. 'As do all parents. Don't we?' It wasn't much of a long shot—he must be a good fifty, so surely he'd be married and with a family. Most Greek men seemed to be. Perhaps he'd launch into a recital of his own sons and daughters. And his grandchildren. With photographs.

But he just said noncommitally, 'Indeed.'

She started to walk off in the direction of The Twins' House, and he fell into step beside her. For some time he didn't speak, but then he said,

'You like Twins' House?'

'Yes, thank you, we're very comfortable.'

She was aware of his eyes on her. And, as they waited to cross over a road, of his fingers touching her wrist, as if to say, wait a minute. He's being kind, she thought. It's nice of him.

'You have a problem?'

She didn't know what he meant. It was what he'd said outside the airport, when he'd offered them the house.

At a loss, she asked, 'What do you mean?'

'You have a problem?' he repeated. 'In the house. You have—' he screwed up his face in his efforts to think, '—tap that drips? Light that has no light? Cooker won't work?'

She realised he was going through a sort of check list. Finding out, solicitously and somewhat laboriously, if she had any complaints.

'Oh, I see!' she said, smiling up at him. 'No. No problems at all.' She didn't think there was any point in mentioning the crack in the lavatory seat or the ill-fitting plug in the basin. 'Everything's fine.'

For some unfathomable reason, he looked disappointed.

They were coming into the square where The Twins' House was. It was very quiet; an old woman sat dozing in her doorway, and on the far side two little children played in the shade.

He walked up the steps with her. 'I check,' he said.

'Check?' She paused, key in the front door.

'Né.' He gave her a calculating look, as if assessing how she'd react. 'Before, last month, big problem. Cockroaches.' *Cockroaches!* He must have seen her shudder. 'I spray, I kill. And now, I check.'

'Yes, goodness, yes, please do!'

She had the door open, was hurrying into the house. Into the kitchen—wasn't that where cockroaches would go? Looking for food? Oh, what a good thing I've kept everything covered, she thought, and that we've tried to clear up the spills and the crumbs as they happen! He was right behind her, pushing past her into the kitchen, and she watched as he got rather breathlessly down on to his hands and knees and began opening cupboards.

'Are there—is it okay?' she asked apprehensively.

He didn't answer. He opened another cupboard, then slid the cooker out a few inches so he could look behind it.

'Is okay,' he said.

She was vastly relieved.

'Do they go anywhere else?' she asked. 'What about the bathroom?'

'I check.'

He rumbled out into the hall, and she heard his heavy tread on the stairs. He was puffing alarmingly, his ruddy face now scarlet and beaded with sweat.

Poor man, she thought, he's really concerned. Fancy having to poke about in cupboards and dash up stairs on a hot day like this!

'I'll be in the living room,' she called up to him. 'Come and have a drink, when you've finished checking.'

She heard his noise of assent.

147

She took a bowl of ice, a bottle of tonic and one of beer from the fridge and carried them through into the living room. The shutters were closed, and the dim light was welcomingly cool. She polished a couple of glasses and put them on the tray by the drinks. What would he like? she wondered.

He seemed to be taking a long time. She thought, he's found some! Oh, *no!*

She went out into the hall and shouted, 'Is everything all right?'

A door banged shut. She thought it might have been her bedroom door. She put her foot on the bottom stair, about to go up and see what he was doing, when to her relief he appeared on the landing.

He came heavily down the delicate curving staircase.

'All is okay,' he said. 'No cockroaches in bathroom, in children's room, in your room.' So you've had a good nose round, she thought. Then berated herself for being ungrateful.

'Thank you for taking so much trouble.' She turned, leading the way back into the living room. 'Now, what would you like? Beer? Lemonade? Gin and tonic? Whisky?'

She heard the door shut.

She felt him right behind her. His hands closed on her, one huge hot heavy palm either side of her waist, and he was pushing her forwards. Towards the sofa, over its solid stuffed arm, pressing her face down into the dry dusty cushions so that the breath she drew to cry out was stifled. He was panting, the air rasping in his throat as if there were some constriction. She tried to turn her face, to free her mouth, to look at him and shout out, but before she could think how best to escape him he had her wrists in the tight grip of one hand, and, bending her arms up behind her back, was holding her face-down with the same hand.

He felt as if he were made of bricks. As hard and as unmovable.

His legs pressed against the backs of her thighs. She crossed her ankles, feet straining tightly side to side, knees clenched so fiercely together that her muscles creaked.

With his free hand, he reached down and released her feet from each other as easily as if they were two tumbling puppies.

He forced his fist between her knees, and as her strength gave out, pushed himself into the gap. His thighs were iron. She felt them slide along the inside of her legs. Nearer. Nearer.

He grabbed her knickers in his fist and tore them off her. Then she heard the death-knell sound of his fly zip opening.

Felt his first desperate, inaccurate stab as he thrust himself against her.

She wanted to scream, but couldn't. Raised her eyes in an agony of supplication, to somebody, *anybody*.

She saw those two paintings. Horrible, she'd thought them. Worrying. Was this why they'd disturbed her, because by some strange precognition she'd foreseen this moment? Been aware that she'd be here, with this terrible man poised to enter her, and would look up at the paintings in her helplessness?

Aphrodite, please!

No. No good calling on her. She'd be egging him on.

He made another stab. Closer, this time, but not close enough. His muted bellow of frustration hit her like a blow. She could feel wetness leaking on to the inside of her thigh.

Ares! You could do for this bastard with one hand tied behind you! *PLEASE!*

He was pulling away slightly. Touching her, touching himself, providing guidance, this time.

She closed her eyes and waited.

A sound rang out through the hot breathless silence. Loud, deafeningly loud. Indefinable.

And he was off her. His hand let go of her wrists, the dreadful heat of his thighs and his loins was suddenly wrenched away, leaving her skin shivering and crawling with sweat.

Drawing in her legs, curling them up tightly underneath her, she raised her head.

Ares had stepped down from his painting. He was standing, huge and majestic, in the middle of the room. Arm extended, the splayed fingers of the hand pointed at the Bull in a gesture of dreadful power.

She looked over her shoulder at him. He was cringing, arms up to his face, trousers and pants falling round his knees so that she could see his genitals, shrunken and withered beneath the thicket of coarse red hair. Sick, she swallowed the water rushing into her mouth. The room swam before her.

Ares was moving in a slow semi-circle. Arm still held out, it seemed as if the Bull, following the progress of the great hand, was attached to the ends of the fingers by sharp-hooked wires. The red head drooped on the heavy shoulders, like a doomed beast who feels the whispering edge of the sacrificial axe slice into the first layer of skin and sinew. Cowering, apparently trying to push himself out bottom-first through the wall, he slithered round towards the door.

She could hear him whimpering, like a beaten bully.

Another sound. Distinguishable, this time, as a voice. Just.

She didn't understand what it said.

But the words were full of meaning for the Bull man. He gave a great gasp, then, as if anticipating some frightful agony, moaned in pain. She saw him clutch at his clothes, falling towards the door. Opening it, he

150

threw himself through. She heard racing footsteps, then the banging of the front door.

He was gone.

Slowly she rolled on to her side, clutching herself, arms wrapped tightly round her body as if she were giving herself the comfort of a hug.

She felt her skirt being pulled down around her. And Aaron's voice, gentle now, said, 'I will pour you a drink.'

He sat beside her for a long time. Not talking, not touching. Holding for her the glass of brandy which her own hand was too numb to grip.

She said, the words shuddering, 'He must have thought I was encouraging him. I smiled at him, because he was nice about the boys. Well, about children, in general. He seemed to understand.' She was aware she wasn't explaining very well. 'Then when he said he'd come and check for cockroaches, I offered him a drink. He'd got all hot and bothered, and I thought . . .'

Disgusted, she realised why he'd been panting. It had nothing to do with the heat or his exertions.

Aaron said, 'You have nothing for which to reproach yourself. You did no wrong.' He paused. Then added, the words sending a chill right through her, 'The offence was his. And he knows what retribution will be exacted.'

An image flew through her mind. Blood. Lots of blood. And that didn't seem right, either, that the Bull man should suffer so appallingly. 'I don't . . .'

'It is not for you to decide.'

She shrank from him. Instantly his hand was on hers. Warm, its touch tender. Do not think about it, his voice said in her head. The image faded, to be replaced by a scene of wavelets running up a smooth shore. And, distantly, she seemed to catch his thought. I must be more careful, with you!

151

The waves in her mind were soothing. Making her feel sleepy. He said, 'I think you should rest, now. I shall take you to bed.'

You're making a habit of taking me to bed, her dreamy mind reflected as he carried her upstairs. But why do you keep rushing off?

Amazed at herself, she tried to snatch back the thought before he should pick it up. His low, soft laughter indicated she was too late.

He didn't undress her, merely laid her down and spread the bedcover over her. Then he sat on the edge of the bed, his dark eyes on her face.

'I will find your boys,' he said. 'I shall bring them home, eventually. Tell them that you are sleeping, not to be disturbed. In the morning, everything will be fine. Nobody will ask you any questions you cannot answer.'

He put out his hand, fingers brushing across her forehead. It was a loving thing to do. She looked up at him, and saw that he was smiling faintly. Heart full, she wanted to thank him. To tell him all sorts of things that she couldn't even put into words.

'I know,' he said quietly. 'There is no need of speech, between you and I.'

He bent down and kissed her, his lips touching hers and resting there for some moments. Her body stirred as if she were preparing to welcome him in. And in her mind he said, yes. But not now.

He stood up. Walked across to the door. And, leaving it ajar, disappeared down the landing.

Sleep was invading her. But she fought it, for there was something she had to think about . . . What was it? . . . Aaron. To do with Aaron.

She smiled, for thinking about him filled her with gladness.

Then the thought stuck up its head, defiant. Look at me! it said. Not all perfect, is it? Listen to me!

Weak, unable to fight anyone or anything else, she had no choice.

And the thought expanded from a pinhead to a mushroom cloud that encompassed all her mind. I love him. I've fallen in love with Aaron, because he's nice to me. Treats me like a real person, one who needs consideration and kindness just like everyone else, who wants sometimes to be the weak one instead of always having to shoulder everyone else's burdens.

And because the touch of his fingers, of his lips, drives me wild with the promise of what is to come.

Desolate, for didn't the pain and the sorrow of love always outweigh the joy, she wept at her own folly.

Part Two

THIRTEEN

In the Shadows

With Barry's return, Fay's steadily-crystallising plan for what to do with the rest of her life went straight out of the window.

They hadn't been able to let go of each other, after their incredible and very public embrace at the back of the hall during the graduation ceremony. They'd slid into a pair of seats in the last row, whispering, hugging, trying to remember where they were and not allow the joy of reunion to spill out and ruin other people's concentration on their own supreme moments.

By the time they were back on campus, Fay was beginning to come down to earth. Not entirely, but a bit.

'I've got to return my gown and mortar board,' she said anxiously when they were back in her room. Barry had worn the mortar board all the way home on the bus—'I'm practising,' he said when she told him he wasn't entitled to wear it, yet. 'You wouldn't want me looking silly next year, now, would you?'

'Give it back, for heaven's sake, before you damage the bloody thing.' She stood on tiptoe and made a lunge in the direction of his head, knocking the mortar board to the floor.

As her body swayed against his, he put his arms around her. Pulled her to him. Looked down into her face with an expression that was suddenly serious, the fun and the laughter wiped away.

'Fay,' he whispered. 'Fay, it's been so long.'

She stared up into his eyes. In his tanned face, they were unbelievably blue. The whites were clear, and the flesh around them had lost its puffiness. His body in her arms felt strong, the muscles toned. She couldn't remember when she'd seen him look so good.

He bent to put his mouth to hers, an exploratory kiss, as if he were savouring the different stages all over again, familiarising himself, unhurriedly, with what it felt like. Then, as her own leaping desire made her clutch him to her, his tongue went deep into her mouth and she heard him give a sort of moan. His hands were on her breasts, fingers pulling at the row of buttons down the front of her crisp white blouse, dragging her bra straps down over her shoulders until, her chest bare, he could bury his face against her flesh.

He pushed her backwards on to the bed, reaching down to swing her legs up, parting them with his knees and lying down on top of her so that she could feel his hardness pressing against her. And he said, before the physical sensations took over and talking was no longer appropriate, 'I've never made love to a woman in a gown before.'

She'd had to sponge and press it, before racing across to the Registrar's building just in time to give it back. She was aware of her pink face and her still-pounding heart as she stood at the desk and waited to reclaim back her deposit. She felt faint: it surely wasn't good, she thought wildly, to make love with such fervour, come galloping to such a climax as that—the best, oh, the best ever!—then have to set about ironing a voluminous serge gown and returning it where it belonged before her breathing had even returned to normal.

Barry, oh, Barry. Not back five minutes, and already you're turning my world upside down.

'Name?'

'Morrison,' she said, jumping.

The woman seated at the desk seemed to Fay to look suspiciously at the gown. Don't be absurd, she told herself sternly. How could she possibly know?

She picked up the envelope containing her deposit cheque and hurried away.

'I don't want you to be down in London while I'm stuck up here,' Barry said over their second drink that evening.

'It's where I have to be,' she said quietly. And without much conviction.

'Don't you want to be with me?' His hand on her thigh squeezed. She felt a slight trembling begin, deep inside her. You're exploiting my weakness, you rotter, she thought. But she didn't think that with much conviction either.

'Yes, naturally.' Oh, I do! 'But I want to do this course, too.' One year, it was going to be. And at the end of it she'd have a diploma which, added to her psychology degree, would qualify her to start working as a therapist.

'You haven't got a place on it, yet,' he pointed out.

'But I'm almost certain to get one, they said anyone with a . . .'

'Do it next year, Fay.' His mouth was right up against her ear, warm breath on her neck transporting her straight back to earlier, in her room. 'We'll go to London together.'

'That's all very well, but...'

'I'm going to live off-campus, in October. Get a place with a couple of friends. Living in hall has lost its appeal, after Berlin. You could live there with me. We'd be together, always.'

She saw them. Waking together every morning, going their separate ways for the day's work, returning in the evening, full of love and eagerness, for the evening in each other's company.

And the night.

'I'd have to get a job.'

'You will! You can do anything, Fay!'

She smiled. His unshakable faith in her was one of the things that most touched her. A job. Something mundane, boring, when she could be embarking on her course. London tugged once more, hard, at her sleeve.

'Barry, I don't know. It seems such a pity, to throw away this chance.'

'You won't be throwing it away! If they're prepared to offer you a place this year, they're bound to hold it open for you next year!' She opened her mouth to ask how he could be so sure. But at the same instant he leapt in with his humane killer and administered the death blow.

'Besides, I need you.' His voice was low, urgent. The hand on her thigh moved to seek and clasp hers, tightly, like a child finding his mother in the alarming dark. 'It was all right, in Berlin. But here, where my bad habits are leaping out with open arms to greet me like long lost friends . . . Fay, I don't think I can stay on the straight and narrow, without you.'

What's a year? she asked herself as they moved into their new abode in the autumn. It was too run-down and shabby to be called a home, with nothing at all then, at the beginning, that was homely. One year. One *scholastic* year, which was only October to June. Not even a twelvemonth. Maybe it'll do me good to have a break from the academic life. I went straight from school to University, so it's been years since I wasn't preoccupied with learning, and books, and lectures, and exams. A year off will be nice!

Isn't this new, fit, *sober* Barry worth giving up a year for?

And besides, I love him.

Don't I?

Barry's friends Dave and Martin were sharing the house with them. They too were in their final year. Fay wondered how it'd be come the spring, living under the same roof with three finalists. Dave had a girlfriend called Sally who lived on campus, and quite often he stayed there with her. Martin was a bit of a loner, who tended to pick up wildly unsuitable women, fall heavily in love with them and then mope in his room playing miserable music when inevitably they ditched him.

Fay and Barry, as the house's most permanent couple, took up residence in the master bedroom. It had a double bed that sagged in the middle like the dip between two hills, until Barry hit on the idea of removing the shed door and putting it under the mattress to make up in firmness what the bed base lacked.

'Won't they mind?' she wondered. 'They' were the landlord and his wife, a singularly unpleasant couple devoid of charm and indefatigably nosey.

'They won't know,' Barry said confidently. 'We'll make sure they never go in the garden.'

It wasn't very likely, she had to agree. No-one, apparently, had gone in the garden since God was a lad, judging from the height of the nettles and the awesome amount of junk.

She resurrected her grandmother's patchwork blanket, and treated them to new sheets. And a mattress cover—she didn't think she could bear to look down on other people's stains every time she changed the bed. One Sunday she and Barry painted the walls and the ceiling white, immediately making the room look twice as big, and she bought lengths of bright material in the market to make cushion covers and new curtains. She had to skimp on the curtains, and they didn't quite meet in the middle. But they looked fine, drawn back. Barry went along with her orderliness, co-operating in keeping his things under control when she pointed out how little space they had, and how much more welcoming the room looked when it wasn't littered with books and discarded clothes.

The room was a haven. She could ignore the rest of the house, and its occupants, as long as she and Barry had their little room. It was just as well: as the only resident woman, she was firmly in the minority, and the male attitude seemed to be, leave things wherever they happen to fall out of your hand. Never wash up a cup. Hoover? What's a Hoover?

She was determined not to become, as the only person who *cared*, the one who kept it clean and tidy. So she spent more and more time upstairs, and in the rest of the house the sordidness increased as the weeks went by. Dave's mother had let him bring her car back to university with him for his final year, which turned out not to have been very generous of her as it didn't go, after the first month. Dave brought the engine into the house, working on it in the evenings when he wasn't studying or entertaining Sally, and even if Fay had wanted to Hoover the living room, she couldn't, since the floor was littered with bits of Fiat 500 innards.

Dashing out of the house early one morning, late for work because Barry had knocked the alarm clock on to the floor in the night and it hadn't gone off, she snagged her new tights on Sally's bicycle in the cold, dark, early-morning hall.

And, in that moment, hated the four people sound

asleep upstairs for being warm, comfortable and oblivious to her torn tights and her anger.

She had found an office job, with a firm that sold to garages the wherewithal to repair damaged cars. She got to know all about door sills and wing panels, and could have lectured on the subject of industrial paint, if anyone had been prepared to listen; the other people in the house tended to look down on her as a humble office worker, and when the conversation turned to intellectual matters, as so often it did, talked *round* her. Barry, lovely Barry, had reminded both Dave and Martin more than once. 'Fay's got a degree, you know! She's not stupid! She's as capable as you are of discussing a Marxist interpretation of the Chinese revolution!' But they kept forgetting.

The staff in the office didn't seem to know quite how to treat her. The sales reps chatted her up, and when she didn't respond—or responded with a remark which they thought was probably sarcastic, which was worse—left her alone. The boss sometimes kissed her hand when she'd typed his letters especially quickly, which she rather liked. The other girls—clerks, assistants in the shop downstairs and delivery van drivers—quite clearly thought her a snob. She would hear them mimicking her Southern speech, which sat ill on their basic broad Midlands. They have the cheek to imply *I've* got an accent! Fay thought indignantly.

But the pay was reasonable. And it was better than the biscuit factory.

Sometimes, coming in to find Barry still out, Dave fiddling with his engine and Martin shut in with his misery, she wished for a warm, welcoming hearth and a home full of love. Sometimes she wondered what Steph was doing, and fantasised about him drawing up outside No. 8, Furnace Street in a borrowed

Daimler and taking her out somewhere really nice for dinner.

Finals came. In the preceding weeks, Barry abandoned even the small amount of drinking he still did—to keep his hand in? Fay wondered—and devoted himself to his studies with a dedication she wholeheartedly admired. Hurrying home each evening, she'd race upstairs to join him, typing out notes for him on the ancient typewriter he'd liberated from the philosophy department, throwing herself into a discussion of whatever it was he needed to discuss. She was, she knew, more a sounding-board for his own soaring ideas than a contributer in any real sense to their development, but she didn't mind. He was *working*, really working, that was what mattered. And she was prepared to do all in her power to help him.

Dave moved in with Sally during the weeks of the exams, and Martin turned in on himself so that they hardly knew he was there. Fay saw Barry up, bathed, dressed and ready for the day each morning before she left for work. The way he'd look at her as she left— eyes glued to her till the very last moment, as if he were drawing his strength from the very sight of her— was almost more that she could bear. But she'd manage a cheerful comment: 'Knock 'em in the aisles,' or 'Break a leg.' And a smile, to which he'd respond with pathetic eagerness.

He worked steadily through his papers. She thought he seemed fairly confident, but she wasn't sure she could tell. Then it was all over, and in the huge relief it seemed quite natural that he'd find a release in drinking and pubbing. Hadn't she done that very thing herself, when it had been her turn?

On the day the results were posted, remembering Steph, she went with Barry to the Union Concourse and held his hand. Followed his shaking finger tracing

164

down the long list of names to LEARY, Barry Seamus, German and Philosophy.

He'd got himself a IIi.

Instantly, he turned to her. Stared down at her, the blue eyes fixed to hers dimmed with tears. He said, in a husky voice that broke on the words, 'That's you, my Fay. That's your IIi.' And, ignoring the crowds of anxious students trying to push him out of the way so they could see the lists, wrapped her in his arms like a drowning, desperate man holding a life jacket and kissed her till her lips bruised.

They had money saved. Quite a lot: she'd had to bite her tongue, sometimes, to stop herself pointing out how much richer you were when you didn't spend all your cash on drink which you then peed up the wall. Barry had fifty pounds left from a cheque Liam had sent him, and she had nearly two hundred in her account. But she didn't tell Barry.

They both had something lined up; she was going to embark at last on her course, and he had a job with the export department of one of the manufacturing giants. They would move to London and, with any luck, find somewhere suitable to live. They'd rent somewhere, Fay supposed. Nobody bought, just like that. You had to save first, to afford the down payment on the mortgage.

You had, usually, to be married. But she didn't let herself think about that.

She was all for going down to London straight away. Moving into a hostel or something, while they found a flat. And found their feet—neither of them had lived in London. Sidcup didn't count.

But, 'Let's have a holiday,' Barry said. 'Just for the crack, Fay me love—it's been a tough year on both of us, and don't we deserve a bit of fun before we settle down to being boring working people?'

She forebore to say that she'd been a boring working person all year.

'What sort of a holiday?' she asked cagily. You couldn't do much with two hundred and fifty pounds, even once you'd convinced yourself you were prepared to do *anything* with it other than leave it sensibly in the bank.

'Greece! Back-packing!' He had it all worked out. 'We'll get a flight to Athens, then we'll get on a boat to an island. Any island—first destination we see, that'll be for us!' It sounded marvellous. 'Sunshine, Fay, warm blue sea, retsina, ouzo, ancient temples, magical sites... can't you just see us?'

She could. All too clearly. The sordid house, the oily bits of Fiat engine, the squalor—the *smell*—of living with people who didn't wash, the boredom of a daily nine-to-five job that only used ten per cent of her intellect at most, rose up and clocked her on the head.

'We'll go,' she said firmly. 'Soon as we can.'

Barry looked at her, mouth open. She laughed—he'd obviously expected to have to use several big-gun persuasive arguments before she caved in.

'Right!' He had a great ability, she reflected, to recover fast. 'Tomorrow morning, we'll find us a bucket shop and a couple of the cheapest tickets anyone ever bought.'

FOURTEEN

Sacrifice to Poseidon

In the hot, still Corfu night, Fay dreamt of sacrifice.

She saw the great curve of a soaring pair of horns, silhouetted shadow-black against a hard blue sky. Saw a figure—sexless, ageless—hold aloft a broad, flat knife whose fine-honed edge caught the light and winked like a diamond. Heard voices, chanting hypnotically in unison.

There was movement, on the periphery of sight, and she was looking at the sea. It was heaving, the deep secret waters humping up as if there were some great disturbed creature beneath the surface. A bull, perhaps, a bull of the sea. As the catastrophic waves broke against the shore, their motion seemed to be continued on the land, which rippled and arched like an angry snake. There were cracking sounds, as the earth split into black trenches. Thumps like distant explosions as man-erected masonry fell in the face of nature's challenge. Screams, as puny men were crushed.

And the secret creature was coming up from the depths. Its horns spanned wider than the reach of a man's arms, and its head was fierce and frightening. Neck, shoulders, emerged from the sea, cloven hooves struck the stones of the shore, even as the hind quarters seemed still to meld with the water.

It flowed ashore.

Across its back, face-down, was draped the figure of a woman. Dead, or dying, it was hard to say. Victim, blood on the long white skirt of her robe. Blood soaked into the hair of the creature's underbelly. On its horns, scarlet dripping into the hot red eyes.

The scene changed. Now the bull was penned in a wide golden courtyard, and its bellows of fury held the first hint of fear. Men were running, confusing the great beast with nets and ropes until its roars split the air. The diamond-bright blade was held aloft in ceremonial gesture, the sun glinting sparks of fire from its cruel length. There was a whistle as it flashed downwards, then a fountain of scarlet blood arched up, spouting in five powerful but diminishing surges as the creature's huge heart beat its last.

At the last, the creature's head came into sharp focus. And it bore not the features of a bull, but of a thick-necked, red-faced man.

People scampered around the body, frantic to catch the blood, spreading it on the ground then returning to plunder the carcass, hacking, dismembering, disembowelling, castrating, desperate not to let an iota of the sacrifice go to waste.

The figure with the knife stood apart. In some way, it looked like Aaron. A different Aaron, his anger manifesting itself into the vision she was picking up.

Fay cried out.

Like heavy curtains drawn across a lighted window, the scene was hidden away, and she was excluded. On the outside. In her head she seemed to hear his voice: This is not for you.

Deep sleep was beckoning her. Come, rest, relax, and let your worries fade from your mind . . .

When the morning sun and the cooing pigeons woke her, the memory was so faint that she could scarcely catch it at all. And it was hard to distinguish what had really happened, last night, from what had been confined to the mystery of her dreams.

The boys, just as he had predicted, asked her no awkward questions. They seemed to think she'd felt unwell the previous evening, and this morning were solicitous. They tip-toed into her room, faces anxious.

'Are you awake, Mum?' Rupert whispered.

'Yes.'

'Are you feeling better?'

'I—yes, thanks. I'm fine. I was just rather tired.'

Oliver sat on the bed beside her, looking earnestly into her face. 'Aaron said we had to leave you alone,' he said. 'He brought us home, in his Range Rover. He made us a sandwich, 'cos I said I was hungry and I can't go to sleep if I'm hungry, and he said, you must go to sleep 'cos you mustn't disturb your mother.' His eyes were wide with amazement, and she wondered if his surprise was at a strange man coming in and making him a sandwich or at the even weirder phenomenon of someone proposing he should be considerate towards her.

He leaned towards her and gave her a loving kiss. 'I'm glad you're all right, Ma,' he whispered. 'I was worried about you.'

And she felt a heel for having misjudged him.

'Did he—what did he say when he left?' Even to herself, the question was absurd. 'I mean, did he say anything about plans for today?' Thank God they're still young, she thought. Young enough not to see through my words to what I'm really asking.

'He just said goodnight,' Rupert said.

'No, he didn't, he said good*bye*,' Oliver corrected.

Goodbye. How very final. But perhaps he didn't realise it was, and hadn't meant anything by it. On the other hand—

169

She made herself stop, before her unproductive, futile thoughts should drive her mad.

What was there to do but go on as usual? Send the boys out for bread, set out the breakfast, watch as they ate it and then clear away the mess. Fetch her bag from upstairs, trail after them to the lido. Take up her position on her bench, get out her book and her suntan oil.

Pretend that today was just like yesterday. Like any of the days, before she'd admitted to herself she was in love with him.

The boys and a gaggle of their local friends were involved in a noisy game in which they all in turn had to go right to the rear of the lido's sunbathing area, then run as hard and fast as they could, between the lounging people and out on to the old wooden pontoon, accelerating right up till the last moment when they flung themselves into the sea. It seemed compulsory also to shout as loudly as possible while running. Fay looked around at the group of Corfiot matrons who, as usual, sat in their enclave facing inwards and engaged in continuous conversation. They seemed to be able to ignore the racket their offspring were making; why couldn't she?

Perhaps I could, she thought, if I had someone to talk to. Some nice normal motherly type, who'd discuss with me the ups and downs of pre-adolescent boys till the cows come home. Fay smiled: the image was attractive. Then I could tell her about last night. About that awful man. And what happened afterwards.

About my dream.

NO!

She fought it. Tried to blot out the memory, which with equal determination was trying to get in. They killed him! Tied him down and cut his throat, to punish him. Watched the blood spurt from his severed artery till his heart gave up and stopped beating. 'He knows what retribution will be exacted,' Aaron said. And it was because of me! It was *my fault!*

'Guilty,' she whispered.

She knew all about guilt.

Deeply distressed, she could no longer bear to lie there with the excited sounds of the happy children all around her. Leaping up, she hurried down the steps and into the water, pushing herself on till it was deep enough to swim, breaking not into her sedate breast-stroke but into a fast efficient crawl which shot her rapidly through the warm sea. When her breath finally gave out and she lifted her head, she found she'd almost reached the little marina at the foot of the Citadel where the rich people moored their yachts.

She trod water, panting. Feeling slightly dizzy, it seemed for an instant that the sea was heaving, arching its back into an enormous wave . . .

Panicking, she lunged towards the shore. Here under the rocky Citadel mound, there was no welcoming beach but instead a harsh line made up of the remains of ancient fortification walls. Eyes searching for a haven, she failed to notice the wash from a distant passing boat until the first wave smacked her on the back of the head. It was followed by another. And another. And, her face under the water, she was taking the burning brine into her mouth, her nose, so that she coughed and choked and, eyes streaming, was unable to see.

Her foot struck against a rock. The sea's motion pulled her back and threw her forwards, and she hit her foot again in exactly the same spot. Crying in pain, she swallowed another mouthful of water. Black spots floated in front of her eyes.

Something nudged her in the small of her back. Something smooth. Into her confused mind flew images of dolphins. Rescuing drowning men, supporting them till they were safe on dry land. Turning, she saw—thought she saw—a friendly snout with a mouth that seemed to smile, and the sun flashed on an arched back that curved out of the water before plunging into the depths and out of sight.

A hand encircled her wrist, pulling her out of the sea as if she were a small child. Rubbing the water out of her eyes, she saw Aaron.

He'd obviously been swimming. He was wearing trunks, and the water was streaming off him. He studied her for a moment, then said gravely,

'It is customary to give thanks to Poseidon, for such a delivery from his domain. Are you able to walk?'

She put her weight tentatively on to the hurt foot. In response, the long cut opened and she watched her own blood seep out on to the rocks.

'No.' Looking down with her, he answered his own question. Then he picked her up in his arms.

'You'll never do it!' She was staring in alarm at the steep slope that reared up behind them. 'You'll . . .'

He laughed. 'I am not proposing to carry you up there.' He glanced down at her, his dark eyes full of amusement. 'I know my limitations. We shall go along to the Marina.'

She turned her head to see what he meant. There was a path, of sorts. Relieved, she relaxed against him. Then, anxious again, said, 'We can't go there! It's for yachting people, there's a sign that says it's private!'

'It's not private for yachting people,' he said calmly. And carried her straight past the 'Private' notice and along the quay to a sleek white-painted motor launch whose aggressive, sweeping bows suggested a fair turn of speed.

She said, 'Good Lord.' And then, as he negotiated the gangplank and set her down on the varnished wooden planking of the deck, 'Mind I don't bleed all over the floor.'

He had found a towel, which he put under her foot. He was frowning, and she thought in embarrassed distaste at herself, I'm being a damned nuisance. But he said, 'I believe there is a word other than "floor", when one speaks of a boat. But I am afraid I cannot think what it is.'

She wanted to laugh at the absurdity of it.

He sat her down while he looked at her foot. Then he fetched an impressive-looking first aid box and began tending to her.

'I do not think it must be stitched,' he remarked. 'The cut is not as deep as it looks, and already the flow of blood is lessening.' His hands around her foot were strong, and appeared very brown against the white skin of her instep. He pressed in with his fingers, and a mere trickle of blood seeped out.

She hardly noticed. His action had brought back a similar movement of his fingers that she'd seen before. On the marble breast of Aphrodite.

She felt horribly faint, and thought she might throw up. 'I'm so sorry,' she began. And couldn't continue.

He looked up from her foot. He put his hands on her shoulders and manoeuvred her till she lay down along the bench she'd been sitting on. The darkness raced through her head, and the black spots before her eyes joined up till there was no more light.

When she came to, she was still lying down. There was a pillow under her head, and, despite the sunshine, a thin blanket covering her. Her injured foot, bandaged, was propped up on another pillow.

He was standing over her. In each hand was a glass of dark-red wine.

'Will you drink?'

She shook her head. It didn't seem a very good idea.

'Then I shall offer a libation for you.'

Libation? Was that what he'd said? Still muzzy, she watched. He put one of the glasses down, then, holding the other in both hands, walked to the seaward side of the deck and slowly poured half the contents into the water. She saw that his lips were moving, but could not hear what he said. Then, staring out at the far horizon, he drank the rest of the wine in a single draught.

He came back to her, and crouched down on the deck beside her. The light caught on the heavy medallion round his neck, and, staring at it, she saw it was a ram's head. But, as compelling as if he'd physically put out his hand and lifted her head, came the message, look at me!

She raised her eyes to his face.

He said, 'It is well.'

What was? What did he mean? She didn't understand. There was so much that she didn't understand.

'Please,' she said. It was barely more than a whisper.

He leaned towards her, his hand touching her forehead, stroking the wet hair.

'Please, what?' he said softly.

'Tell me what I want to know.' It was a tall order, that he'd understand what that was when she scarcely did herself.

But he smiled. And said, 'To begin with, I must stop amusing myself at your expense—which is difficult, you must appreciate—and reveal to you that it was I who pushed you out of the water.'

'No dolphin?' She didn't know whether to be relieved or disappointed.

'No dolphin. No magical deliverer sent by Poseidon at the very moment you needed one.'

She thought, you're wrong. *You* came. You arrived, at the very moment I needed you.

And, nodding, he said, 'Yes. That is why we thanked the god.'

His voice was so matter-of-fact that he carried her along with him and she, too, found herself thinking it was nothing out of the ordinary.

But then her sense and her logic rose up. It *is* out of the ordinary! she protested silently. So is everything else! I'm not going to be seduced into thinking it isn't, even if he is charming and wonderful and I love him and I'm prepared to go along with anything he says because . . .

Her mind was pulsing, out of control. Eyes fixed on his, she saw him recoil slightly, as if she'd hit him. For a split-second she saw a considering expression cross his face. Perhaps, she thought, he's wondering how best to deal with me.

Then, apparently deciding, he put his arms round her and kissed her.

At the outset she was angry. Thinking, this is unfair, to use such a method to stop me! But anger could not last. Could not be sustained, when the effect of his warm, enclosing mouth on hers was arousing so strongly in her other, lovelier emotions.

His lips were firm, and he took control of her totally. She had no motivating force of her own, but merely followed where he led. Mouth opening to his, her tongue met his in a welcome, thrilling excitement unlike anything she'd ever felt before. Yet simultaneous with the wonder of novelty came the thought, I know him. We have kissed like this many times.

And, the unease and the mystery and the anxiety flooding back to disturb her, she broke away.

His face right above her, she could see deep into his eyes. Read in them things which, although she told herself it was her imagination, she felt instinctively were really there.

He moved away. Took his supporting arm from behind her head, laid her back on her cushions. And said, with a sigh, 'Very well. I did not want to speak of such things, when the day is so beautiful and you are here with me.' He stared at her, his expression suddenly severe. 'And when in any case it is none of your business.' He turned away, shaking his head. 'I do not know why you are picking it up.' He spoke almost to himself. 'You are not meant to.'

His eyes were on hers again, drawing her into him. Just to see if it would be possible, she tried to look away. Realised, with a tremor of fear, that she couldn't. She heard his voice loud in her head: This is not a game. This was what you wanted, this is what you shall have. And in the dark eyes the darker pupil dilated until the brown iris was nothing but a thin ring, and she seemed to be poised to plunge into his very being.

Right on the brink, she found she could hold back. And saw in him an instant's admiring recognition.

In her mind he said, as he had done before, It is well. Now I will tell you what you want to know.

How? she wondered. How can he distinguish the one pressing thing from all the rest?

She didn't know if he'd received the thought. Probably he had, and had ignored it. He said, I shall tell you about the Bull man.

FIFTEEN

Flight to the Sun

She was back in her dreams. The great beast captured, bound, severed flesh pouring blood on to the hot golden stones.

Her fault.

Her hands flew up to cover her face, palms pressing hard against her cheeks as if she could crush the images from her head. She waited, trembling, to receive what he should impart.

After a long moment's silence he said, 'He works for me. I have property, and he manages the letting of my houses to visitors.'

Her hands dropped into her lap. *What?*

She couldn't believe what she'd heard. But the echoes of his words were still ringing in her ears. He works for me. He manages the letting of my houses.

And with another shock she realised he'd spoken out loud.

Nothing mysterious about *this*.

She knew she ought to be making a response. 'I—er, I imagine that's why he was at the airport, then,' she said. 'He came up to me because he was looking for a tenant for The Twins' House.' She risked a look at him. But he was standing before her with his back to the sun and she couldn't see into his eyes. 'Your house.'

He made no response.

'It was pure chance that it happened to be me,' she whispered. 'Probably he saw that there was some difficulty—he might even have heard me talking to the taxi driver—so of course he'd come over and offer us the house.'

Her vague, unexpressed and thrilling thoughts that the Bull man had been sent specially to find her, to make absolutely sure that she and no other woman took up residence in The Twins' House—Aaron's house—suffered a brief death agony and expired.

She was just another tourist, and he was only after her money.

Hastily she turned away from him, kneeling up on the seat and leaning her elbows on the rail. Before he should pick up her hurt, she summoned anger.

'Well, your blasted manager almost raped me, last night!' she said vehemently. 'Remember? What have you got to say about that?'

She sensed him, close behind her.

'I remember.' His voice was neutral. 'I also remember that I came in time to stop him.'

Yes. You did. And you were so strong, so kind, looked after me so well, that I realised I was in love with you.

No! You mustn't think that, with him standing not three feet away!

She rallied her defences.

'That's not the point!' she shouted. 'What if you hadn't been there? What are you thinking of, employing a man like that who goes around raping people? Taking advantage of women alone, conning his way into their houses then attacking them? Good God, I've a good mind to report him to the police! That'd serve him right, *and* you!'

Now he was angry. She felt it blast against her like

a shock wave. And she wondered if she'd gone too far. *And* you!

Yes, she had. For what on earth had she to serve him right for? It was her fault she'd fallen for him. Not his.

'I'm sorry.' Her voice wasn't steady. 'I shouldn't have said that.'

She heard him sigh. Turning, she watched as he sat down beside her.

Unwillingly, she raised her eyes to his.

'The police would listen politely,' he said coldly, 'agree that, yes, it was indeed an appalling thing to happen, say that yes, they would make every effort to apprehend your rapist and punish him. And that would be the last you would hear, for the police would probably think, we have only her word. Perhaps she was leading him on—after all, she asked him into her house, offered him a drink. Perhaps she changed her mind at the last minute.'

'Now hold on! It wasn't like that, he...'

'And besides,' he went on, as if she hadn't spoken, 'even if the police scoured the island for him, they would not find him.'

His words sent an icy chill of horror through her. He's killed him! I was right all along! The blood, the knife, Aaron standing watching, it really happened!

In her head she thought she heard him laugh. And he said aloud,

'I have sent him away. He flew out this morning.'

'Where to?' It was totally irrelevant, but all she could think of.

'To Athens. I have an apartment, and a tenant who wishes that I do some redecoration.'

The thoughts and the words, the dreams and the reality, whirled in her head like manic dancers, pairing, separating, flying away with new partners. What was true? What was illusion?

She had no idea.

She sat back, letting the tension drain out of her. Then, taking a steadying breath, said,

'Well, all I can say is, I hope he doesn't try to rape her too.'

For a moment he didn't answer. Again, she wondered if she'd gone too far. I've relaxed too well, she thought, lost what small ability I had to pick up what he's feeling . . .

But it was all right. Because he'd started to laugh, and already she was joining in.

'He will not,' he said. 'The tenant is an elderly man. Not beautiful, and quite without allure.'

When she'd stopped laughing, she realised that in an upside-down sort of a way—for whoever wanted to be beautiful and alluring if it meant men trying to rape them?—he'd been paying her a compliment.

He took hold of her hand. 'I will take you back to the lido.'

She had forgotten about the rest of the world. Guiltily, she leapt up. 'What time is it?'

He shrugged. 'Midday, perhaps.'

She was pushing past him, towards the stern of the boat where steps led down into the water. 'I must fly!' she muttered, anxiety driving her on. 'They'll be frantic!'

He caught hold of her arm. 'I said, I will take you.' He sounded amused. 'You need not repeat your record-breaking swim across the bay.'

'But it'll be quicker,' she protested. She looked up at the Citadel, rearing up behind the Marina. 'It must be miles round, by road, and I'm not sure I should walk all that way, on my foot.'

'If you are unable to walk, you are unable to swim,' he said unequivocally. 'But I have my car. I shall drive you.'

'Oh.' She hadn't thought of that. 'That's very kind

of you.' He's going to drive me, through those crowded streets, and all I'm wearing is a bikini. 'I suppose you couldn't...'

He had bent down to reach under the seat. Straightening, he was holding out to her a golden-brown sweatshirt. She pulled it on, and it was long enough to cover her to her thighs.

She caught his eye. She didn't think she needed to say anything else.

On the way back to the lido she suddenly burst out, 'I keep getting confused, here. There's something about the island—it's as if two worlds existed, side by side, and I seem to stray into the other one sometimes.'

Straight away she wished she hadn't spoken. What a stupid remark!

But then he made a reply. In the noise of the crowded lunchtime streets she didn't quite hear. But it sounded like, 'Many more than two.'

He drove down the track and pulled up outside the lido's gates. As she got out of the car he said, 'If your foot does not incapacitate you, perhaps the twins might be prevailed upon to look after your boys tonight so that I may take you out to dinner.'

Dinner. What a wonderful prospect.

She stared at him. Deep into his eyes, which there in the bright sun had taken on a golden tone. Remembered how it had felt when he kissed her. Wished he'd do it again, there and then.

It was unlikely, in the middle of the day with people looking on.

Turning her head away, she stepped down on to her good foot. And wondered fleetingly if she'd hurt that one too, for as she walked towards the gates both feet felt as if they belonged to someone else.

*

Barry's bucket shop's cheapest tickets flew them out of Luton at eleven-thirty at night. She wondered, sitting in the crowded and shabby lounge with another forty minutes to wait, if she'd have preferred to spend a bit more and leave at a civilised time. From a civilised airport. But then Barry got the guide book out of his rucksack and she was distracted by his happiness.

'Athens at dawn, Fay!' he said. 'Can you imagine it?' She could. Her picture didn't seem to be as rosy as his. 'We'll climb the Acropolis! Watch the sun creep up to wake the sleeping city!'

She was sure there must be a flaw somewhere. But she was catching his optimism, and thought, why worry?

Athens airport in the small hours, bored sleepy officials, nothing open but the loos. And a plane-load of British tourists vanished into the night as if they had never been.

'I'm scared, Fay,' Barry said. 'What do we do now?'

It was lonely, the two of them in the empty airport. She felt scared too.

'We get a taxi to the Acropolis,' she said. 'We wait there for your precious sunrise.' She grinned at him, and his face lightened immediately.

'That's what we'll do!' He was mercurial. Happy again. She didn't have the heart to wonder aloud how they'd fill the remaining small hours till dawn.

The taxi, one vehicle in a silent city, dropped them at the foot of the Acropolis. They walked hand-in-hand up paths beneath pine trees, disturbing cats which slumbered curled up on top of ancient pillars. They found a bench, and Barry lay down with his head in her lap and slept while she sat wide awake with her thoughts. First light, and the thrill of climbing a narrow track to emerge from the wooded slope and see the Parthenon rise up ahead.

Such things she could never forget.

By nine o'clock it felt like afternoon. Spirits were flagging, and she knew she must act.

'Where's this place we get the ferry?' she asked him.

He shrugged listlessly. 'Depends where we're going.' He sounded as if he didn't much care.

'What was the island you were telling me about the other evening? The one that's very quiet, with hardly any tourists?'

'Kea.'

'Well, how do we get there?'

He handed her his guide book. Don't worry, Barry, she thought ironically, I'll do it.

'We have to get the bus to a place called Lavrion,' she said after a while. 'Look.' He glanced across to the map she was pointing to. 'The bus goes from near the Archaeological Museum.'

'Wherever the hell that is.'

She ignored him. 'And that is...'—she flipped through the book till she found a street plan of Athens—'here!'

He frowned, and she thought he might be about to make some remark about it being too far. 'We'll take a taxi,' she said decisively. And before he could comment, stood out on the edge of the pavement and hailed one.

They had an early lunch in Lavrion, having a couple of hours to kill before the Kea ferry went. They discovered a local bottled beer that was just right with the food and the heat, and after drinking the lion's share of several bottles, Barry's depression was behind him. On the boat he was at his best, witty, entertaining and loving as only he could be, and she thought, it's going to be all right. Everything's fine.

As the ferry docked, they leaned on the rail to catch the first eager glimpse of this place they'd come to. There was a big hotel at the end of the waterfront road, which they thought looked promising till she noticed—and pointed out—that it was still under construction.

'But that's good, because it means there won't be masses of tourists staying there,' she added.

Barry said morosely, 'Where the fuck are *we* going to stay?'

She couldn't believe he'd said it. That just one place not being open to visitors should cast him down like that.

'There'll be other places!' She hugged him violently. 'Cheer up! We probably couldn't afford a hotel, anyway—we'll find rooms.'

They did. A double room with its own shower and lavatory, opening out on to a balcony where you could dry washing. She thought it was perfect. After a few more beers, he did too.

They pushed the twin beds together and lay down. Too tired to make love, they slept deeply and apart, wakened eventually by laughter and footsteps in the alley behind their room and finding it was quite dark. They showered and went out to find supper, but with only a few drachmas left from the small amount they'd brought with them, the meal had to be cheap.

'We'll find a bank, tomorrow,' she said. 'Cash a traveller's cheque. It'll be all right!' He was looking depressed again.

They discovered that when you ordered ouzo, a plate of snacks accompanied it. Salami and bits of cheese, on slices of white bread. Olives. Nuts. And with each round of drinks, you got another plate of snacks.

'I don't know about you, Fay me love,' his hand was on her bare thigh, stroking up under her skirt, 'but this'll do me.' He lifted his glass and drank the last inch of ouzo. He took it neat; she'd had the carafe of water all to herself.

She'd been hungry when they came in. So hungry that she'd felt the beginnings of a headache. She was still hungry now, for all that she'd eaten most of the snacks.

But there was no money left. And this little bar didn't look like the sort of place that would cash a cheque. 'Do not ask for credit,' she thought vaguely, 'as a refusal often offends.'

'It'll do me, too,' she said. 'Let's go to bed.'

The washing she'd done earlier was dry. Lovely heat, she thought. Wonderful climate. Barry used the bathroom while she stowed her clean underwear in a drawer, and she went in when he came out. Cleaning her teeth, she thought of him in the bar, putting his hand on her leg. Hidden under the table, stroking upwards. Reaching her knickers, his fingers slipping inside to touch her flesh. She found she was trembling.

It was hardly worth putting on her nightie, but she did so anyway, not liking the idea of walking naked into the bedroom. It'd be blatant, she thought, he'd prefer to think he was going to have to persuade me. She smiled. If he only knew!

He was curled up in his own bed, the sheet drawn up under his chin. He was sound asleep.

She stood looking down at him, and the excitement slowly ebbed from her body.

Tomorrow, she thought as she got into her bed. And lots of tomorrows after that. It'll be all right.

Following his example, she closed her eyes and told herself to go to sleep.

SIXTEEN

Island in the Sun

He was up before her in the morning. She woke to find him sitting on her bed with a loaf of fresh bread, from which he was tearing chunks and spreading them with butter and honey.

'Good morning,' he said.

She looked up into his eyes. His expression—slightly apologetic, very loving—made her heart leap. 'Hello.'

'I smelt the bread.' He handed her an inside slice, still warm, the butter and the runny honey seeping into the soft dough. 'And I realised how hungry I was.'

'Mmm.' She didn't want to answer; the sensation of the food in her mouth was too good to interrupt. Then she had a thought. Swallowing, she asked, 'What did you do about money?'

He shrugged. 'I told the woman I didn't have any, but that I'd pay her next time we go in.'

'And that was all right?' Obviously it had been. Barry's charm must work as well on Greek women as on those of every other race.

'It was.' He was preparing another couple of slices. 'Fay, there's a place up the end of the waterfront where you can hire motor bikes. Shall we get one?'

'I can't ride a motor bike.'

'I can. I'll drive.'

186

Just as she was about to remind him about having no money, he said, 'The bank's in the next town. Up the hill there.' He pointed vaguely inland. 'There's a taxi on the quay, maybe you could go and get some money while I organise the bike?'

It seemed a great idea. She was happy, suddenly, to find he'd been so eager that he'd got up, bought food, found out about the bikes and the bank. She leaned forwards, wrapping her arms round him and snuggling up close to him. He smelt of fresh air and soap.

He responded to her hug, turning her face up so that he could kiss her lips. His mouth felt as sticky as hers did. He said as they broke away, 'What was that for?'

'Just because.' She pushed him away and got out of bed. 'Now, if I'm going to be presenting myself in a bank and persuading them to part with some money, I'd better have a shower and dress in something respectable.'

She found she needn't have bothered. The ancient grey Mercedes taxi drove her sedately up the steep road to the little town at the top of the hill. The driver apparently understood when she said she was going to the bank and would he please wait, and waved a hand to show her where to go.

If she hadn't remembered from Barry's guide book that *Trapeza* meant bank, she would have missed it. There was no counter, no cashiers, no buzzing of phones or atmosphere of quiet efficiency: the bank was simply a fat old man in a stained shirt sitting at a rickety table in the corner of a hardware shop. He sat looking at her traveller's cheque for a good three minutes before eventually coming to the decision that it was all right to cash it. Stuffing the thick wad of dirty drachma notes into her bag, she left the shop feeling glad Barry hadn't been with her: it was easier to hold back your laughter on your own.

He'd acquired a bike—though he said they'd have to drop in a deposit before they could ride off—and a map. He'd also packed their swimming things and a towel in a bag, which he'd fixed to the bike's carrier.

He stood looking at her, smiling happily. He said, 'Let's hit the road,' and there wasn't anything she'd rather have done.

When she stopped thinking she was about to fall off, and had consequently released her stranglehold round Barry's waist, it was all right. Better than all right— she knew they couldn't be going very fast, but the warm air zipping past her cheeks and the noisy roar of the little engine gave the illusion that they were racing along. Barry said over his shoulder, 'Anywhere special you'd like to go?', which was so absurd that she laughed aloud.

They followed a road that led roughly south-west down the coast of the island. Occasionally they passed local people, who looked up from whatever it was they were doing in their fields to give cheery waves, but the place lived up to its description in Barry's book and they didn't see one tourist.

'I want to stop soon,' Barry shouted back to her after a while.

'Why? Had enough?'

'No!' He removed one hand from the handlebars and reached back to clasp it around her thigh. 'I want to make love to you.'

She couldn't think how to respond. For a moment she felt as if she couldn't breathe, as if her lungs had been paralysed and she was never again to draw in. Relax. Calm down. It's not that unexpected, is it?

She said, in a surprisingly level voice, 'Let's stop at the next place we come to and get some food. Then we can have a look at the map and see if we can spot a beach.'

He squeezed her leg in response. 'Okay.'

A collection of houses loomed up on the road ahead. One of them had rusty tin tables outside, where three very old men sat in front of tiny cups of coffee, silently gazing out at the empty vista before them. The dim interior seemed to be stocked with provisions, and Fay went in and bought bread, feta cheese, olives, fruit, and two big bottles of beer. The bottles had crown caps, but she knew from long experience that Barry never went anywhere without a bottle-opener.

When she came out he was studying the map.

'What about that?'

She read where he was pointing. 'Pisses! How charming!'

'Do us, do you think?'

'Perfectly.'

Twenty minutes on, they came to another collection of houses, slightly bigger, which apparently was Pisses. A track led down from the road to a long sandy beach backed by pine trees.

Barry stopped the bike and switched off the engine. In the utter silence he said, 'We'll be lucky to find a space to sit down.'

There wasn't a soul in sight.

They left the bike in the shade of the trees and walked right along to the far end of the beach. Among a jumble of rocks they made their own place, spreading the towel on a little patch of sand where, when they lay down, they couldn't be seen unless someone walked right up to them. He made a pillow from their t-shirts and put it behind her head. His hands on her were gentle and loving. As he came into her the soft sea sounds and the distant insect hummings seemed to sing with her and share in her joy.

They drank the first bottle of beer as an aperitif, eating the black fleshy olives and spitting the pits over the rocks to the sand.

'We'll come back, in a few years, and there'll be our own olive grove,' he said. 'We'll turn our backs on the rat race and live here. How do you fancy being a peasant farmer?'

'Not much.'

'No.' He sighed. 'Me neither.'

She sensed there was something he wanted to say.

'What is it?' she asked softly.

'Fay,' he whispered. Then, 'Fay, I do love you. You know that, don't you?'

She couldn't speak. She nodded.

'I've been a bastard. Last night. Hundreds of nights, when I've let things—*drink*—get in the way. Haven't I?'

Yes, she thought. Yes you have. You have been a bastard, of the first water, quite often. She looked into his face, about to put her thoughts into words. But his eyes were full of pain, and she couldn't. She reached for his hand. 'It's a pity, when something gets in the way,' she said quietly.

'It's more than a pity. It's hurtful, to you. You shouldn't waste yourself on me, Fay. You should let me get out of your life and find yourself the sort of man you deserve.'

Let him get out of my life? Oh, *God!* Is that what he wants, that we part? And this is a kind way of telling me?

Her eyes were full of tears. To contemplate life without him, even fleetingly, showed how totally, irrevocably, he was a part of her. And how agonising it would be to cut him out.

'Fay?' His voice sounded amazed. 'Fay, what's the

190

matter?'

Dumbly she leaned against him, face pressed to his bare chest so that he must have felt the drenching of her tears. 'I don't want to live without you.'

His arms were round her, one hand moving in gentle slow circles across her back as if she were a baby and he was winding her. He said into her hair, 'Sorry. I'm sorry. I'm useless at this—that wasn't what I meant. I don't want to live without you, either, and I was sort of working up to saying so.' He hesitated. 'It's just that—I suppose I was saying—I want to be able to think, in the future, that I gave you the chance to get out while the going was good.'

She saw through the tangle of his words to what he was telling her. And said, 'I hear you.' Then lifted her face to receive his kiss.

*

Until the telephone rang out, she hadn't noticed that The Twins' House had one. She was in the kitchen, grilling beefburgers for the boys' supper, and had to follow the sound to find it.

It was on a little corner table in the living room.

She picked up the receiver. 'Hello?'

'I am sorry to make you go back in there,' said Aaron's voice in her ear, 'but I needed to tell you that I am delayed and will not be able to collect you until eight-thirty.'

Knees suddenly weak, she leaned against the wall. 'It's okay,' she said. 'I'd have had to do it, sooner or later.' Having him know what she was thinking, and be understanding enough to mention it, was making her feel very happy. Then she remembered what else he had said. 'Half past eight's fine. Thank you for letting me know.'

'Don't be *polite*,' he said. 'Not with me. See you later.'

And was gone.

She went slowly back to the burgers, hurrying the last few yards when she saw that the grill was turned up too high and fountains of fat were being sucked out and ignited, shooting out like the burn-off on an oil rig. Thank goodness the boys were used to a fairly hit-or-miss standard of cuisine, and ate things with gusto even when they were burned.

She made an effort, putting salad prettily on to the two plates, spreading butter on the bread and cutting the slices into triangles. Calling the boys, she dished up the hot burgers.

Oliver arrived first, his hunger-inspired run brought up short at the table. 'What have you done to the tomatoes?' he asked.

She'd cut them into fan shapes, and sprinkled them with oil, vinegar and herbs. 'Oh—just dressed them up a bit.'

Rupert, sitting down, picked up a tomato in finger and thumb. He looked doubtful.

'What's the matter?'

He looked up at her and grinned. 'Just checking,' he said. 'Usually when you mess things about, it means they're going off.'

'Now, look . . .' she began indignantly. Then remembered slices of bread cut into funny shapes to disguise the holes where she'd removed the mouldy bits. Pies, smothered in warm custard to make the crust less like armour-plating. She said, 'Yes. I'm sorry, it's not my strong suit, is it?'

Rupert got up and came across to her, throwing his arms round her in a mute and intense hug. He muttered, 'Like you as you are,' then went back to his supper.

Oliver said, 'What's a strong suit?'

*

192

The twins were taking the boys down to the Esplanade for a while before bringing them home to bed, and arrived to collect them in time to give Fay an hour to herself before Aaron was due. She came out of the shower to see them all off, hair in a towel and dressing-gown tied tightly round her.

Even so, the twins stood looking at her with that same contemplative, admiring look. Responding, but trying to persuade herself she wasn't, she thought tritely, maybe I should go out to dinner like this and see if it has the same effect on Aaron.

'Have a good time,' she said at the front door. The boys were already leaping down the steps, calling out to her as they went. 'There are beers in the fridge,' she added to the twins, 'please help yourselves. I don't suppose we shall be late.' *We*. I said *we*. Damn. Like some teenager with a new boyfriend, suddenly everything's got to be *we* and *us*, as if you can't bear to pass up an opportunity to remind the world you've latched on to someone.

And besides, it was a stupid thing to say when she had no idea where he was taking her or how long he'd want to keep her there.

A shudder of anticipation ran through her.

The twins were patiently waiting, standing a couple of steps down from her so that their incredible eyes were for once on a level with hers. As if they recognised that her dishevelled thoughts had ground to a stop, they said together, 'It does not matter.' And one added, 'We hope you will enjoy your evening.'

If the twins ever winked, she thought, going back inside, that would have been a winking moment.

She stood on the balcony, looking out over the square so that she would see him as soon as he arrived. She had positioned herself in the shadows, in case he saw her. It wouldn't do to look too eager.

But then she thought, what's the use? He'll know I am. I can't hide from him what I'm feeling.

It was an overpowering thought. And frightening—it means I'm exposed, she realised. At his mercy. Nowhere to hide.

Against her will, an unrecognised, quite unfamiliar feeling snaked up from her depths. A feeling of intense sexual excitement, whose origins, she knew—although it was not a welcome knowledge—lay in the concept of him having power over her. Making her do things she wasn't sure she wanted to do. Holding her, forcing her on down into the depths of herself, arousing the beast that lay inside her so that it roared in triumph.

A tiny element of control came back to her, and she clung on to it. Drove the awful, wonderful, thrilling fantasies away.

Looking down into the square, fixing her attention on the old lady in black—who was still sewing, still keeping one eye on the small children playing at her feet—Fay wondered how long it would be until the images came thundering back.

SEVENTEEN

Warning Signs

For almost two weeks they were under Kea's spell, a magic which was composed partly of the island's natural beauty, peace and charm, partly of the love and the new-found harmony which existed between them. The days took on a simple routine: lazy breakfast—with several slow cups of coffee—in one of the little waterfront bars, then down to the beach for sea and sunshine until whatever time either of them felt like doing something else. They'd return to their room for a shower later, then go out to stroll and, eventually, to eat. Before turning in, they'd often go back to the beach to sit in the quiet darkness and listen to the gentle sounds of the sea. Barry lit a little driftwood-and-paper fire on a couple of occasions, but the local policeman, with whom they were on nodding acquaintance, came down on to the sand and rather apologetically asked them to put it out.

When at last it was time for bed, it was, for Fay, the most magical time of all. It seemed to her that Barry understood, that he was determined to show her he *could* put her first, above the demands of going out with his mates, of gallivanting in some pub till all hours, of drinking, drinking, drinking till he was sodden and incapable. Now his only intent was to make her happy, and she responded to his care like a flower blooming in the warm spring rain.

On Kea, it was perfect.

On Kea, there were no gallivanting mates. And no pubs.

The morning came when it was time to move on. Barry said over breakfast, 'The ferry goes at ten-thirty this morning. Shall we be on it?', and she smiled as she said yes because it was exactly what she'd been thinking.

Leaning on the ship's stern rail, she watched as Kea was left behind. Bit by bit, the little town where they'd been so happy was hidden by a spur of land as they sailed away. There came, inevitably, a moment when she couldn't see it at all, and she was struck with a deep sorrow, as if not being able to see the location any more meant that it had never really been there. That the magic hadn't happened, either.

Stricken, she looked round for Barry. A hug, a touch of the hand, would have reassured her.

She couldn't see him. Running along the deck, leaping down the steep steps to the snack bar, she found him, having a glass of ouzo with a seedy-looking sailor.

But he must have seen her dismay, because he got off his stool and came to greet her. Ordered her the coffee she asked for and, as once long ago he'd done with his half-pint of beer, gave her his ouzo to share.

It was all right. The magic was still there after all.

On the bus back to Athens they browsed through Barry's book. So many islands sounded attractive, and they had no way of knowing which would be the best.

She had a thought.

'Remember what we said?'

He smiled. 'We've said quite a lot. Especially recently.'

She reached out and took his hand, pleased that he should have commented on that. It had been part of the magic, how much they'd talked. Endlessly. About everything. He must have thought it was good, too.

'I meant, back home.' No. Not home any more. 'In Furnace Street, when we were planning this, we said—*you* said—we'd go to Athens and get on the first boat that was leaving, whatever its destination.'

'I said that?'

'Yes.'

He looked at her dubiously. 'And you agreed?'

'Yes.' She was laughing now, at his expression which said so clearly, *that* doesn't sound like you!

He closed the book with a snap and pushed it back in his rucksack.

Piraeus was dozy in the afternoon heat, and for a time there didn't seem to be any boats going anywhere. Then one of the small ticket-offices that lined the quay opened its shutter, and in the shady interior they could make out a man in a vest licking his thumb and flicking through a book of tickets. In his own good time he got up, came out of his little hut and propped a blackboard against the front wall. Then he wrote in chalk, πωρωσ, and beneath that, for the benefit of those who only read the Roman alphabet, POROS.

Barry said, 'It looks like we're going to Poros.'

The man in the vest indicated they could go on the ferry, which left in an hour and took two and a half hours, or wait a further forty minutes and go on the much faster hoverfoil. Since it cost twice as much to zip across the water by hoverfoil, and since Fay preferred ferries anyway, they opted for the cheaper transport. The man pointed down the quay to where the boat was tying up, and as soon as the gangplank was down and the disembarking passengers had come off, Fay and Barry went aboard.

197

Before they sailed, the hoverfoil swept into Piraeus and tied up alongside them.

'Show-off,' Fay said as its bow-wave creamed round them and set them bobbing.

The hoverfoil passengers were show-offs, too. Disdaining the shabby old ferryboat, they stalked aboard the hoverfoil in their smart suits and their high-heeled shoes, serious-looking business men and their dressy wives, sometimes even a maid in tow to look after the children.

Barry said, 'I hope we're going to like Poros.'

'Why?' The note of doubt in his voice made her instantly anxious.

But it was all right—he was smiling. He nodded in the direction of the hoverfoil. 'It's okay,' he said. 'I was joking. I just meant, that lot don't look like our sort.'

'What day is it?' She'd had a thought.

'Friday, I think. Why?'

'Then we needn't worry. They're probably only weekend visitors. You know, rich Athenians with villas on the island, getting away from the city for a couple of days. Wouldn't you think?'

Slowly he nodded. 'Yes. It sounds likely. Rich Athenians with villas,' he repeated. He glanced at her. 'Maybe we could get taken on as gardener and housemaid, and stay for ever.'

She was about to protest that she didn't want to be anyone's housemaid, even in a rich villa on a Greek island, but he was looking so wistfully out to sea towards their distant destination that she didn't have the heart.

Poros was quite different from Kea. Smarter, busier—nowhere on earth, Barry remarked, could be *less* busy than Kea—and, even with the hydrofoil-load of Athenians dispersed to their various destinations, obviously more sophisticated and a lot richer. There were expensive-looking yachts and motor launches tied up at the marina which they passed on their way into town from their lodgings, and in the evenings the pavement cafés and tavernas were full of a type of Greek quite different from the slow and insular people on Kea.

Their room was in a new building on the edge of the town, across the water from what appeared to be a naval college. Tied up in front of the college was a battle cruiser, and sometimes hectoring voices on the tannoy, or snatches of amplified martial music, would come floating across the still water. A little way along the road was a stony beach, and they took to spending as much time in or by the water as they'd done on Kea.

On the beach one morning, they got into conversation with a girl from Exeter who asked them if they knew of any rooms to let. When Fay had told her where to enquire, she didn't immediately set off to get herself sorted out, but instead flopped down on the pebbles with every appearance of staying all day.

'Bloody hell, you don't know how nice it is to talk English again,' she said with some fervour, peeling off her Indian cotton dress to reveal a faded blue bikini. 'I've been away six months—I was in Turkey, most of the time, right out in the wilds—' she rummaged in her large patchwork bag and got out a towel and an inflatable pillow, 'and it's been an experience, I can tell you!'

Fay watched as the girl half-inflated her pillow and, lying back, made herself instantly comfortable. She realised she was staring; despite the dark glasses and the hat pulled down over her eyes, the girl might have noticed.

'What were you doing in Turkey?' she asked hastily.

'This and that.' Into Fay's mind flew torrid and highly unlikely pictures of harems and slave girls in bondage. Drug trafficking. This girl cramming pounds of heroin into her homely patchwork bag. 'Talking to gypsies and fortune tellers, when I could find them.'

Curiouser and curiouser. 'Do you speak Turkish?' Silly question, Fay thought.

'Do now,' said the girl. 'Who's that?'

Fay looked to where she was pointing. Barry, coming towards them with two bottles of Amstel in his hands.

'That's Barry.'

'He's with you?'

'Yes.' Oh, yes. She thought she heard the girl mutter, 'Pity.'

She looked up at Barry as he squatted down and opened the beers, nodding a greeting to the girl. 'This is—sorry, I don't know your name.'

'Charlotte.'

'She tells fortunes,' Fay added baldly.

The girl snorted with laughter. 'No I don't. I read horoscopes.'

Fay could see the scepticism break out on Barry's face. Before he could say anything rude, she said, 'What's Turkey like? Any good?'

And later, when Barry had finished his beer and gone for a swim, she said, 'Now would you tell me about horoscopes?'

'Libra and Scorpio,' Charlotte had said musingly, staring after Barry as he swam out to sea and then switching her gaze to Fay. Then added, ominously, 'Jesus.'

Fay, lying in bed with Barry fast asleep beside her, couldn't get it out of her mind. She'd tried to laugh it off.

'As bad as that?' she said, forcing a smile. 'And for every Libra who's foolhardy enough to take up with a Scorpio?'

'Depends,' Charlotte said. 'Trouble is, you've got everything different that could be different. You're air, see, and he's water. You're cardinal, he's fixed. You're positive, he's negative. You're ruled by Venus, him by Pluto. Get what I mean?'

'Sort of,' Fay said cagily. She didn't like the idea of this complete stranger putting such a blight on her relationship with Barry. And why should I listen? she asked herself, angry suddenly, when everything's going so well? I don't need someone pouring poison in my ear! 'I'm not sure I believe in it,' she added. 'I've never understood how you can possibly be affected so greatly by something as nebulous as where the planets happen to be when you're born.'

'Believe what you like,' Charlotte said, in the sort of tones that suggested she didn't care what Fay thought. But then abruptly she raised herself on one elbow, her face up close to Fay's. 'What about the moon?' she hissed in a sharp whisper. 'The moon makes the tides. Even in a puddle—even in the fluids in your own body—the moon's influence can be detected. There's a place in America where they treat irregular periods by making you sleep under an uncurtained window, so that the moon shines on you. If the moon can do that, why do you dismiss the power of the planets?'

'Good grief!'

But Charlotte hadn't finished. 'They're alive,' she said quietly. 'The planets. Pulsing with electro-magnetic energy. Why do you think man's studied them through so many millenia?'

'I've never thought about it. I know the planets are called after the ancient gods—Venus, and Jupiter, and Mars, and the rest, and the gods figure in the myths, but...'

'Ever wondered why the names are the same?'

Fay felt as if her mind were expanding to meet the

challenge. But not widely enough, nor quickly enough. Charlotte was speaking again.

'Perhaps it was the other way round.' Her hypnotic voice in Fay's ear was like an incantation. 'And the gods were named after the planets.'

Now, in bed in the dark, Fay found that those words still had the power to shock. Why? she wondered for the twentieth time. What does it matter which came first? Why is it significant?

She couldn't come up with an answer.

It's her, she thought, punching the hard pillow in an effort to make it more comfortable. She's put stupid thoughts into my head, and made me worry about them. She's a charlatan. Charlotte the charlatan. No wonder she hob-nobs with gypsies and fortune-tellers, she's probably busy learning how to make gullible people like me part with the maximum amount of money in the minimum amount of time. I'll probably get her bloody bill, tomorrow.

Resolutely she told herself to stop being so silly and go to sleep. But, drifting off, she heard again Charlotte's voice.

Libra and Scorpio. Jesus.

The end of the summer was near. Each day there seemed to be fewer people on the beach, and across the bay the villas of the rich Athenians were being shuttered-up for the winter. Time for us to think of going, too, Fay thought. She tried to discuss home with Barry, but evidently he found it too daunting a proposition.

'Not now, Fay me darling,' he said. Sitting beside her on the beach, he was staring out to sea. 'Not yet.'

'When, then? We fly back in three days, and we have absolutely nothing planned beyond landing at Luton.'

He ran his hands through his thick dark hair. It had grown a lot while they'd been away, and she loved the way it curled on to his shoulders. She moved closer to him, her own hand pushing his out of the way, her fingers twining and smoothing. 'You'll have to get this cut off,' she said inconsequentially.

'I know.' He sounded so mournful that they might have been speaking of his head rather than his hair.

'Don't worry, it'll grow again!'

He turned to look at her, eyes full of misery. 'When? When will it have the chance? It's a symbol, Fay. Isn't it? Go home, get your hair cut, start the new job. Start being sensible.' He paused, his gaze sliding away from her and back out to sea. He added, very quietly, 'I'm not sure I want that.'

She felt as if a great rift were opening up inside her. Going home, getting a place together—getting on with this new phase of their life—had seemed so obvious a next step to her that she'd hardly given it a thought. What else were they to do? Stay here? Bum round Greece for another six weeks? Go further afield? India? Australia?

And what then?

She thought of the place waiting for her on her postponed course. Of how much she was looking forward to work again, real cerebral work worthy of her mind and her enthusiasm.

Some devil of determination in her made her say, '*I* want it.'

'You do?' Still he was staring out to sea.

'Yes.'

The moment stretched out till it hurt. He said, on a sigh, 'You don't fancy staying here a bit longer? Going to look at some of those places in Turkey that Charlotte was raving about?'

Bloody Charlotte. 'No. I don't.'

She didn't dare say, do you?

After a while he said, 'Okay, then.'

But his voice was so defeated that she didn't feel in the least bit triumphant.

The island was at its most beautiful the day before they had to leave. Fay thought she'd never seen a more glorious sunset: from the little balcony of their room, she watched the sun set behind the great bulk of the Peloponnese to the west, the range of mountains called the Sleeping Woman showing up in black silhouette against the pink and gold sky. The light breeze had fallen with the fading light, so that now the air was completely still. In front of her, the narrow channel between the island and the mainland was flat calm, and the lights from Galata and Poros reflecting in the dark water reached out towards each other long straight arms whose fingers touched in mid-channel.

She thought, *now* who doesn't want to go home?

But it was a fleeting doubt. Barry was singing in the shower, happy again, and as soon as they were ready, they were going out for a last meal. 'We'll go somewhere nice,' he'd said. 'Somewhere expensive. We can afford to blue our last bread—I'll be earning next week, and you'll be picking up your grant cheque.'

He'd seemed quite resigned to the idea.

We'll talk about home tonight, she told herself. I reckon we could find digs, to tide us over while we look for a place. The Y, if it comes to that. I'm sure it's not as daunting as all that—everyone else seems to manage, so we shall too.

She realised even as they walked into town that Barry wasn't in the mood for serious plans. Full of sun and happiness, he was loving, silly, and charmed her into being the same. Passing the long row of boats moored in the marina, he asked her which one she'd like. Volunteered to steal it for her, sail off with her into the night.

'Where shall we go?'

He stopped, pulling her close to him in a sudden intense hug. He said against her hair, 'I don't care. As long as I'm with you.'

And then planning where they were going to live when they got home didn't seem so important after all.

He chose the most expensive-looking taverna, where the tables had cloths and the diners wore well-cut, fashionable outfits. She was aware of the crumples in her dress, which, pretty under better circumstances, was showing distinct signs of having been dragged in and out of her rucksack once too often.

'You look lovely,' he said to her across the table. 'I think you're the loveliest woman in here, and all the other men agree with me.'

Embarrassed, she tried to hush him. 'Don't!'

'You are,' he insisted. 'And they do. They're all staring at your body and wishing it was them and not me that's going to make love to you later.'

'*Barry!*'

He was summoning the waiter, impatient to have an opened bottle on the table. Feeling herself blush, she kept her eyes down. It would be awful to look round and find he was right and all the men *were* looking at her. Even worse if they weren't. She wanted to laugh.

'Ouzo? Retsina?' he asked. A smiling waiter stood at his side, pad and pencil at the ready.

'Both,' she said recklessly.

I've never got drunk with him, she thought. I've always been the responsible one, who made sure we got home all right. The one who looked after the key, who made sure he cleaned his teeth and got undressed before falling into bed. What would happen if I got smashed too?

They had two glasses of ouzo each, then, when the food arrived, shared a bottle of retsina.

'Another?'

She focussed on him. He was holding the bottle upside-down over her glass, the last drops slowly falling.

She nodded.

But when the new bottle came, she didn't want it any more. She let him pour her out a glass, knowing it would stay untouched. That, eventually, when he'd finished the bottle on his own, he'd drain her glass too.

Not your fault, Barry, she thought. Not this time— you asked me if I wanted more, and I said yes. And it's a shame to waste it. Waste not, want not.

Already she felt strange, as if nothing around her were quite real. Barry was chatting happily about everything and nothing—about other people in the room, about the food, the drink—and she realised he was too far gone to notice she wasn't giving him more than a very superficial response.

Barry, oh, Barry, she cried silently. Can't you see? Help me! I'm slipping, drifting, and I need you to come down here after me and pull me back. Do you know me at all? Are we so distant, that I'm calling out to you and you don't hear?

She wasn't being fair, and a still-sensible part of her recognised it. But as the trance took hold and grew in strength, the sensible part waned.

We're different! the sobbing voice in her head said. We want totally opposite things! I want to go home and settle down in a nice little flat, start my course, get my qualification and throw myself into a job which I think I shall love and which I'm sure I'll be good at. You, darling beloved Barry, want to grow your hair, drink yourself into a permanent stupor, lie in the sun, go through Turkey on a rattly bus and ride the hippy trail till you're so far out you never come back.

What in God's name are we doing together?

What am *I* doing, throwing in my lot with you?

Terrified, her eyes raced round the room for an answer, as if one of the wordly, sophisticated diners might leap up and say, it's all right, Fay! No need to worry, he'll change when you get back, just you wait and see. Help! shouted the mute panicking voice. Someone, help!

For a split second, it seemed that someone had responded. But not with help, for what entered her mind was no comforting platitude but a stab of black despair. As if someone were warning her. Giving her a glimpse of a future so bleak that it didn't bear thinking about.

She covered her face with her hands, and the invasion went away.

Shaking, she looked up. Stared here, there, not caring what she should see or who should see her staring, desperate in her need to *know*. Who was it? What was it?

From somewhere—her glance was moving too quickly to be sure where—she caught a subliminal impression of eyes, steadily watching her. With difficulty, as if she were trying to pull to a halt a galloping horse, she turned back. To that table? That one?

Between her and the far corner, just at the wrong moment, a group of people got up to go. Talking, laughing, kissing each other on both cheeks, they seemed to take forever about it. When the very last of them had moved out of the way and she could see the one place in the room she hadn't checked, there was nobody there.

Tears were pricking in her eyes. Reaching across the table, she found Barry's hand. Took it, squeezed it hard, so hard that his shocked face was staring right into hers as he said, 'Ouch!'

She had wondered, with what capacity remained to her for wondering, how he'd react. If, now, he'd perceive that something was wrong. What she'd do if he didn't.

'Barry, I'm sorry, I . . .'

He was on his feet and coming round to stand behind her. Saying gently, 'It's all right, me love. I'll look after you,' with love and concern so clear in his expression that the threatening tears pushed nearer. One arm round her waist, he was reaching in his pocket for money, throwing it on the table.

Helping her outside, to the blessed fresh air and the dark, tranquil night.

Leaning into him as he held her, she whispered, 'Barry, take me home.'

EIGHTEEN

Into an Older World

Fay and Barry were married on the last Saturday of July, a couple of weeks after she had graduated from her course and earned herself a distinction. A year's hard and satisfying work was behind her, a brand-new and challenging job in a special school waited for her when the new term began in September: her professional future was assured.

He had started as long ago as the previous October to refer casually to, 'When we're married...' The first time—he'd been musing aloud about wanting to get to know more of England, and said, 'When we're married we'll get out of London for weekends now and again,'—she'd felt a small jolt, half of pleasure, half of apprehension. But as the months went by, she too found herself saying it. 'When we're married.'

I love him, she thought. No man has ever matched him, for me. She suppressed the thought that there hadn't really *been* any other men. We've been together for a long time—six years, in October, since I first set eyes on him!—and I'm not happy when we're apart.

Isn't that a good reason for getting married? That you're happier with someone than without them?

It was. She told herself with conviction that it was. And he'll make a fine husband, my Barry. He works

hard—too hard, sometimes, tires himself out, especially on those trips to Germany which seem to crop up
so often—and his company think highly of him. Highly
enough, anyway, to have promoted him and given
him that brand-new car he's so pleased with.

Suddenly she thought of the mini-van. And the
money she'd set aside for petrol, which he'd been
quite prepared to spend on drink. It wasn't the best
moment in the world to remember that.

But he doesn't drink, now. We've had that half-
empty bottle of gin in the cupboard since Christmas.
And when we have a beer with supper, he drinks no
more than I do. And I can't think when was the last
time I saw him drunk. He's grown up, at last. Become
the mature sort of man that women marry. Sensible.
Responsible. And very, very loving.

Barry.

The next time he said, 'When we're married,' she
moved from where she'd been sitting curled up in the
corner of the sofa and went to crouch beside him on
the floor. The flat's little living room was too small for
a big table, and he always read the evening paper
sprawled out in front of the fireplace.

'Shall we?' she said tentatively.

'What?' He was still concentrating on the property
page which had sparked-off his thought. When we're
married we'll probably want to move out of town.

'Get married.'

He lifted his eyes from the paper and, rolling over
on to his side, looked at her. After a moment he said,
'It's what I've always wanted.'

She didn't know how to respond. He had sounded
so wistful—sad, almost—as if he knew he'd been
wanting something he was never going to be given.
She moved closer, putting her arms round him,
tightening the hug as he dropped his head down on
to her breasts.

'I want it, too,' she whispered.

He made a sound in his throat, and clutched her to him convulsively. She felt his shoulders shake, and realised he was weeping.

'I love you so much,' he said, the words muffled and barely audible.

She stroked his hair. She felt calm, and a part of her wondered why, when he was so moved that surely she should be, too.

'I love you, too,' she replied. 'I always have.'

'Have you?'

Have I? She didn't know. 'Yes.'

They lay side by side for some time. After a long period of silence, he suddenly said, 'I'll make sure you never regret it.'

They opted for a register office wedding. Fay told her parents the date and time, but thought afterwards that she needn't have bothered since the only notice they took of their elder daughter's marriage was to send her a cheap little card wishing her 'Joy on this your special day.' Her family was represented by Julie, who attended the brief ceremony but said she couldn't go on to the lunch party afterwards.

'It's Mike, see,' she told Fay. 'Saturday's his training day. He said he'd have the kids this morning if I'd be sure to get back dinner-time so he could go out.'

'You could have brought the children along.' Fay, shocked at herself, realised she couldn't remember how many children her sister had.

Julie gave a rueful laugh. 'No I couldn't,' she said. 'They're a handful. Best off having beans and burgers at home where it doesn't matter.' She hesitated. 'But thanks for the thought.'

They stood looking at each other. Fay couldn't think what to say, and she imagined Julie felt the same. She studied her sister. The well-upholstered but shapely body of her teens had spread a bit, and the short pink dress and the hat like a marshmallow didn't do her any favours. But she was still a good-looking woman, and there was something else about her—a sort of contented confidence, as if she were saying, this is me, and I'm okay.

Fay said suddenly, 'Are you happy? Is marriage nice?'

Julie laughed again, but this time with real amusement. 'Having doubts already?' she said. 'Don't you. Marriage is fine. And yes, I am happy.' She leaned forward, arm round Fay's shoulders in the sort of wrestling-hold hug she used to give her when they were small. 'So will you be. He's a right hunk, your Barry.'

Fay watched as Julie went over to kiss her new brother-in-law goodbye.

It fell on the Learys to make the lunch party go. And they took up the challenge with a vengeance, Liam and his wife and his teenage children, a couple of Barry's uncles and their families, and a stern aunt whose special job was apparently to take care of Barry's frail widowed mother. Fay had only met Mrs. Leary once before, on a flying overnight visit to Liverpool of which her clearest memory was sleeping on a horsehair sofa which prickled her bottom till she gave up and slept on the floor, where a smelly Yorkshire terrier took exception to her presence and tried to nip her ear.

Mrs. Leary, although living the life of a semi-invalid, had still been sufficiently in command to insist that her beloved son slept in the spare room so that it was his 'lady friend' who had to make do with the sofa. And, today, she was making no secret of her disapproval of the register office ceremony. 'Good Catholics marry in church,' Fay heard her say. Many times. 'Dey speak their vows in Our Lord's hearing, and then dey take the sacrament.' The very way she said the word—

'saaacrament', as if it had about a hundred 'a's, irritated Fay.

She wasn't predisposed to like her mother-in-law. It was just as well, she reflected, watching the look on the old girl's face while Barry made his speech, that Liverpool and London were too far apart for regular visits.

When the speeches were over and the cake cut and distributed, Fay began to think it was time to make a move. The Learys had started singing, and it might be an idea to break the party up before the various friends from work whom she and Barry had invited got the wrong idea. Or the *right* idea, she corrected herself as she slipped away to take off her hat and comb her hair. And in any case, she thought, I've had enough. Liam, cornering her, eyes bleary with emotion and whiskey-encouraged tears, had started to tell her how much Barry meant to him. To all of them. How it was now up to her, as Barry's wife—he managed to make it sound almost holy, as if by assuming the role she'd suddenly been elevated to sit one step below the Virgin Mary—to take on the mantle of 'Keeping Barry Happy'.

She'd wished fervently that Julie had come after all. With a bit of prompting, she might have retaliated, what about him keeping Fay happy? Isn't that important, too?

She went back to the dining room, pushing against resistant inebriated backs, disliking them all, thinking how nice it would have been if just a few of them had been *her* kith and kin.

But then a clutch of bodies cleared and there was Barry. Looking out for her, saying firmly to an uncle holding out to him a large glass of whiskey, 'No, thanks. Fay'll be here in a minute, then we're going. We've got to . . .'

He caught sight of her, and, as the frown and the

213

tinge of annoyance were wiped away, his face was lit with an expression of radiant love which she knew she'd never forget.

I don't need kith and kin. I've got Barry.

*

At twenty-nine minutes past eight, Aaron's Range Rover pulled into the square. Fay was seized with a momentary paralysis: it seemed to her she'd been standing there on the balcony, hidden back in the shadows, for a very long time, so that now, when the waiting was over and the next thing on the agenda was going to happen—had to happen almost—she wished the waiting would continue. It was, ran the abstract thought in her brain, a bit like coming to the final moments of a long journey, when the travelling has become an end in itself and you're reluctant to get off the train, or the plane, and face up to your destination.

She stared down at the roof of his car, parked directly below. Watched as the door opened and he got out. He looked straight up at her, eye to eye contact in an instant of such intense communion that she felt herself tremble. Then, watching her own actions as if from above, she saw herself go in from the balcony, close and lock the door, pick up her bag and cross the hall. Slam the front door. Walk down the steps.

And come, at last, to stand before him.

He reached out and touched her hair. He said, 'I like it, swept up this way.' His eyes ran down over her body, and, even though his hand did not follow, she felt the caress. She swayed slightly.

But somewhere within her, a small part of her spirit that wasn't yet under his spell awoke and prodded her into life. Hey! He's not going to have this all his own way! Gathering her courage, she raised her head and stared back at him.

214

For a split second, her mind joined with his. She could see herself from his viewpoint, and she caught the very edges of the profound, shadowy depths of all that was him. It was too much, far, far too much: her eyes screwing up tight as if at a sudden brilliant light, she turned away.

He touched her arm, gently. And said, 'Get into the car. I shall take you somewhere quiet for dinner.'

He drove out of the town, around Garitsa Bay to its southern point, pulling off the road to park on the edge of the sand. She had no idea where they could be going; in front of them a paved path led down on to the beach, where there was a bar with a small amusement park for children and tables and chairs set out on the sand under umbrellas. Music came loudly from inside, and a group of young men and their girls sat in one corner, watched somewhat apprehensively by some holidaymakers who just had to be British.

It didn't look like Aaron's scene at all.

He said, and in the darkness she could hear he was smiling, 'We walk from here.'

He took her arm as they crossed the road. Although they had forked off the main road a few hundred yards back, quite a lot of traffic seemed to want to drive south via this seaside route, and they had to wait for several vehicles to pass. On the far side they walked beneath trees down a path which was bordered by walls, high and overgrown with flowers: tall blue lilies, white marguerites, pink and purple stocks, fragrant roses. Beyond the trees, she could see the sloped terracotta roofs of a clutch of houses.

The path turned an abrupt corner and opened out into a square. In front of them was a Byzantine church, and around the square were flower beds, slightly overgrown but vibrant with life and colour. Beyond, holding the church, the square and the crouching houses in a protective, concealing grasp, was a barrier of tall leafy trees.

She felt, just as she'd felt in the Old Town, that she had walked into another world. She turned to him, about to comment, to ask, but he held up his hand and she heard him say, wait.

They stood on the edge of the square and watched.

The doors of the church opened, and a grey-robed, black-bearded priest emerged, with him a scent of incense from whatever late-evening service he had been conducting. He took up a position just outside, and one by one he blessed the members of his small congregation as they filed out. An old woman in black gave him a small bottle—wine?—and he clutched it to his breast like a holy relic as he continued with his valedictions. The light from within the church was golden and warm, and it seemed to Fay that as it spilled out into the night it brought with it a benevolence. Her eyes followed the worshippers— most of them were female, and all of them were elderly—as, talking quietly, they formed into small groups to disperse and walk home. She was ready to smile, to utter a greeting, but as one they passed her with no acknowledgement at all.

Strangely disappointed, she whispered to Aaron, 'Can't they see us?' And was instantly ashamed that she could have said anything so silly. But then, she thought, it doesn't seem silly here.

He laughed quietly. 'Yes, they can. But we are not relevant to them. This is their place, and they turn inwards on themselves, away from those of us who inhabit the rest of the world. Our life is not their concern—they don't care about us, and so it is natural for them to ignore us.'

'Who are they?'

He shrugged. 'Just people. Ordinary people. Their little suburb happens to be situated in such a way that

216

they are cut off. You saw how the roads run, either side of the village?' She nodded. 'Chance brought that about. Had the road run through the middle, then this place would have been lined with bars, apartments and tourist shops just like everywhere else.'

There was no bitterness in his tone, but still she wondered how he could accept so calmly the total despoilation, other than a little pocket here or there, of the whole of his island.

He put his arm round her in a warm hug. 'Do not worry,' he said into her ear. 'The little pockets have a very strong resistance. They will never succumb.'

'How can you be so sure?'

He sighed. 'Although it is not my island—I keep telling you, the island belongs to no-one—I know it. I know its past, and what will happen in its future.' The protesting question rose in her mind, but he arrested it. 'There are places on the island which, as you have detected yourself, are apparently of the modern world yet belong to a wider time. When you walked in the Old Town, you felt it, I think. You were aware that it had hidden itself away and wanted no part of the rushing anxiety of today.'

'Yes. I did feel that.' With the memory, the trance-like state she'd fallen into at the time was reawoken. *Narnia*, she remembered. *I thought it was like Narnia. And when I was back in the noisy present and couldn't see where I'd emerged from, I wondered if, also like Narnia, you couldn't get back into that other world unless someone called you.*

Is it Aaron?

You found it by yourself, he answered in her head. *I hoped you would, and by making sure you stayed in The Twins' House, on the edge of the Old Town, I increased the chances that you would.*

A great joy welled in her. *He did want me to be there! I was right, oh, I was right!*

217

The thought came, and she didn't know if it was from him or herself, aren't you going to ask why?

Why?

She frowned, trying to work it out. She shook her head. 'I have no idea.'

He said, 'Try to think what else you felt about the Old Town. What you are feeling about this place, too.'

Its apartness? Sense of isolation? No, we've covered that. She went back over the past few minutes. Saw again the opening door, and the good light flowing out into the darkness.

'It—these places help you, somehow,' she said eventually. 'Make you feel…' Trying to say what she'd felt, she was inarticulate. 'I don't know. Better, somehow.'

'Did you not think in the Old Town,' he prompted gently, '"This is a refuge, offering help to the wounded"?'

The memory came, bright and sharply in focus. She'd been watching the little cat stretching in the sun. Thinking how peaceful it was. She said, no longer even surprised that he should know, 'I did.'

And are you not wounded?

No! *NO!* I'm not wounded, I'm fine! I get by, I manage my life, the children, don't I? How can you say I'm wounded! I'm not, I'm not!

Peace.

The hurt, angry protests stilled and died. Holding her hand, he led her slowly out of the square. Peace. As they walked, he began to speak, aloud, but softly, hypnotically. Soothing her. 'We leave the church behind,' he said, 'and we go deeper into the past.' They were going out of the square by another of the walled paths, and flower scents were heady on the air. 'We are approaching Palaeopolis. Do you know what that means?'

218

Palaeo. Palaeolithic means old stone age. Palaeo is old, then. Polis? Metropolis. 'Old city.'

'Yes.' He smiled at her briefly. 'And you arrived at that with no prompting from me. Palaeopolis is where the city of Kerkira stood of old. An element of it remains today, for its stones are incorporated in the church you just saw.'

They had come to the end of the path and stopped on the edge of a dip of waste ground, in whose hollow could be seen, dim in the light of a street-lamp, the ruins of some ancient building. She was assailed by a sense of the past, a sudden certain awareness that all that had happened here, everyone who had lived their lives, eventful or uneventful, in this small corner of the island, was still alive in the air around her. *If I could only reach out, I could touch them, make contact, understand . . .*

Beside her Aaron waited. Not speaking, not putting out his thoughts. Quite still.

The ruined stones before her assumed a pattern. She saw the shape of a temple. Rows of pillars, now only marked by their bases but making an unmistakable outline. Then, as if she were looking from high up, she perceived another form beneath the temple. Smaller, its orientation slightly different. *An earlier temple?*

And what, could she only look, would she see beneath that?

The world is so old, she thought, an awed fear beginning to take hold of her, *and we're just the top layer. All that mankind has thought, felt, believed, he has poured into the fabric around him. He has moulded the land to his purpose, used and abused Mother Earth to suit himself, and now, today, we sit above thousands of years of our own ancestors.*

Thousands of years.

It was too much, and she turned her mind from it

even as she turned her face away from the bleached, cracked stones half-hidden in the brittle grass and the faded flowers.

His arms went around her, and she felt the balm of his presence wash over her. After a minute, as if he'd been waiting and now judged the moment right, he said, 'I recall that I invited you out to dinner. Now, I think, would be a good time.'

And, hand in hand, they walked back along the walled paths to the car.

NINETEEN

Epiphany

She had hoped as they drove away that he wouldn't break the mood by taking her somewhere violently loud and aggressively twentieth-century. I insult him, she thought contritely as he drew up in a village up in the hills behind Corfu Town, he knows far better than to do that.

They'd eaten a simple meal, beautifully cooked, and the quiet company around them had been exclusively Greek.

Back in the car afterwards, he drove on up a winding and increasingly narrow road. Higher and higher, glimpses of the lights of the town appearing sometimes through the thick trees, the faint scent of pine on the air...

'I know where we are!' Her exclamation shot out just as he was turning into the drive. As the steep track loomed up ahead and the green gates came into view he said, 'I wondered when you would recognise it.'

As before, he bipped the horn and the small boy came out to undo the padlock. As before, Aaron regally lifted his hand in thanks.

She was puzzled. 'But... We came here to eat, last time.' There was no way to say it except bluntly. 'And we've just eaten, down in that village.'

'This is not a place solely for eating.'

'No, I realise that. It's a club, isn't it? For—' She was at a loss. What on earth could it be for, out here in the wild hills with a locked gate to ensure its privacy?

He laughed, a burst of sound which suggested he'd been enjoying her thoughts too much to hold in his delight any longer. 'For unspeakable vice?' he suggested. 'For old men to paw and slaver over beautiful young girls in provocative underwear? Beautiful young *boys* in provocative underwear?'

'Well, it could be!' It wasn't fair of him to laugh. How was she to know? And there were those statues, out on the terrace—as well as the modestly-clad Muses, there'd been quite a lot with nothing on.

He said, not laughing now, 'If I came to admire young women or young boys, ask yourself if it is likely I should bring you with me.'

No. Of course you wouldn't. I'm sorry.

And *I* am sorry, for teasing you.

Then he added aloud, 'It is not a club, of any kind.' And, just as he'd said before when he first drove her back to The Twins' House—sounding amused, as if he remembered just as well as she did—he added quietly, 'It is my house.'

I realised he was rich, she thought, mind still reeling in shock as they got out of the car, but this, this is something else! He *owns* this incredible place. She repeated it a couple of times, as if that might help her believe it. And he has a motor launch, and The Twins' House, and various other properties God knows where which that awful Bull man looks after for him. What *is* he?

He was leading the way up the steps, opening the tall porticoed front door. No butler to admit him, tonight, she thought suddenly. They walked across the marble slabs of the hall, footsteps loud in the silence.

She followed him down a dimly-lit passage, and waited as he opened a door at the far end. He switched on a lamp that stood on a low table, and the soft light shone out on a long room whose many windows looked out on to the terrace. She could see the backs of the Muses, and beyond them the black and white flags of the terrace, like some giant's chess board.

He must have switched on the stereo, too, for there was music in the room. A woman's voice, singing something hauntingly poignant that seemed to reach inside her and touch against her saddest thoughts. She wondered what it was. Why he should be playing it.

He said, 'It is "Beim Schlafengehen".' He spoke the German words as easily as he spoke English. And Greek. And whatever strange language it was in which he addressed the Bull man. '"Going to Sleep". One of the *Four Last Songs* of Strauss.' He added quietly, 'Music can sometimes unlock, where other things fail.'

Slowly she turned to face him. He was standing behind her, hands in his pockets. He didn't feel threatening, or overwhelming, or powerful. He felt reassuring.

She moved closer to him. Several things flashed through her mind as possible conversation starters, but in the end she simply said, 'Why have you brought me here?'

He stared down at her, as if in contemplation. Then he said, 'A question with many potential answers.' From nowhere, a shiver of pleasure rose in her, trembling its way right through her before dissipating and fading away. 'To begin with, to attempt again what I was trying to impart to you in the museum.'

He took her hand and led her to the far corner of the room, where a copy of the Aphrodite statue stood on a plinth. Or perhaps, she thought—much more likely, really—the museum has the copy and this is the original.

223

'Aphrodite,' she said. It was almost like greeting an old friend.

'Have you yet appreciated why I showed her to you?' He was standing back from the statue, not touching her this time. 'Do you not allow yourself to realise why the twins look at you as they do?'

'I—' What was she to say? What was he talking about?

'The resemblance is faint, but it is there for those who will see it.' Now he was touching, his hand on the marble head as if in blessing. In exactly the same spot, she felt a corresponding pressure. When she had finished gathering her resources to cope with that, it dawned on her what he meant.

ME?' The word came out as an undignified screech. 'What rubbish!' And that was downright rude. 'I'm sorry,' she added. 'But—'

'But?' he echoed. 'I told you, after you had run away and out of the museum, that Aphrodite is woman, that you must accept her. You could not take it, then. But perhaps now you can.'

I can't, she thought bleakly, any more now that I could then. And how on earth can I explain? 'It isn't— I'm not what I appear to be.' It was a form of torment, to say what she had to say. But with him only honesty would do. 'You also said something about accepting sexuality,' she plunged on, 'and that was why I had to get away. You're wrong, about that. Quite wrong, because . . . because . . . '

Even for him, she couldn't go on. But the memories, the shame and the remorse, the humiliation of what had happened and the horror of what it had led to, ran riot in her head, blundering painfully into her tenderest, most vulnerable places like the heavy footsteps of a tribe of giants, all the more violent for having been so long penned up. In dumb pain she shook her head—no! no! go away!—but it was no

224

good. A tight spiral was screwing down into her brain, tormenting, torturing, as the things she had buried so deep, for so long, were dug out and squeezed forward into the light. She saw herself, hurt. Saw the children, crying. Saw herself lash out in her pain to wound in her turn, but far, far more deeply.

Felt the hurt again, and the blind wild impulse to hit back.

Felt, devastatingly, the guilt.

Aaron's arms were round her, Aaron's mind said direct to hers, let it go. Put it aside. Not for ever, but for now. And indomitable came his command: *Forget*.

She fought with him, screaming from the mortally injured part of her, I can't! I mustn't! I did wrong, and I have to bear it, carry it round with me always! It's unforgivable, and I don't expect to be forgiven!

Let it go! he shouted again. It was not your fault, you need not bear all the guilt.

Yes I must! It *was* my fault, all my fault, and I can never make amends, never have the stain wiped from my soul!

What arrogance, resounded his chilling thought, to think you are the one penitent in the whole long history of the world who is not to be absolved!

Everything came to a halt. In the silence that rang in her head she heard his words echo, once, twice.

And even as she realised he was right, she appreciated how clever he was, to have hit on the one thing she'd never thought of. The one thing that might, at long, long last, bring her peace.

She said, in a whisper, 'Aaron.'

The strong hold of his arms round her waist lessened in intensity. Became less like the grip of a strait-jacket, more like a hug.

He said again, 'Let it go.'

And, this time, she did.

He swept in to fill the vacuum. Overwhelmingly—

now that she was letting him in and no longer fighting—he was there. His arms crushing her against him, his body hard against hers, were only the outward, physical signs: beyond them, deeper, unstoppable, his mind and his soul flowed into hers, strengthening her, pouring into her like a draught of cool life-giving water to a body dying of thirst.

She wanted to laugh, wanted to cry. All she could do was say his name, over and over, until his mouth finding hers in a profound and bonding kiss silenced her.

A great surge of delight raced through her, awakening her like sunshine bursting in to bring a new day. It's you, she thought wildly, it's all you. Thank you.

As if he heard, he lifted his lips from hers, pulling away slightly so that he could stare into her eyes. He looks happy, she thought. How wonderful, that I can make him happy. Is it the kiss, or is it the thoughts? Or both?

I've come home. I'm where I belong. And it's going to be all right, now.

She said—not aware if she spoke aloud or not, for it didn't matter—you don't know how awful it's been.

She knew he understood, that she need say no more; it was in his eyes. He went on looking at her, as if drinking in the full measure of the awfulness, as if he knew, just as she did, that it was never going to be as bad again.

Then he bent his head, and this time the kiss didn't have to stop.

She was drowning in him, in the feel of his lips, his tongue, against hers. His hands were on her, one slipped inside the opening of her dress, touching her neck, fingers in the hollow above her collar-bone, the other on her chin, as if he had to hold her face exactly where he wanted it. Even in the intensity of her

226

pleasure at his kissing, she became aware of his fingers moving upwards over her cheek—long fingers, their touch delicate—and coming to rest, questing, at the edge of her eye. She heard his summons and, obeying, her eyelids reluctantly came open.

Right above her, his dark eyes stared down into hers. She felt the shock of his nearness—not his physical nearness, but his very soul glancing against hers, meeting, merging, until she felt herself drawn into him, willingly, the world beginning and ending in him. Entranced, she felt a new joy begin, for his hand at her neck was going down, inside her clothing, fingers playing over the curve of her flesh, arousing her to an unknown pitch of excitement, melting for him, flowing into him, to culminate in the moment of perfection as he touched her nipple.

She was dizzy, knees weak, and she was afraid she would faint. He said, do not worry, I will not let you fall. She leaned on him, and he was strong, supporting her as he moved her backwards until there was a cool touch against her legs and she found herself lying on the yielding smoothness of a leather sofa.

With no fumbling, not even any apparent effort, he was undressing her, undressing himself, and his hands, his mouth, running down over her breasts, her stomach, her thighs, set her on fire, every inch of her skin warming to his touch, warming to him, lifting to him, wanting to be close, closer to him than to anyone, ever, before. With no idea where it came from, she felt her own sexuality rouse itself, grow tall, exert its power until, coursing through her with her racing blood, she gave back to him what he was giving to her. The moment came when the touch of his hands on her—of her hands on him—was no longer enough: poised above her, she knew he would enter her.

Images flashed in her head. The twins, beautiful in their swimming trunks. Their blue eyes on her,

227

admiring. Aaron, holding her wrists down in her lap in an iron grip. The twins on the beach, lying either side of her as the waves ran up over her body and left her weak and satiated. Aaron, carrying her to bed. Looking down on her near-naked body. Aaron, tending her foot. Fingers pressing into the white skin as now they had pressed into her. Aaron kissing her.

Aaron.

Now he was inside her. They were one, united in body, united in mind, their two souls combined, one running into the other so that she no longer knew where her consciousness ended and his began. His movements were her movements, his impulses hers, and, as the ecstatic sensations accelerated faster, faster towards their climax, his joy was her joy.

Lying against him, head resting on his chest rising and falling with his now-peaceful breathing, she wondered if he'd fallen asleep. I wouldn't be surprised if he had, she thought dreamily, after an expenditure of energy like that, any man could be excused for...

'No, I haven't,' he said.

Smiling, she hugged him. Said against his smooth skin, 'Do you *always* know what I'm thinking?'

He hesitated, then said, 'I always *can* know. But, sometimes, I think I should not—intrude. Then I try to resist temptation and turn my attention elsewhere.'

'I don't suppose you'll tell me how you do it?'

'No. I would tell you, but it is not something that can be explained.' His hand came up to stroke her cheek. 'There is no mystery about it. It is a human ability, like speech, or hearing. Once, thousands of years ago, our ancestors depended on non-verbal communication. How do you think they managed, before there were words? It is simply that the skill has fallen into disuse.'

She thought about that. 'So you mean anyone could do it? I could do it?'

'You more than anyone. You already possess abilities which you do not recognise.'

Good grief. 'Such as what?'

He was silent for some time, and she wondered if perhaps he wasn't going to answer. But then he said, 'On one or two occasions—perhaps more than that—I have been tuned into you, thinking that it was without your knowledge, and you have surprised me by sensing my presence. And, although I do not like to admit it, I believe you have had some awareness of what I was thinking.'

'And other people don't do that? Don't know you're there, I mean?'

She felt him shake as he laughed shortly. 'I cannot think when someone last knew I was there.'

It was a lot to take in. Amazing, really, to be told something so fundamental about herself of which she'd had no inkling. Because she was still not quite convinced—or, she admitted honestly, more likely because she wanted him to give her a specific instance so that she could be proud of herself—she said, 'Could you give me an example?'

'I could.' She knew from the way he said it that he didn't want to. 'There are two—no, three—occasions that I remember particularly. But two of them are to do with the person whom you persist in referring to as the Bull man, although he is known to everyone else by the less colourful but more acceptable name of Angelos.' Angelos! she thought. How highly inappropriate. 'And I am sure,' he was saying, 'you do not want to talk about him.'

'No. I don't.'

She thought, but couldn't quite say, what was the third occasion?

And met with a blank wall.

Before it had time to start hurting, he was shaking her. 'Come on,' he said. 'We'll walk on the terrace. The cool night air will feel good.'

He pushed her off him, sitting up beside her then getting up and pulling her to her feet. Taking her hand, he led her to one of the long windows.

As he stepped outside, she hung back.

'What's the matter?'

'We've got nothing on!' She felt foolish saying it, even more foolish standing there in the open window stark naked.

But he came back to her. He looked at her, his head on one side, and said, 'Does it worry you?'

She nodded.

'Why? You must realise that there is nobody here besides us?'

'Yes, I do. It's not that, it's...' She made a stupendous effort to overcome her self-consciousness. It was easier than she'd thought, with him. 'I feel vulnerable without my clothes.'

He had his arm round her waist and was leading her slowly outside. 'Vulnerabilty implies you have a weakness which you fear someone will exploit,' he said thoughtfully. 'Is it, do you think, that you worry I do not like the sight of you naked?'

'I suppose it must be.'

They had paused before one of the nude statues. A woman, mature and handsome. As curvy as Fay was. 'Do you remember, I did this before?' He turned to look at her as he ran his hands over the rounded buttocks.

'You didn't do *that*. You only got as far as the stomach, then I ran away.'

He said, 'You're not running away now.'

She stared up into his eyes. 'No. I'm not.'

It seemed to take him quite an effort to get back to what he'd been saying, and it gave her such a keen delight that she was sure he must pick it up. 'I was trying to help you,' he said reproachfully, and she laughed.

'Yes. Please go on.'

'The great majority of men through the ages have admired women like this,' he said, with such authority that she had to believe him. He caressed the outthrusting hip, his hand lingering on the rounded thigh. 'A man—especially a Greek man—does not want a woman who looks like an athletic boy.' Mischievously she thought, very deliberately, of the Greeks of the past and their notorious penchant for the youth of their own sex. And into her head he said, please do not be flippant.

She laughed. 'But these voluptuous Junoesque types you admire imprisoned themselves in corsets,' she protested. 'Squeezed all that flesh away behind whalebones and calico.'

'And what impression were these corsets designed to create?' he countered. His hand went back to the statue's bottom, then to her jutting breasts. ''A large bust and a protuberant rear. No?'

'But—'

'And they did not go to bed in their corsets.' Suddenly the mood between them was charged. 'Did they? What better,'—his hand now seemed to cover the statue in her entirety—'than this, a soft, warm, living pillow?'

You're doing it deliberately. Talking about bed, and pillows, and sleeping with people.

I am.

I can't sleep with you, I have to get back, I have to . . .

Do you want to stay with me?

Yes.

Then do so. The twins are caring for your sons, and they will watch over them until I return you early in the morning.

But . . .

What now?

Nothing.

He drew her to him, and the feel of his body against hers was so fiercely arousing that she would have slept with him, made love all night with him, out there on the marble terrace with the Muses, the other statues, the absent staff, the whole of Corfu looking on.

He led her back into the house. As he reached behind her to close the door, he said, 'It was a nice idea. But, if you do not mind, I would prefer to take you to my bed.'

Part Three

TWENTY

Under the Sign of Gemini

In October 1977, soon after her twenty-eighth birthday, Fay's first pregnancy was confirmed.

It occurred to her, years later, to reflect on how powerful was the reproductive urge, cutting across sense and better judgement like a scythe through ripe corn. Have a baby *NOW!*, Mother Nature kept shouting in her head, loud enough to drown the protesting voice pointing out that a baby would mean giving up the job she enjoyed, moving from the neat and easily-run London flat to a house, somewhere out in the sticks.

Pointing out that Barry was too immature for fatherhood.

She didn't listen. A baby became her sole aim, and, wanting one so much, she assumed conception would happen immediately, so that in the months following abandonment of contraception, she would weep with disappointment each time the evidence of her body indicated that it hadn't happened yet. And when, at last, it did, the shadowy fears—how will I cope? Will Barry really be delighted?—were drowned by the flood of joy.

'Shall we go out house-hunting this weekend?' she would say to him each Friday evening as the autumn days flew by. Once in a while he'd say yes, and they'd drive out of town on an unplanned, inefficient trip that would achieve nothing and end in the early evening in some country pub that sold real ale. Sometimes she thought that'd be the way to persuade him, to point out how much nicer the pubs were out of town.

More often he would have an excuse and they'd stay at home. 'Too tired.' Or, 'I'm going to Dusseldorf on Monday! Had you forgotten?' as if going to Dusseldorf precluded any activity over the weekend except sitting dozing on the sofa in front of the television.

Realising that if they were to accomplish anything, she'd have to do it on her own, she wondered where to start. The list of towns from which they—all right, Barry—could commute fairly painlessly into London was interminable. Do we want to be north, south, east or west?

A friend of Barry's invited him up to St Albans to watch the rugby. Barry went, presumably enjoyed himself—enough to stay the night, sleeping on the friend's floor—and came home on Sunday saying St Albans was great, good rugby side, friendly people. Fay thought there were probably worse ways of deciding on your future abode—sticking a pin in a map?—and, with the aid of a St Albans telephone directory in the Post Office, wrote to a handful of estate agents for details of properties for sale.

With a positive plan of campaign, Barry became more enthusiastic. The friend with the flat—his name was Tom, and he was engaged to a girl called Sophia who was an air stewardess—proved to be a pleasant sort who came with them on some of their viewing forays and added vital bits of local knowledge of the kind that the estate agents were wont to omit. 'Yes, it's a nice house, but there's an overspill estate just over the back and half the kids are Picassos with the spray paint.' 'I know there's a bus stop outside, but the bus only runs twice a day.' 'Miles from the schools, Fay.' Fay's pregnancy was beginning to show.

In February, on a bitter day when Barry was worn out after a week away, she went on her own to look at a three-bedroom detached house which, from the details, she thought just might do. She went by train: one of the symptoms of her condition was a reluctance to drive herself, not liking the proximity of her swelling body—and what was swelling it—to the hard unyielding circle of the steering wheel. And she went resentfully—Barry looked awful, and she didn't believe him when he said he was going down with a cold, thinking it far more likely he was hung-over. Tom met her at the station and drove her out to the house.

'I love it,' she whispered to him as they stood on the upstairs landing waiting for the lady of the house to decide which bedroom to show them first.

Tom was amused. 'Why?' he whispered back. 'It's nice, but so have lots of others been.'

'Oh—I don't know. I like the location, the way it's near the main road yet hidden by the trees. I like the way it's been looked after, too—we could move in without having to do anything at all.'

Tom nodded. 'That's true.' He gave her an understanding smile. 'And pretty important, I should say.' She wondered if the understanding smile was because he, too, had a shrewd idea of who it would be up the ladder with the paintbrush. Not a job for a pregnant or newly-delivered woman.

I gave him the credible, sensible reasons, she thought as the woman finally made up her mind to show off the best first and admitted them into the peach and gold master bedroom. I didn't give him the real one, that I'm bowled over by the address.

She *wanted*, with as illogical a fervour as her desire to have a baby, to live on Watling Street.

She went home with a stern determination to

railroad Barry into agreeing. If you won't make the effort, she rehearsed as she walked up from the tube, then you don't deserve to have a say. And I love it. I want it!

He was looking out for her. He ran down to open the door before she could get her key in the lock, embraced her, then led her upstairs to where an appetising aroma of roasting chicken permeated the flat.

'I've done supper,' he said, pushing her down on to the sofa, putting a pouffe under her swelling legs, 'I hope you're hungry, because I've done a pud too. And I've bought some wine, if you fancy some.'

He was kneeling on the floor in front of her, watching her anxiously. She thought he was flushed, and reached out to put her hand on his forehead. He felt as if he had a temperature. She was remorseful, that she'd ascribed his symptoms to drink. About to say so, he got in first.

'I'm sorry, Fay. I should have come with you, it's not fair to make you do it on your own. We could have gone by car, if I'd come, and it wouldn't have been half as tiring.'

'It's all right.' She put the cool back of her hand against his hot cheek, and he turned towards her touch. 'You don't really look up to it.'

Knowing by her tone that he was forgiven, he climbed up to sit beside her. 'It's not too bad,' he said. 'I'm dosing myself with aspirin.'

'It was nice of you to do the meal.'

'No trouble.'

Now was the moment, when peace was restored, to tell him about the house. When she'd finished, he said, 'It sounds perfect. If you want it, we'll have it.'

They sold the flat remarkably quickly. 'Easy, selling to first-time buyers,' the estate agent said. 'No chain, with them.' But there was a chain with the St Albans lady, and in addition there was the vacillating nature of her husband, who seemed to change his mind from one week to the next whether he wanted to move before or after the summer—'He'll miss his roses, you see,' his embarrassed and apologetic wife explained to Fay, 'and he does love them, they're his only interest since he retired,'—or, sometimes, whether he wanted to move at all. Fay, listening to yet another tale of postponement and indecision on a day when the baby's antics were an all too clear reminder of its imminent arrival, silently cursed the silly, stubborn old bugger and released her anger in imagining where, and with what force, she would like to stick his roses.

They moved in at the beginning of May. The birth was due in three weeks, and Fay sat in immobile frustration watching the removal men, aching to leap up and work beside them. Barry, drawing on some reserve of common sense which, saved for emergencies, consequently came out brand-new and high-powered, got the men to furnish the bedroom first, so that she could go up, shut the door on the noise and the chaos, and lie down. When the pantechnicon at last drew away, Tom and Sophia arrived with a take-away Chinese and a bottle of champagne. They sat in the bedroom, the three of them pampering Fay and insisting she mustn't come down till they'd finished.

Exhausted, even though she'd done nothing more strenuous than sit in the car and lie on the bed, she did as she was told and loved them all for their hard work and their care.

Barry came and woke her up as the sun was setting.

'Tom and Sophia have gone,' he said, sitting on the bed beside her and stroking her hair. 'They thought we'd like to be alone.'

They went up a few more notches in Fay's estimation.

He took her hand and led her downstairs. The furniture was all in place, there was a smell of polish in the living room and a clean aroma of disinfectant in the kitchen. Everything shone. There were vases of flowers from the garden, and two big pot plants, a fern and a rubber plant, stood by the French doors.

'Housewarming present, from Sophia,' Barry said. 'We can put them outside on the terrace, only I didn't tonight as it might be too cold. Is it okay?'

He was so eager to please. So wanting her to like it, to approve of all they'd done. Her heart turned over with love for him.

'It's lovely.' She put her arm round him, and he pulled her as close to him as the bump allowed. 'You must have worked so hard. Thank you.'

He whispered, 'I want to make you happy.' Then, defiantly, as if there were evidence to the contrary, 'I *will* make you happy.'

A week after the due date, Fay was still waiting. Depressed and miserable, she was sick of the whole thing, longing to be rid of the great weight of baby she was lugging around, longing to be *her* again, body to herself, with this energetic intruder, who kicked and punched with such monotonous persistence, in her arms and not in her womb.

Sophia had taken to dropping in most days. Her schedule meant that she was often going to work, or coming home, during the long daytime hours when Fay would otherwise have been alone. Watching her set about the chaos in the kitchen, which Fay had neither the heart nor the strength to do anything about, Fay wondered if all air stewardesses were as capable and *nice* as Sophia or if she'd just struck lucky.

'What about supper?' Sophia said. 'Want me to put a stew together, or something?'

'No, thanks. Barry said not to bother, he'll be late again tonight.' Say it lightly, so she won't think I mind as much as I do.

But Sophia was perceptive. Perhaps it went with the job. 'Bit hard on you, isn't it?' Her voice was sympathetic. Oh, Fay thought, please don't be kind to me!

'He can't help it,' she said, too quickly. 'They're very busy. He's meant to be going to Germany again next week.'

'Don't you *mind*?'

Fay looked up at her. 'Yes, I do,' she said quietly. 'I mind a hell of a lot. I mind the way my life with him has gone, so that I've backed myself into a position I can't get out of. I'm the strong one,' she plunged on, before the impetus should die, 'I hold him up, hold his hand, tell him everything's going to be all right, and I seem to have done it so well all this time that it doesn't occur to him I'm fed up, sick of being pregnant, worried about going into a hospital among total strangers, frightened of the birth, *terrified* I shan't know what to do when I have to bring it home!'

For a moment she sat amazed at all the things she'd been carrying around with her which had suddenly thrust themselves out into the light of day. Then, to her horror, she began to cry.

Sophia's arms were round her, and she was murmuring gentle soothing words. She'd be a marvellous person to hold your head while you were being sick, Fay thought distractedly. 'Come on, love,' Sophia said, 'don't. You're not yourself at the moment, no-one would be, coping with trying to settle in a new place *and* having their baby putting in an appearance a week late. It'd be enough to make anyone upset!'

241

The darkest of the fears subsided a little. Slid back into the corner where she usually kept them penned. 'I suppose so,' she said.

'It'll be better when something starts to happen,' Sophia said robustly, 'you'll see! You won't have time to worry, you'll be too busy doing the breathing exercises and timing your contractions!'

Fay laughed shortly. 'It sounds a bundle of fun.'

'Is Barry going to be with you?'

'I don't know. He won't say. I think—'

'Go on,' Sophia said quietly. 'What do you think?'

Fay shook her head.

'You think that's why he's staying out late every night? To lessen the chances he'll be here when you start?'

Fay raised her eyes to look into Sophia's. 'Yes. That's exactly what I think.'

Sophia stroked her hand. 'It's overrated, you know, this business of fathers being present. Half of them faint and have to be helped out, the other half think they know best and insist on saying so when all that most mums want is to be left with the professionals to get on with it.'

She sounded as if she knew. 'Have you had a lot of experience of births?'

Sophia smiled. 'I used to be a nurse, till the rotten pay and my wanderlust persuaded me there were better ways of earning my corn.'

Fay said impulsively, 'If Barry's not here and you are, will you come with me?'

And Sophia said, 'I thought you'd never ask.'

Late the following morning, Fay passed what the woman at the ante-natal classes had referred to quaintly as a 'show'. The twinges she'd been experiencing since breakfast stepped up and settled

242

down into a rhythm: one minute's twinge, ten minutes' respite.

She went to the phone and called Sophia, who arrived almost immediately.

'What do you want to do?' she asked, her hand on Fay's stomach as another twinge tightened the muscles. 'If the contractions are ten minutes apart, it'll be a while yet.'

'I don't know,' Fay said. 'What do people usually do?'

'They usually go into hospital far too soon and wish they'd stayed in the comfort of their own homes a bit longer.'

'Let's stay here, then.'

'Do you want me to call Barry?'

Fay hesitated. Then she said, 'No.'

They sat together in the living room, watching an Ealing comedy on television. Sophia gave her a thickly-folded towel to sit on—'You don't want the waters breaking all over your sofa'—and, absurdly, because the comedy wasn't that funny, Fay kept wanting to laugh.

The humour went out of the situation as the contractions intensified. When they were six minutes apart, Sophia phoned the hospital to announce Fay's imminent arrival. Standing up, leaning on Sophia, Fay felt the waters break and warm fluid run down her legs into her shoes, overflowing on to the floor. 'Goodness!' she said.

'Don't worry.' Sophia's voice was reassuring. 'I'll come back and see to it, later.'

It was good, to have Sophia with her. She was forthright and efficient, far more so than Barry would have been, and Fay got the distinct impression Sophia was telling the staff what to do rather than the other way round. Most important, hers was a friendly familiar face among a lot of strangers.

'Pity you couldn't have stayed in London till the baby came,' Sophia observed at one point. 'It might have been better for you to be with nurses and midwives you knew.'

'I didn't know them,' Fay replied. 'I saw a different lot every time I went. Had to spend the first few minutes of every appointment telling them the details. One of the doctors...'

She broke off as another contraction soared through her.

And soon she didn't feel like talking any more.

She had a shot of pethidine, and felt as if she were floating. Was aware of it starting to wear off. Wanted to ask for more, because it hurt, hurt, *hurt*.

But then, as the evening sun faded and twilight fell, a different sensation began and deep inside she felt a new, insistent pressure.

'Sophia?' she said dreamily.

'Wait,' Sophia said, getting up. 'I'll call the midwife.'

I don't think I can wait, Fay thought. This seems to be outside my control.

'Don't push yet!' the midwife ordered, appearing at the bedside and leaning in between Fay's legs. 'We must see if you're fully—Oh!'

Then all was hurry and bustle as Fay was moved on to a trolley and wheeled rapidly along to the delivery room, Sophia laughing and hopping at her side, saying, 'Nearly here! Your baby's nearly here!'

'The head's crowning!' the midwife shouted as she and a nurse helped Fay on to the table, 'we got here just in time, you almost gave birth in the corridor!'

Elated, Sophia and the nurse stood either side of her, propping her up, while the midwife commanded, 'Push!' 'Wait—pant!' 'Now, contraction coming—*push!*' and Fay, dizzy with wonder, relief and the light-headed aftermath of pain, tried to comply.

244

There was a rush and a squelching sound, and a sudden gutsy cry.

The midwife said, 'You've got a son!'

She knew she must have been asleep, because now it was quite dark. She was in a bed in a ward, washed, in a clean nightdress, and she felt as if she'd just built a motorway single-handed. She lifted her arm, which felt as if it had dumbbells strapped to it, and looked at her watch.

Half past eleven.

There was some sort of nightlight burning by the bed, and she saw a note propped up against the carafe of water. Reaching out—it seemed to take an age and a disproportionate amount of effort—she picked it up.

'Congratulations! Eight pounds, lots of red hair, and he's lively as a cricket. Clever girl! Have gone to your house to tidy up, but I'll pop in on the way to work tomorrow. Will get Barry to come as soon as he's home. Love and hugs, Sophia.'

Barry. She'd phoned, Fay remembered, Sophia had dialled the number and held the receiver for her. And Barry's office had said he was on his way back from a meeting, that they'd tell him the moment he was there, and wasn't it all marvellous?

Unable to stay awake, even for him, she'd fallen deeply, dreamlessly asleep.

Half past eleven. Where was he? Where was everybody? *Anybody?*

There was a buzzer on a cord on her pillow. She pressed it, and quite soon a nurse appeared.

'How are you feeling, Mrs. Leary?' she asked softly.

'Fine. Where's...?'

'Any pain?' She was taking a thermometer from a

245

little tube over the bed, shaking down the mercury, putting it under Fay's tongue.

'Nmm.' Fay shook her head. Why did people like dentists and nurses always ask you questions just as they were sticking things in your mouth and making it impossible for you to answer?

The nurse took her pulse, wrote a note on the board at the foot of the bed, then took out the thermometer and looked at it.

'Fine,' she said. 'Your son's awake. Like to see him for a moment?'

'Yes.'

The nurse disappeared, to return wheeling a bassinet.

'Here he is.'

She put him in Fay's arms. He was clean now, wearing a little vest with short sleeves and a nappy that looked absurdly large. His eyes were open, and staring vaguely in her direction.

She whispered, 'Hello, little boy.'

Footsteps outside. The nurse, going to see. Coming back. Saying, 'Just a few minutes, and you must be very quiet.'

Barry, standing there, swaying slightly, cheeks wet with tears as he looked down at Fay and his new son.

Meeting her eyes, he said, 'Oh, Fay. Whatever have we done?'

TWENTY-ONE

Evil Spirits

He didn't mean it.

She kept repeating to herself, he didn't intend it to sound like that. As if the baby in its reality were more than he could bear. As if terminal despair were on him, and there was no way out.

He was drunk, she told herself. Definitely. He was swaying, and his eyes were bloodshot, and it wasn't just with tears. I haven't seen him as bad as that for ages. He must have gone out with his friends from the office—yes, I bet that's it! They'd have been so pleased for him, they'd have taken him down the pub and things would have developed. That nice girl I spoke to who promised to give him the message was delighted, over the moon. She'd have told everyone else, and they'd all have congratulated Barry as soon as he got in. Champagne, I expect. Whiskey, anyway, to wet the baby's head.

She saw him again, standing at the foot of her bed. Hardly glancing at his tiny new son. Face ashen, red-lidded eyes deep and sunken and looking more black than blue.

He was drunk.

He didn't mean it.

*

There was much to keep her busy during her short stay in hospital. A baby to get to know, so that she learned to distinguish one sort of cry from another and realise what it was he wanted. Breast feeding to master, which almost defeated her until one of the nurses came to sit with her for an hour one night and between the two of them—and a hungry, desperate baby—they finally got it right.

And, gradually, anxiety and apprehension faded, and in their place love grew.

She kept him with her all the time, cradled beside her as she lay reading on her bed, in her arms as she strolled endlessly up and down the long corridors. The feel of his face pressed to her skin, the weight of his round and solid little bottom resting in the palm of her hand, became imprinted on her physically, just as his dawning consciousness struggling out towards her reached into her mind.

My son.

Barry came again, as she'd known he would. She stopped agonising over his first disastrous visit, and in time pushed it away into that part of her brain reserved for things she didn't want to think about.

Barry was keen to throw a party to welcome her home. Tom and Sophia, he said, and people from the office. The neighbours. At first she was pleased, that he should produce this happy and positive reaction to his son's arrival. She agreed—'as long as you don't ask too many and I don't have to do too much.'

But quite soon she realised it was an awful idea. Life at home with a week-old baby was incredibly tiring, and she hadn't had the time to organise herself—and him—into any sort of routine. And I've got twelve people coming tomorrow evening! she thought in horror. Why in God's name did I say yes?

She wondered what on earth she was going to

wear. It was the least of her worries, but the only one that was small enough to be approachable. She felt fat, with a belly that swelled as if already another baby were growing there. And she was sure she smelt of milk—she was embarrassingly full of it, breasts huge and round like the exaggerated mammaries of some ancient fertility goddess. The milk leaked: whenever the baby cried—sometimes even when she imagined him crying, or simply thought about him—she would feel the instant let-down and the resulting dribble. She stuffed breast pads inside her bra, but still the damp patches would soon start seeping and spreading down her front, like the lap-puddle of an incontinent old man.

She wore a navy-blue maternity smock, loosely pulled in with a belt. She felt the worst frump on earth. Standing in the living room trying to think of new and interesting ways to respond to people's congratulations—so well-meant but so wearisome, when she'd been up half the previous night—she wished they'd all go home.

Soon, quite a lot of them did. They ate the cold buffet—all straight from the supermarket; she'd felt up to no more than putting it out on plates, and sometimes, when the carton was pretty enough, hadn't even done that—and they drank the drink. Then said their polite farewells. Fay, seeing them off, replied, 'Thank you for coming. And for the present— so kind of you.' It *was* kind of them, all of them—there had been some lovely gifts—and she knew her thanks were inadequate.

She hoped they understood.

She sat on the stairs after closing the door on the last of the guests who had only stayed for the early shift; there was a hard core of drinkers out on the terrace with Barry, but she didn't think there was any chance of them leaving yet. From upstairs she heard

249

the soft little whicker that said, I'm waking up. In a minute, I shall be hungry.

'Go up,' Sophia said, coming out of the living room and heading for the kitchen, a stack of dirty plates in her hands. Understanding in her face, she added, '*Stay up. I'll see to this lot.*'

Holding at bay the threatening tears—*stupid!* it's only because I'm so tired!—Fay gave her a heartfelt smile and dragged herself upstairs.

The question of a name was uppermost in her thoughts. Barry, in a permanent state of euphoria—drink-induced?—went all Irish. 'Patrick. Fergal. Seamus. Kevin. Donovan, Dominic, Donan. Liam, after me darling brother.' His eyes filled with the ready maudlin tears of alcoholic sentiment.

Irritated into sharpness, she snapped, 'Oh, shut up!' The baby started to cry. Oh, God, she thought, now look what I've done. Bitten Barry's head off for no reason, and started the baby bawling. Nasty bad-tempered cow. She went to pick up the child, soothing him, crooning to him, then turned to apologise to Barry.

'I'm sorry, I . . .'

But he wasn't looking at her. He was sitting staring out of the window, glass in his hand, humming to himself. Putting a few words to the tune. Something about a handsome rover from town to town. Come all ye young men and lay me down.

The regret died in her throat. She said decisively, 'I want something *English*. I want to call him . . .' She hunted for the English name to end all English names. 'Rupert.' Barry hardly seemed to register it. 'Rupert James.'

Barry was away at more frequent intervals, and for periods of longer duration, after Rupert's birth. A baby in the house didn't seem to suit him: it wasn't, Fay thought, a lack of love, for when he was there he would sit and gaze at his son with great tenderness, and she knew he carried a couple of the best baby photographs always in his wallet. But she sensed in him a basic lack of belief in his own ability to *cope* with it all.

'Fetch the baby, would you?' she'd say. 'He's crying, but I've just fed him so he probably only needs winding. Can you do it?' Or, 'He needs changing, I can smell him from here. Will you see to it? I'm in the middle of making pastry.'

Always, there was a reluctance to comply.

When she had the time, she asked herself, why? And think, poor Barry, when he loves his son so much, not to have the confidence to care for him!

But more often she didn't have the time. Would be bone-weary, fed-up with being fat and milky and never having enough sleep. Would have no patience, and would think, *SOD* Barry, I'll have to do it myself.

She got used to doing it herself. She realised, sadly, that she managed better when he was away than when he was home. He was no help, and seeing him sitting there not being any help irritated her. Then she would be upset at having been irritated.

When he was away she ached for him. Missed him, longed for him to be the sort of father and husband she wanted him to be. For the three of them to be a nice, happy, ordinary family.

But when he was away, she managed.

She wasn't sure exactly when she realised he was drinking again. He'd got through a lot when Rupert was born, but that was acceptable. Everyone did that. But she'd thought that, like everyone, he'd go back to not drinking a lot once they'd all settled down again.

The realisation must have been building up in her unconscious for some time, but unadmitted: when the final irrevocable proof came, there was in her a sense of, I knew it! I knew this all along!

It was a Saturday, a lovely, hot August Saturday, and she'd put Rupert and his pram in the car and taken him to Verulamium Park. He was, of course, far too little to appreciate it—it'd be years before he could join in the rumpus on the swings and roundabouts—but the park was pretty, and Fay enjoyed the company of the other mothers, watching with them, sharing their indulgent amusement at the fathers playing with the children.

Barry was going to a pre-season training session. 'I'll join you later,' he promised. 'Take a picnic—I'll get someone to drop me off and we'll have tea together.'

Today, she thought, glowing with quiet inner happiness, I'm meeting these other families on equal terms. I too have a husband, and he'll be along later, and he's far more handsome and attractive than any of the others. We'll sit over there in the shade, spread the rug, lay out the picnic, and for once everyone will envy *me*.

Three o'clock came. Three-thirty. Four.

At a quarter to five, she ate a sandwich and poured a cup of tea from the Thermos. Then, with sudden violent anger, threw the rest of the carefully-packed picnic into a bin.

He wasn't at home.

She fed and bathed Rupert, put him to bed.

Gave up on the television, and on her book.

Sat in growing fury until, at half-past midnight, he came in.

He stood in the open doorway of the living room, looking at her, a silly smile on his face.

He said, 'Guess what, Fay? I'm second team captain. Roger's backed down.' He burped, laughing, and lurched across to collapse beside her on the sofa.

She said icily, 'Where the fuck do you think you've been?'

He leaned away from her, head nodding slightly as

he tried to hold it still and focus on her. 'Where...? Don't swear, Fay, it's not nice.'

'Not nice? Not *nice*?' She was up on her feet, leaning over him. '*I'll* tell you what's not nice, Barry. What's not *fucking* nice! You, promising to come to the park for a picnic without the slightest intention of turning up!'

Shrinking from her—she realised she'd been spitting—he muttered, 'Things sort of developed.' He dropped his head, and she thought vindictively, guilty! The bastard's guilty!

He said, 'Sorry, Fay.'

She straightened up, turning from him. Walked towards the door. She stopped and said, 'I *hate* you.'

It was a demon in him, the urge to drink. A demon who, having been shut out—more or less—for so many years, celebrated his victorious re-admittance now with ebullient delight. And Barry seemed to have lost the will to fight. It was as if, now that it was out in the open and she knew, he no longer even tried to cover up.

A demon. She could almost see it, red-hot pitchfork in its evil little hand, pushing gentle, loving Barry on down the slope into his own hell. Sometimes it seemed to her that she saw his face looking up over his shoulder at her, heard his frightened voice call out in despair, Fay! Help me, Fay!

She tried. Had tried, she now saw, on and off since she'd known him. Had always succeeded, to a greater or lesser extent, for in that distant country called 'the past' he had wanted the same as she, had met her halfway. Had *tried*, stretched out his hands to grasp hers as she reached out to save him from himself.

But that was in another time. And besides, that man was dead.

Instead she had a new Barry, one whom she hardly

253

recognised. One who grew fat round the middle, whose once broad shoulders seemed to sag in defeat, whose blue eyes were half-obscured by the permanently puffy, reddened lids. Who became, on most of the rare occasions when he dared to put it to the test, impotent.

They now made love so infrequently that she hadn't bothered to fit herself up with another coil after Rupert's birth. The nurse at the clinic had warned her not to believe the old wives' tale that breastfeeding acted as a contraceptive: 'Don't go relying on that,' she said. 'I've seen too many young mums get pregnant that way, and the last thing you want when you're just managing to cope with one baby is to fall for another.'

Fay wanted to say, my husband no longer wants me. I've had a baby *he* can't cope with, even if I can, and he wants to bury his head in the sand and pretend it never happened. And I told him I hated him. In six months he's hardly touched me.

Pride held her back. She said noncommittally, 'Okay.'

They went on holiday, when Rupert was fourteen months old. A week, staying in a hotel on the Gower peninsula, spending their days exploring the little lanes and lazing on the wide sandy beaches. Just once, Barry made love to her, turning to her in the middle of the night, waking her from deep sleep so that, in the morning, she hardly knew if it had really happened or been part of some erotic, desperate dream.

But it must have happened. Because, amazingly, she found she was pregnant. As if her hungry ovum, knowing it was now or never, had sucked up the gush of sperm and pulled one into itself like magnetic north drawing the point of a compass.

Three months after the holiday, in bleak and miserable rainy November, she said to Barry, 'I'm going to have another baby.'

He stared at her in horror. Pity soared through her, agonisingly, that she should have said something—no matter what—to cause that awful look on his face. At the same time, the juxtaposition doing frightful damage to her deep heart, she despised him for his weakness.

Loving him, hating him, she stood at the moment of balance.

He dropped his head on to his folded arms and started to cry.

*

In the little square, the silver dawn light robbed the golden stones of all colour, so that The Twins' House looked unfamiliar. She had a moment's anxiety over how she was going to get in—she'd given her key to the twins and it would be embarrassing to have to wake one of them from profound sleep. She glanced across at Aaron, and saw he was smiling slightly. It struck her that of course *he'd* have a key, since it was his house. She was glad the thought had occurred to her and that he hadn't had to prompt her, either by word or thought.

He drew up outside the house. She felt his eyes on her, and turned to him. She knew with sudden insight that there would be times when this moment of parting would hurt like hell, when she would want more than anything to cling to him, to cry, 'Don't go.'

But those times were not yet: now she almost wanted him to be gone, so that, alone in the silent early morning, she could re-live the wonder and the passion of the night. Absorb the reality of him into herself, so that she could start to believe in him.

He said, 'I will call you, later.' He held out to her a key-ring bearing a single key.

As she reached out to take it, his fingers closed

around hers. The brief touch reawakening in her things which had barely had time to settle down, she pulled her hand away and threw herself out of the car. Running up the steps, she thought she heard him laugh. And was pleased, somewhere amid the confusion, to have this reassurance that her abrupt departure hadn't offended him.

She opened the door and crept into the house. Pulling the key out of the lock, she felt the key-fob knock against her hand. It was surprisingly heavy: looking at it briefly, she saw it was a silver medallion engraved with the sign of Gemini. Twins again, she thought.

Twins. I wonder where they are?

She went quietly upstairs. The door to one of the spare rooms was slightly ajar, and, holding her breath, she peered through the crack. The beds were occupied, on each of the two pillows a fair-haired head. The twins, eyes closed, were apparently fast asleep. On chairs at the foot of each bed were their neatly-folded clothes. Jeans, pants, t-shirts. Identical pairs of trainers, toes towards each other like two people about to waltz.

For some reason, she was surprised that the twins should be asleep. The thought flashed into her head that it was too *human* a thing for them to do.

Suddenly she felt like a voyeur, standing there spying on their vulnerable unconsciousness. She made herself turn away.

Along the landing, she went into the boys' room. Oliver lay curled up, face in his pillow and only the incredibly tousled back of his head showing. Gently she touched the nape of his neck, as she'd been doing since he was a baby, to make sure he wasn't too hot. Rupert lay on his back, and, as if subliminally registering her presence, muttered something. She bent over him, smoothing the hair from his forehead, and watched as a brief smile flickered over his face.

Everything was as it should be.

She tiptoed out and shut the door behind her.

In the sanctuary of her own room, slowly she took off all her clothes and prepared for bed. On her bare skin she could smell Aaron, and the sensation brought him violently, vividly close, a vibrant leap of reminiscent desire surging through her, vortex-like, leaving her trembling.

She put on her nightshirt and slipped under the cool sheet.

Still at last, she lay and waited for the events of the tumultuous night to start flowing through her mind. To prompt them, she tried to remember how he'd looked when he came for her. What they'd talked about, in that little hidden-away village. Dinner. Going back to his house. The moment of confrontation, when he'd touched on those frightening things she kept locked tight away in the corner of her mind...

I don't want to think about that. Something happened—something important—but it was inconclusive. There will have to be more, we'll have to....

Her mind slid off the thought, as if someone were leading her away.

And instead she remembered him kissing her. Touching her, arousing her, making love to her again and again until she was full of him, overwhelmed with him, and there wasn't room for anything else.

Aaron in her body, in her mind, in total occupation, she felt herself falling helplessly asleep.

TWENTY-TWO

Aries the Ram

It was almost midday when she woke, and unsurprisingly the house was empty. There was a note on her bedside table, in Rupert's writing:

> '*Dear Mum,*
> *Me and Oliver and the Twins have gone to the lido. They were still here when we got up and we all had breakfast together. We finished the fruit juice, hope that's all right.*
> > *Love, Rupert.*'

Oliver had added a P.S.:

> '*There's a ginormous bunch of flowers for you, Castor put them in a buket. Love you, Oliver.*'

B-u-*c*-k-e-t, she thought absently. And Oliver and I, not me and Oliver.

Then she realised what she'd just read.

Leaping down the stairs, she raced into the kitchen. On the cleared and wiped top of the table stood a red plastic bucket in which flowers—roses, lilies, delphiniums, carnations, and great fronds of some ferny thing with tiny white blooms whose name she didn't know—were crammed so tightly together that there was barely room for the water.

Propped against the bucket was an envelope with her name on it. On a thick piece of card he had written:

'You will know who these are from without being told. Thank you for the evening, and for the night.'

She reached out and touched his flowers as if she were touching his body. Then, for the urgent need was suddenly on her for something to *do*, she searched through the cupboards until she had found enough vases to accommodate the full wealth of her bouquet.

By the time she had gathered herself together sufficiently to set out for the lido, the house was full of the scent of roses.

I ought to go back, she thought in the middle of the afternoon, he said he'd call, and I might miss him. It occurred to her to wonder if 'call' had meant telephone or call round, and the thought of him arriving to find her not there was so unnacceptable that she leapt up off her bench, reaching out for her bag, all set to run home that minute.

Then, subsiding again, she realised she was being stupid. He'll know I'm here, I'm always here in the daytime. If he goes to the house and finds me out, he'll come to find me.

Would he need to do that? Or does he *know* I'm here, in the same way that he *knows* what I'm thinking?

The thought was vaguely alarming.

Why? she demanded. It seemed imperative that she answer herself. Why should I worry that he can read my thoughts and is perhaps able to be aware of where I am at any given time? And anyway I'm not sure about that, I'm only speculating. And why should it matter?

What else does he know?

Last night. Something about last night. Aaron, shouting into her mind about guilt. Yes! 'Let it go,' that was what . . .

He was there again, back in her mind. Blanking out the thought, so thoroughly that it was gone and she couldn't remember what it had been. And she was aware of surprise in him, perhaps self-accusation, that he'd allowed her to come close to thinking about something he was determined she shouldn't.

Then all of that was driven out by a fresh amazement, that apparently he now could enter her mind even when he wasn't with her. Now that *is* alarming, she thought, it really is, because I . . .

A hand on her shoulder, stroking up her neck and under her hair. Arousing in her a faithfully-remembered delight. Aaron's voice, saying quietly, 'I went to the house, and as you were not there I knew you would be here.'

Wanting to laugh—with relief? With joy?—she turned to him, and just for an instant he drew her head against his chest. Then he let her go, and, moving away from her, pulled up another bench and sat down beside her.

She wanted him to go on touching her. Into her head he said, I know. I want to touch you, also. Do you think that one night could have been enough? But here there are too many people.

She looked up into his eyes. Very deliberately she thought, when will you touch me again?

She knew he'd received it; for a split second his eyes widened, as if having her put thoughts into his head were a different matter, here in the daylight, from the almost mystical thing it had been last night. But then, recovering, he answered: Tonight.

Aloud she said, 'The twins were asleep when I got in. And by the time I woke up, they'd brought the boys down here. Which means they're spending all their time looking after my children.'

260

He looked at her, head on one side. A contemplating look. Then, as if her concern for the twins were hardly worthy of consideration and he was surprised she'd even mentioned it, he said, 'They do as I tell them.' And added, 'Your sons are well-behaved. And the twins would be here at the lido in any case, whether your boys were here or not. Castor and Pollux do not mind.'

That, she was aware, was the end of it. She knew better than to pursue it any further. Conscience salved—*he* says it's all right, so who am I to question?—she was filled with a guilt-tinged relief that the presence of two such pleasant, suitable and ever-available child-minders meant she was free to do whatever she wanted.

Standing up, he said, 'I shall come for you earlier this evening, at seven-thirty. There is a place to which I want to drive you, and there are questions connected with it which I wish to discuss with you.'

A drive. Some place they were going to visit. Things they were going to talk about.

She fought against the thought, bit down hard on it, but it was no good. And this, she was quite sure, wasn't one of those times when he would—what was it he'd said?—turn his attention elsewhere.

She was right. He hadn't. Laughing, he reached out to ruffle her hair. He said into her mind, warmly, affectionately, his words full of an erotic promise: No, of course that won't be all.

She took the boys home early, determined that for once she was going to remind them of what you were meant to do when you showered because, left to their own devices, neither of them seemed to remember that the purpose of soap and shampoo was for getting you clean. Then, to make up for being so bossy, she gave them some money and let them go down to the supermarket to choose something nice for tea.

'We're having things on sticks for supper tonight,' Oliver announced, dipping a biscuit covered with lurid pink icing into a huge pot of yoghurt.

'*Souvlaki*,' Rupert said, nonchalant tone not disguising his pride at remembering the Greek word. 'Like kebabs. You know.'

'Are you? With the twins?' She made a mental note to make sure they took some money with them, and wished she hadn't been so generous over funding tea. 'That'll be nice.'

'What are you doing, Mum?'

Innocent question. And Rupert, who had asked it, was still tucking in to his tea. She said, 'I'm going out for a drive with Aaron.'

'In his Range Rover?' Oliver sounded envious. 'Wish I could come.'

'We're going to look at the sights,' she said quickly. 'Churches, statues, I expect. That sort of thing.'

'Oh.' She heard him mutter, 'Bor-ring.'

'Mum, how do you do this?' Rupert had reached into the supermarket bag and was holding up a huge watermelon. He added, 'You *said* we could have one.'

'I did. You're quite right.' She was sorry he'd noticed her dismay. 'It's only that I'd forgotten how big water melons are. We'll be eating it for days.'

'We could throw it out, if we get sick of it,' Oliver suggested.

'Not allowed,' Rupert said. He looked up and caught her eye. '"I spent good money on that, you'll have to eat it up."'

She recognised herself. And was glad he could make a joke of it.

'Give me the knife,' she said, and as he did so she patted his hand to show him she didn't mind.

She cut a third of the melon into slices, wrapping the rest in the plastic bag and putting it in the fridge. Rupert de-pipped the pink flesh, and, watching them take the first bite, she wondered which one was going to say he didn't like it.

It was Oliver.

'*I* like it,' Rupert said. He reached out for Oliver's discarded slice. 'I'll have his.'

As she opened her mouth to bite into her own slice, she felt a pain in her jaw. On both sides a sharp stabbing sensation, at the hinges of her jaw-bone. Instantly she thought, what is it? Oh, God, I'm ill, I've got mumps or something, and we're miles from home, stuck here where the doctors won't understand and I'll have to pay a small fortune, what the *hell* am I going to do?

'What's the matter, Ma?' Oliver asked. 'Don't you like it either?'

'No, no, I love it.' She smiled at him. 'I—actually I don't think I'll eat it now, I'll save it for later.' She got up, wanting only to be alone, to think what to do next. As she left the room she heard Rupert say, 'It'd be better if she had a fresh slice. I'll finish hers too.'

Upstairs she went into her bathroom, staring at herself in the mirror. Her hand on her jaw, experimentally she opened her mouth again, and the pain shot out in protest. Alarmed, she felt for the glands in her neck. Nothing. No swelling, no tenderness. I *can't* be ill, she thought frantically and absurdly, I feel too well!

She went through into the bedroom, throwing herself down on the bed. As she did so, another pain hit her. But this one was in the muscles in her thighs. It felt as if she'd been riding a broad-backed horse.

And then she knew what was the matter with her.

Knew that the pain in her jaw, just like the stiffness in her thighs, was because of unaccustomed exercise.

Kissing. And making love.

For the first time in over nine years, she'd made love. Many times, with a man who knew exactly what he

263

was doing and who didn't hesitate to sweep her up with him, making her do things, feel things, she'd never experienced before. Making her alive, the blood pulsing through her like the first onrush of spring. Making her use, at long, long last, the potential that had been in her all along.

She lay back, weak with relief—no wonder I hurt! I'm just not used to it!—and as the anxiety went, it was replaced by an altogether different feeling.

Because she'd just thought, tonight we're going to do it all over again.

She was ready too early, and, knowing that standing on the balcony looking out for him for twenty minutes was a sure way to make her feel anxious, she went down to the kitchen, where the boys were sitting at the table with the twins, the Travel Trivial Pursuit spread out between them.

The laughter had been an almost-unnoticed background to her showering and dressing: as she went into the room, Oliver was picking himself up from the floor, pink in the face with merriment. She hadn't realised Trivial Pursuit could be so funny.

'Come on, Castor,' Rupert said, 'you've run out of time.' He looked down at the card in his hand. '"What is the largest train station in Britain?"'

It didn't seem fair to expect a fairly unsophisticated Greek youth to know the answer to a question like that. She wished she knew what it was—it would have been nice to lean down and whisper it in Castor's ear. But then Castor closed his eyes, and, opening them again, said, 'Waterloo.'

'You're *cheating!*' both the boys shouted together, Oliver leaning against Castor and punching him. Rupert, noticing Fay in the doorway, said, 'Mum, did you tell him?'

'No!'

264

'They *must* be cheating,' Rupert said, 'we keep asking them things they can't possibly know, and they keep getting them right!'

She was amused at his indignation. He liked to win: probably it had been he who had proposed they play, reckoning that beating the twins would be something of a formality. Castor, unperturbed, was throwing the die again, moving his token. He said, 'Green, please, Rupert.'

Rupert drew out the next card, and looked for the green question. He frowned. It must be one he knows Castor'll get, she thought.

Rupert said, ' ' "What is the first sign of the Zodiac?" ' '

Instantly Castor said, 'Aries.'

Was that right? she wondered. Aries was April, wasn't it? Surely the first sign would be the one that applied to January? Aquarius, wouldn't that be?

But, grudgingly, Rupert said, 'Correct,' and Castor reached for the die.

Aries, the first sign. Aaron, first High Priest of the Israelites. Ares, first son of Zeus and Hera. Interesting, she thought idly, that the names all sound alike and that they all hold a connotation of 'first'. I wonder why? Wonder if . . .

The fascinating thought faded and died. And, capturing her attention so that she scarcely noticed, simultaneously Rupert exclaimed disgustedly, 'Castor's *won!*' and Aaron's quiet voice right beside her said, 'Good evening.'

She hadn't heard him come in. She turned to him, aware of a tingling sensation on her skin, as if her very flesh were responding with joy to his nearness. Her eyes meeting his, she said, 'Hello.' Once, not very long ago, she thought wildly, I'd have said, sorry, I should have come down to let you in. Or some other conventional remark. Might even have apologised for the untidiness of the kitchen—*his* kitchen—until he told me not to be *polite*. 'Not with me.'

She looked into his eyes, as close now as last night so that she felt, just as then, that she was on the edge of his soul, his consciousness stretching out in front of her like unfathomably deep, dark water into which she was about to step.

He was right, she thought, feeling herself tremble slightly. You don't have to be polite, to someone you're so close to.

The twins had got up and come over to Aaron to greet him. Almost ceremonially—they stood before him and, one after the other, solemnly embraced him. Fay said, 'Boys,' and Rupert and Oliver said together—and with no ceremony at all—'Hi, Aaron.'

'It is time to go,' Aaron said to her.

'Right. Rupert, tidy the game away, will you? And here—' She got her purse out of her bag, and, managing to turn her back on everyone except Rupert, gave him some money. 'Buy the twins a drink, or something, if they won't let you pay for your souvlaki,' she whispered.

'But Mum, I can't—'

'*Please*, Rupert!' She could sense Aaron right behind her, and didn't want him to see. To complicate the moment, perhaps, by saying, there is no need for you to do that. 'Just do it!'

Rupert had a way of occasionally—very occasionally—giving in quite suddenly with no further argument. To her enormous relief, this was one of those moments. He pocketed the notes and said, 'Okay, Mum.' As an afterthought, he whispered, 'Thanks.'

'See you later,' she said to the four of them in general. And Aaron took her arm and led the way across the hall and down the steps.

TWENTY-THREE

On the Mountain

Alone with him, there was no longer the distraction of other people to dilute his impact. Walking across the pavement, she felt his mind reach out for hers, and once inside the enclosed little haven of the car, it seemed that the world, simply, was the two of them.

He didn't speak. And she received no thoughts from him, other than a general sense of benevolence, as if he were bolstering her confidence, telling her everything was as it should be. Covertly she watched him as he wove through the evening traffic, patient with the wandering and the indecisive, politely allowing other drivers to pull out in front of him. He didn't look at her, but she was uncomfortably aware that he knew she was looking at him.

But I must, she thought. I want to absorb him through my eyes, remind myself of him. Of the way his hair grows, of the lines in his face, of the smooth skin of his throat and his chest. Which I have kissed. Where I have lain my head in the exhaustion that follows love.

Her heart was thumping, and she felt slightly queasy. Lovesick, she thought. I am sick of love, like the woman in the *Song of Solomon*. She concentrated, trying to remember the words. His left hand is under my head, and his right hand doth embrace me. Stay me with flagons, comfort me with apples, for I am sick of love. Sick *with* love, she amended, surely the translation is wrong and should be sick *with* love? She's not saying she's fed up with it, but that it's so strong, so overpowering, that it's almost an illness.

She looked at Aaron's hands on the wheel. 'His right hand doth embrace me.' In her mind she saw his hand on the white body of Aphrodite then, as if that had been merely a preparation, saw it again on her own breast, brown fingers against pale flesh, enclosing, containing, holding her so that he could take her nipple in his mouth. Watch me, he'd said.

The memory she had evoked was too forceful. Shaking, she made herself turn away from him, made her mind think of the crowds in the streets, the orange evening sky, the lights shining on the water.

Anything, other than songs of love.

Suddenly he spoke. One single word, which she didn't recognise but which, both from the way he uttered it and the destructive effect it had on the atmosphere in the car, had to be a furious swear word.

'What is it?' She looked all around, trying to see what had so angered him. What had happened? Whatever could it be, to disturb him, of all people, so much?

Running along the pavement, jumping into the road when slow pedestrians got in her way, was the dark-haired woman whom Fay had thought was Aaron's wife. And she was waving, calling out to him. Even, as they drew level, planting herself in front of the car so that he had to stop if he were not to run her down.

Instantly she had the passenger door open and was leaning across Fay to address Aaron. 'Where are you going?' she demanded, ignoring Fay as absolutely as if the front seat had been empty. 'You are driving in the wrong direction, we are meeting in the restaurant on the Listón!'

268

Aaron said quietly, 'I told you, Virginia, that I was not coming.'

'Oh, that's nonsense!' She waved a dismissive hand, heavy gold bangles jangling. 'It's Leo's birthday, you have to come. Turn round, you can take me with you.' For the first time she looked at Fay, a challenging glance full of enmity. 'I have to ride in the front seat, I get car-sick.'

Fay started to move, but Aaron's hand shot out, his arm across her thighs pinning her in her seat. 'I said no,' he repeated. 'You will all have to celebrate without me.'

Her black eyes, heavily made-up, narrowed as she stared at him. Fay was aware of her perfume. Heavy, and sweet. The sort of smell that would linger long after its wearer had gone, a perpetual and unwelcome reminder of what it was like to have her around.

She said wheedlingly, 'Aaron, we miss you! We don't see enough of you these days.' Suddenly her voice changed. 'People are talking. Wondering where you are.' Don't! Fay thought in alarm. Don't *threaten* him!

But Virginia, oblivious, was not to be stopped. 'People suggest,' she went on ominously, 'that you ignore your rightful duties in order to pursue too far a course that you should not be following. And I—'

She felt his rage like an approaching storm, her flesh creeping and contracting into goose-bumps as if a huge charge of electricity were about to be detonated. The words, when they came, were incomprehensible, falling against her ears like hard heavy raindrops on the baked earth. She shrank from him, hands over her face, and behind her closed eyes seemed to see forks of white fire.

She heard Virginia whimper, the small defeated sound reminding her of the Bull man when Aaron ordered him out of The Twins' House. She felt the

touch of silk against her arm as Virginia drew herself
back and out of the car, then a crump as she banged
the door.

Through the open car window Aaron said
conversationally, 'Go to your restaurant, Virginia.
Apologise to the others for my absence, and wish them
from me a pleasant evening.' Then he put the car into
gear and they drove off.

Fay spun round, eyes on Virginia. Her face was white,
the black-circled eyes panda-dark in contrast, the
brilliant red lips incongruous now that the expression
of haughty sophistication had collapsed into fear. She
looked, Fay thought, like a child who has been
punished for playing with her mother's make-up.

She said, 'What will she do?'

Aaron, driving fast now, blasting the horn to get
people and cars out of his path, didn't answer for a
moment. Then he said, 'She will do as she is told.
Perhaps she will also learn what things she may
question and what things are forbidden.'

The silence that fell as he finished speaking was as
final as a steel door closing.

They drove for a long time. She didn't dare to say
anything, and he sat enclosed in his thoughts,
whatever they were—he permitted no inkling to come
through to her. She had no idea where they were
going, whether he was still taking her where he'd been
going to before the ugly scene with Virginia or whether
that had sparked off some different plan.

After a while he pushed a tape into the cassette
player—she thought it was Mahler—and she wondered
if she should take this as an indication that the mood
was lightening. Then, like a hand reaching out, she
felt him on the edges of her mind again.

Before she could think, she was rushing to meet him,
to welcome him in. And, twisting round so that she

could look at him, she saw he had the beginnings of a smile. He said gently, 'I am sorry.'

Not knowing how to answer, she tentatively touched his thigh. Do not think about Virginia, he said into her head. She is not important. Think instead about where I am taking you.

But I've no idea where that is.

Somewhere very, very old. A special place, where the power of the earth is strong and where, if you approach it in the right frame of mind, you may be healed.

Her mind tried to bounce out the word. But he re-introduced it. *HEALED*.

She said out loud, 'What is the right frame of mind?'

And he answered, 'Open.'

How do you open your mind? she wondered as they sped on through the darkness. It was some time since she'd spotted any road signs, and even then they'd been to places she hadn't heard of. They seemed to be climbing steadily, and the afterglow of orange in the sky behind them and to their left suggested they were going north-eastwards.

To be open-minded is to shed your preconceived notions, he replied. To put away prejudice and pre-knowledge. To be as a child, a clean white page on to which impressions may inscribe themselves.

It seemed a tall order. She made herself relax, breathing steadily and deeply, and quite soon began to experience the sensation that the great collection of memories of her life so far was being . . . not destroyed, she thought, nothing as drastic as that . . . more . . . *obscured*, behind a soft and gentle mist that whirls and billows in my head. So prettily . . .

She felt drowsy. No, that wasn't right—it was as if a trance were falling on her. A trance? Is *he* doing it? And ought I to worry?

271

She didn't seem to be able to summon the nervous energy to worry.

And, he said in her mind, you have no need to be anxious, for do you not realise that my intention is only to help you?

I do.

She sensed his approval. Then let it be, he said. Let the mood come upon you, welcome it, for then it will deepen and the ultimate benefit will be the greater.

It felt good. She was aware of her own breathing, of the flow of her blood through her body. She felt serene, yet at the same time vitally alive. And she knew, somehow, that this was exactly how he wanted her to feel.

She closed her eyes, enjoying the marvellous state into which she had fallen. Then, an unguessable time later, he said, 'We are here.'

Blinking her eyes open, reluctantly, she looked out.

They had left the metalled road and were climbing very steeply, up a rutted, dusty track. Alarmed, she shot forward in her seat—surely this was too much, even for a four-wheel drive vehicle? Confirming her fear came the sudden loud sound of all four wheels spinning. But then as abruptly it ceased, and once more they were moving steadily upwards.

As the incredible climb continued, olive trees gave way to cypress and to pine, and there was a smell of resin on the air. And, soon, they were too high even for pine trees.

On the bare rocky mountainside, a flat plateau spread out before them. And on the edge of it, where the long rough track at last came to an end, Aaron stopped the car and switched off the engine.

Silence.

At first it seemed total, beating against her ears in invisible waves of blackness. Then as her hearing adjusted she perceived that the night was full of noise. Sounds and sweet airs. In the distance, far below now among the pine trees, the rounded melodious hooting of the scops owls. All around her a quiet exhalation of a breeze, soft as a baby's sigh, making the dry grasses rustle. And another wind-made sound—a sort of hollow moan, as if somewhere out of sight metal, or stone, was vibrating as the air blew across it.

Aaron had got out of the car and was walking round to open her door.

'Come.'

She got out, taking his outstretched hand. He led her through the crackling grass, and she felt brittle stems scratch her legs. There was no path, no sign of human beings at all: if this place had ever been frequented by men, it was long, long ago, and now nature was back in command, running wild and rejoicing in it.

The undergrowth thinned and then gave out. As if this was were a sign, and he had reached the spot he was searching for, he stopped. They stood side by side on the bare rock.

After a moment he said, 'Look up.'

She tilted her head back a little. Then, as she caught a first glimpse of the sky, gasped in amazement. Arching back, she tried to look in every direction at once, for in the great black bowl above a million, million stars flared with a brilliance as if they were new-born.

She could see the Milky Way, clear as a shining snowy path. See the great procession of the constellations—the Plough, Cassiopeia, Orion, the Pleiades—so vividly that she could almost make herself believe there were lines between the stars showing the shapes, like a child's join-the-dots picture.

And for a moment she felt a part of it, part of that great, unknowable, unfathomable *out there*, as if something from within the earth on whose bare rock she stood were prompting her with the intelligence, you belong. You are a part of this vast mystery.

She felt a deep joy well up in her, uncontainable, bursting out of her in tears and in laughter and yet far too profound to be adequately expressed in any such human means of relief. She opened her arms, wanting to embrace the earth, the sky, the whole universe, and for a split second of ultimate, sublime ecstacy, it seemed that the universe embraced her in return.

It was gone. Too intense, yes, to last for more than an instant. And even so, even after so brief a contact, she was shaking, trembling, and dizzy.

Aaron's arms were round her, holding her up physically just as, mentally, his mind supported hers. You are all right. All is well. And, stroke, stroke, went his hand across her back, calming, smoothing down the tiny fine hairs along her spine which had risen animal-like at the dark thrill of the unknown.

After a long time, he said, a deep satisfaction in his voice, 'You felt it.' He let her go, standing back from her a pace so that he could look at her.

And, not knowing why she did but rejoicing with him in every fibre of her being, she said, 'I did.'

'I knew that you would. From the moment I first saw you, I sensed in you the right—' he paused, searching, '—material. The open-mindedness to be receptive.'

She struggled to understand. Failing, she asked instead, 'Why me?'

She felt his mind invade hers, searching for what lay behind her question, firing off questions of his own. Why you that I chose to put in The Twins' House? Why you that I have tried to help? To heal?

She replied against the flow, yes, all that.

That is easy. Because men and women should use the good that is in them to aid one another.

So this is something you make a habit of? She

couldn't stop herself, the vital question had to be asked. You regularly pick out life's walking wounded and mend them?

She felt the rush of triumph in him, and realised too late what she'd said. Not that I need mending! she cried. I'm not wounded!

But the foils that had glittered between them were abruptly lowered. As if someone had cut off a power source, suddenly he was quiescent. Shocked, for in this state he wasn't *him*, she reached out.

What is it?

His hand clasping hers, slowly he shook his head. Not like this, he said. Never before like this. Healing, helping, yes. Living with my people, watching them evolve a system that works, struggling with them, growing with them. All this, and more, has long been a part of me.

He was different. Something was out of place. Mind racing, she struggled to seek out what it was.

Me. He said me. For the first time he was talking about himself, his *deep* self, beginning to reveal to her, unbelievably, what he was.

Look at me.

Her eyes met his, and she saw—felt in her mind— that he knew. That he found it as strange as she did.

Yes, he said. You understand. *This*, this reciprocal exchange by which you come into my mind as I come into yours, this is something that has not happened before. That is outside the pattern.

Drawing her to him, cradling her head against his chest, arms tight around her as if he were trying to meld her with himself, he said aloud, 'But then the pattern does not include loving. Not in the way that I love you.'

TWENTY-FOUR

The Power of the Earth

Her mind was confused. Echoes of words were sounding in her ears, but they were fragmented and made no sense. They had been speaking—no, *thinking*—of him. He'd been about to reveal something; she'd got the distinct feeling they were on the verge of a major breakthrough, that he was going to tell her things he never told anyone, that she hadn't expected ever to hear.

And he spoke, didn't he? Said something out loud? Why can't I *remember*?

He was standing close beside her, not touching. She sensed that he was very tense, as if he were waiting for something in great anxiety. What? What was it?

She couldn't think.

She shook her head violently, and the jumble and the confusion seemed to clear. She said, 'What is this place?'

From him came washing over her a huge relief, strong as the incoming tide. Then it was gone, and before she could wonder about it, he was speaking.

'It is a place of worship.' He took her hand, leading her on out across the plateau. 'Men came here, in the oldest of days. When they first came to the island, they found this place.'

'Why?'

'Because it is sacred.' He smiled, forestalling her question. 'No, not sacred *to* anyone, or anything. Just sacred in itself.'

'I don't understand.'

'I know. I shall explain.' Ahead was a row of stones that marched across the rocky ground, so straight that, unless they were part of some geological demarcation line, they must have been put there by man. He leaned against one of the biggest. 'Stand here beside me, your back against the stone.' She did so, and the rock was warm, the sun's energy absorbed over the long hot day stored up and now being given out into the cool night. The heat through the thin fabric of her dress felt good. Restorative, like a therapeutic heat-pad or the touch of massaging hands.

'Nice?' She nodded, and, turning to him briefly, caught his answering smile. Beyond him, she noticed idly, the sky still showed a faint tinge of red. The very last of the sunset. Interestingly, the row of stones against which they stood pointed directly into the west.

The thought seemed to float around in her mind for some time before she understood its significance. Then she said, 'It's man-made! This wall, or whatever it is, was built by men, wasn't it? Because it points due west?'

'It points east,' he corrected. 'Although I suppose it amounts to the same thing. But the men who built the edifice of which it was a part had in mind to make it face the east. The sunrise.'

'So this line was orientated east-west,' she said, hardly taking in his last words. 'Orientated! Like oriental! Meaning, siting something with reference to the east!' It was so logical that she was surprised she'd never worked it out before.

'The sun was a perfect reference point, yes,' he was saying, 'but—'

'Churches!' she shouted. 'Churches always point east, with the altar at the east end, because of Jesus.' She dredged in her mind for the words she'd learned so long ago. 'Christ is the dayspring, the Sun of Righteousness.' They built churches to face the dawn, and the men who put this thing here did the same.'

Unexpectedly—for she'd thought she was doing so well—he sighed. And said, half under his breath, 'Such a long way still to go.'

'What?'

He seemed to gather himself. 'When was the earliest church constructed?'

'Oh, I don't know—first or second century AD, I suppose.'

'And just how long, would you imagine, have these ancient stones stood here?'

She felt foolish. 'Rather more than two thousand years.'

'So?'

She was already there. 'Yes, yes, I see,' she said, impatient with herself. 'You're saying that man's instinct was to build to face the sunrise long before Christ.'

'I'm saying more than that. Don't you see? I'm pointing out to you that the convenient pun of 'Sun' and 'Son' was made clever use of by the early Christians. That, as do the followers of each new religion as it occurs, they utilised man's existing beliefs as the groundwork on which to place their own.'

Her mind was racing. As understanding grew, she wished it hadn't, because what he was proposing was beginning to sound suspiciously like blasphemy. She said coldly, 'I'm not sure you should say any more.'

But he did. 'The major feasts of the Christian calendar were set to coincide with age-old festivals,' he went on relentlessly. 'And their timing depended solely on nature, for what you would call Christmas was the celebration of the winter solstice, just as your Easter was originally man's thanksgiving for the springtime.'

'It was when Christ died!' she cried.

And, unmoved, he said, 'Coincidentally.'

His mood changed. As if he recognised this was not the way, he said more gently, 'You must understand the power of symbols. Does the date matter? Is it not more forceful to be told that your god was reborn at a time of year when such things occur naturally? Will you not believe more readily in something new if it is grafted on to something you already accept?'

Intelligence fought with a childhood of incantation. The bright flame of comprehension that he was nurturing in her flared high, then, as an image of a different sort of fire soared through her brain, abruptly it was annihilated. Across the years she heard the voice of Sister Bernard.

'Pray every day, every hour, for the poor souls in Purgatory!' Fay could see the intense pale eyes, alight with a passion that her childish mind hadn't understood and, consequently, had feared. 'Think of them! Think of the flames, hear them crackling, smell the burning flesh! Feel the awful pain of those souls, think of them knowing that they must endure years, tens of years, *centuries* of this agony before their souls are seared clean and they may go into the presence of Our Lord!' Sister Bernard had possessed the natural ability of the storyteller: like the bards of the ancient oral tradition, she understood instinctively the power of repetition and the effect of escalating exaggeration.

And the heartstopping capacity of the dramatic pause.

She would walk slowly up and down between the rows of desks. The children, transfixed, dared not turn round but waited for the swish of the long habit, the faint footfall, to tell them where she was.

Waited to see if it was to be their own shoulder on to which that strong bony hand was going to fall. Their ears that would receive the full force of Sister Bernard's rhetoric as she burst out once more.

'One day you too will be souls in Purgatory!' It was almost a relief when the great cry came: at least the waiting was over. 'You too will be undergoing the cleansing fire—' she would pause again, and, voice suddenly soft, add half under her breath, '—for I cannot, will not, believe that any of my precious charges in this class would be so sinful, so wicked, as to earn for themselves the eternal punishment of Hell.' She would look around, resting her unblinking stare upon three or four hapless children, one after the other. 'No. But the fires of Purgatory are every bit as agonising!' The voice had returned to full volume. 'Will you not hope with all your hearts that somewhere someone is praying for *you*, to lessen your centuries of torture? Will you not thank, with all your wretched being, the man, woman or child who spares a few minutes of every hour—a few seconds of every minute—to pray for you?'

Silence. Echoes of that impassioned voice fading and dying.

Then, timing as perfect as an actor's, the gentle injunction that came with the force of a field-marshall's command: 'Pray.'

Praying regularly in school hours was easy, for every lesson had begun and ended with the class turning as one to the statue of the Virgin in her corner. But at home it was more difficult. She made herself a little altar in her father's greenhouse. A cross made out of hardboard, and a jam-jar in which she would put wild flowers, for she knew she'd get an early foretaste of purgatorial punishment if her father caught her picking flowers from his garden. For some weeks she'd tried to go to her altar three or four times each day, kneeling down, running off a Hail Mary and an Our Father, then trying to address a god she hardly comprehended—if he was loving, why did he torture people? Why did he make poor Jesus suffer so badly?—and ask him if he'd please give a few souls in Purgatory a couple of days' remission.

After a month or so, she'd gone to the greenhouse less often. Then Julie had hit a badly-aimed rounders ball through a pane of glass in the door, breaking Fay's jam-jar into the bargain and snapping one limb off the hardboard cross. When the furore had died and Julie could once more sit down, Fay hadn't found the heart to start all over again.

Beside her Aaron said softly, 'The Inquisition lives on.'

Recalled, with relief, to the present, she said, 'What?'

'I would have professed belief in any religion, were the alternative torture and death at the hands of its priests. Your nuns may have used subtler weapons, but the principle is the same.'

'But they—'

'Fear.' He might not have heard her interruption. 'Present such a frightful alternative that you terrify your followers into doing what you tell them. Over a superstitious, uneducated medieval peasant—' he paused, looking suddenly at her with an expression of deep compassion, 'or over a little child—you have the power, literally, of life or death.'

She had the sensation that something in her head had moved over. As if a dark shutter which invisible hands had inexorably held in place was being pushed out of the way by a stronger power. Allowing her to see, for the first time, the bright sunlight beyond.

She thought he must know exactly what was happening, for he waited, silent and quite still, while she came to terms with it.

281

Eventually she said, 'It was only their opinion, wasn't it?'

Right with her, he said, 'Of course. Every man who has ever been born starts with the same incomprehension and the same striving to understand. Beliefs arise as men touch the infinite and try to turn it into accessible, human terms.'

The dark shutter was folded back on itself, and she seemed to hear the noise of it falling, broken, to the ground. She said wonderingly, 'What now? Do I begin again?'

His hands were on hers, grasping them tightly. 'Yes, but not in the way you're thinking. You must identify the good in what you used to believe,'—how unequivocal he is! she thought admiringly, what I used to believe! Up till all but a few minutes ago, and he's referring to it quite categorically as in the past!—'and that you must keep. But you must look at it with new eyes.' He paused, studying her. 'What was the greatest commandment of Jesus?'

She said automatically, 'That ye love one another.'

And, with a pause as well-timed as any of Sister Bernard's, he waited to let it sink in.

'No Hell?' she asked presently.

He smiled. 'Plenty of man-made hells, yes. But no, no fiery furnace manned by demons with pitchforks.'

By direct association of ideas, she said, 'No devil?'

'The devil is the personification of evil, and that, too, is largely man-made.'

'But how can you—'

'The universe is neutral. The highly-developed consiousness of man imposed upon it ultimate good and deepest evil.'

'Man-made,' she repeated in a whisper. Then, aloud, 'But the universe isn't man-made! Who made the universe?'

'The creative force.'

'And what is that?'

He said, the words slow and thoughtful, 'An amalgam, perhaps, of spirit and physics. A tight mass of energy, triggered by an unknown power into an explosion of heat and light.'

'And, eventually, us.'

'If you must bring it down to the personal, yes.'

'Light and heat,' she said suddenly. 'The sun. Building to face the east. We're back where we started, aren't we?' She turned to him, alive with the joy of discovery.

'Yes. The sun gave life to the world, so isn't it right to worship it as a deity? The early civilisations each invented their own name, but it was always the same god. *Shamash*, *Mithras*—the word means 'friend', by the way—*Ra*, *Tezcatlipo*, *Helios*, *Sol*. The sun.'

The names seemed to roll across the new bright light in her mind, golden and clear, melding with some understanding which, although she'd never known it, must always have been there. Waiting, perhaps, for this moment. She felt the pull of the past, perceived for a brief instant her place at the end of an immeasurably long line of human forebears who had puzzled, concluded, thrown out, puzzled again.

And eventually discovered, some of them, the ultimate truths.

She felt weak. Letting her legs bend, slowly her back slid down the warm supportive rock until she was sitting on the ground. She looked up at him still standing above her.

'Don't you want to sit down?'

He had closed his eyes, head resting against the top of the stone. 'No. I am not tired. And the energy enters the body more efficiently with the whole spine pressed to the rock.'

He spoke so matter-of-factly that it took her a moment to take in what he had said.

Then she asked fearfully, 'What energy?'

Unbelievably, he was laughing. He said, 'I am sorry. I should not tease you. It is not fair to lead you into the realms of the sublime and then bring you so suddenly down to earth.' He came down to her level, putting a companionable arm round her. 'Except that down to earth is an apt expression, because in answer to your question, earth energy.'

'Ley lines,' she said. Anything seemed credible, tonight. 'Is that what you mean?'

'Yes, that is a part of it. The lines join together points where the power is strong. Like Avebury, or Delphi, to give you two examples.'

'Like here.' She knew without his affirmation that she was right. Then she asked, 'Is that why we've come?'

'The power heals,' he said gently. 'Remember, I told you that on the way here.'

And I didn't want to hear, she thought.

Now you are hearing. He was in her mind, and the wordless communication immediately put them on a deeper level of intimacy. Are you now also accepting, after all that we have spoken of, that you require healing?

The bright new sun in her head had reached the far corner, where it was shining on the last locked place, a veritable iron fortress. I can't! Can't open up that bit, even to you.

You can, if you want to.

I don't want to. I can live with it, I've got used to it.

Perhaps so. But now you know that life can be better without dark corners.

Haven't we done well enough already? Can't I pretend that bit's not there?

But she knew already what his reply would be.

You could—she noticed his change to the

conditional—but then you would never become whole again.

He was right. In a stab of realisation, she saw her psyche as he did. Fractured, labouring along like a cart with a cracked frame bearing a load that was increasing the depth of the crack with every mile.

Do I want to become whole? she asked, no longer knowing if she looked to him or herself for reply.

Perhaps there wasn't any difference anyway.

From the consciousness of one of them—both of them—came the single word, yes.

Falling from Grace

It seemed to her she was walking uphill. Struggling, each step a great effort. Ahead was the locked iron door that hid the buried past.

Behind her, like the sun on her back, was Aaron. He said into her mind, I am here. I will not leave you.

And his presence gave her the strength she could not summon from herself. Pushing on, until the darkness filled her whole horizon, she perceived that the door wasn't as solid as she'd thought. Pinpricks of light permeated its surface, and somewhere there must be a gap because she could feel a breeze blowing, carrying evocative smells . . . baby powder . . . wet clothes . . . the sharp reek of vomit. And she could hear voices . . . Rupert's, high, trembling with the onset of tears. Oliver, crying for her in the night, desperate with ear-ache.

Barry. Barry? Where are you?

She was in their room, and his side of the bed was empty. On the floor were the pieces of a broken glass, a trickle of whiskey seeping into the carpet.

Then she knew exactly where she was. *When* she was. They'd broken more than one glass between them in the years of marriage, but that particular breakage stood out in her memory like a folly on a bare horizon. She'd thrown it at him. She'd picked it up from the dressing table where he'd left it and, aiming for his head as he tried to sit up, hurled it with all her strength. He had ducked, and it smashed against the wall.

And in the instant of reprieve when she realised she'd missed, she didn't know if she was glad or sorry.

It was Rupert's birthday. His fifth. He and little Oliver, dressed in new shorts and sweatshirts with their names on them, had sat waiting in trembling excitement for their father to arrive, because he was taking them out for a joint birthday treat. He'd told them all about it, catalogued in detail what they were going to do, and she would overhear her sons chatting excitedly before they went to sleep. Daddy says this, Daddy's going to do that.

They didn't see all that much of their father, by then. His absences were beginning to join up into one long absence, and from the state of him when he did come home, she found it hard to believe that it was work that took him away. Maybe things would begin with a legitimate business trip. But then at some point, she imagined, the demon took over and the drinking started, so that meetings were missed, flights took off without him.

She didn't know what to do. Barry wouldn't talk to her, and she was afraid to go over his head and appeal to his bosses for fear that she'd bring to their notice something they'd so far overlooked.

They *can't* have overlooked it! Oh, God, he's not Barry any more, he's dirty, shambling, forgetful... goodness, how does he ever manage to do anything?

Then back would come the horrors. Imagination running riot, she'd see him crawling home to confess he'd lost his job. Telling her they'd have to relinquish the car, sell the house, move somewhere smaller while he looked around for employment.

It was all so credible that sometimes she couldn't believe it hadn't happened already.

He'd said he was working in Manchester. Some long-term project that he had to oversee. Staying there during the week, he'd ring up on a Friday, late, and tell her he wasn't coming home: 'It's not worth it, I'm working all day tomorrow so I may as well stay up here for what's left of the weekend.'

She wondered fleetingly if he had a woman. Then chucked the idea out as absurd—what use was a mistress to a man who couldn't get an erection?

He can't with *you*, her own demon would whisper. But perhaps that's your fault. Perhaps it's different with someone more attractive. Someone kinder.

She still didn't think it likely. What kept Barry in Manchester—if that was where he was—was more likely to be golden-brown and come in bottles.

'I'm coming home to take the boys out,' he said on the phone one day. 'I'll come on Saturday—which one's birthday is that?'

'Rupert's,' she replied expressionlessly. 'Oliver's was three weeks ago.'

She heard him mutter, 'Oh, God.' Then, brightly, 'I'll make it up to him, Fay. I promise. I'm going to give them the most marvellous day out they've ever had. We'll go to the zoo—where's the nearest zoo?— or to a theme park, or swimming, and we'll have hamburgers and chips and ice-creams. It'll be grand!. Just leave it all to me.'

She did as he'd asked and had them ready by twelve.

They sat by the window, excitement seeping out of them like air from a badly-tied balloon, for two hours. Then they finally understood he wasn't coming.

The pain of watching her sons' happiness fade and die was the worst pain of all. The picture of two little boys in their best clothes, waiting for something that wasn't going to happen, having to realise it wasn't going to happen, broke something inside her.

'I'll take you!' she said, making herself sound cheerful when she wanted to bury her face in a pillow and wail. 'It's a shame to waste any more of the day—come on! Get your shoes on,'—don't cry, Rupert, not in that quiet, adult way. I can't bear it—'and bring the swimming things. We'll stop for lunch on the way, then go to the fair, and by that time our food will have gone down and we'll be ready to swim.'

She got them through the day. Oliver at three was relatively easy to distract, but then he'd never really known Barry all that well. Rupert was different. She knew, then, that one parent wasn't going to be enough, for Rupert. And he loved his dad so much.

They got back late. Deliberately: she'd reckoned it'd be easier to get them to bed in some degree of contentment if they were worn out. She washed them, put them into their pyjamas, gave them drinks and biscuits and at last took them upstairs and settled them down. Oliver went straight to sleep, but for some time she was aware of the soft sad voice of Rupert, muttering to his teddy.

She sat in the living room, in the darkness, without the television on. A time later, she dragged herself upstairs.

Barry was lying sprawled across the bed. Naked except for his underpants and one sock, as if the process of undressing had defeated him before he'd finished. There was an almost-empty bottle of whiskey on the dressing table, beside it a half-full glass.

She thought coolly, he must have been far gone, if he didn't even wait to drain the glass.

She went out on to the landing and closed the boys' door. Then she closed the bedroom door behind her. And said, sharply, 'Barry!'

He could only have been lightly asleep—if he's been

here since we got home and for some time before that, she thought, he's probably slept off the worst of it by now—and he stirred at her voice. She said again, 'Barry! Wake up.'

He rolled over on to his side, and one puffy eyelid opened. His mouth, wet at the corner where he'd been dribbling, stretched into a floppy smile.

'Fay, me love,' he croaked, hoarse-voiced. 'Where've you been?'

'I have been taking my sons out for their birthday treat. The one they expected to have with their father.'

'Ah, now, don't look like that, I—'

'Their father!' she cried, leaning forward to aim a punch at his groin. 'Although I'm amazed, looking at you now, that you ever managed to get it up!'

'Fay!' He was shocked into movement, drawing up his knees to defend himself. 'What's wrong? I've never seen you like this, not my Fay, my strong Fay, who—'

'*Shut up!*' It was a screech, violent and loud, expressing all the pain of coping with the boys' misery and disappointment. 'You *bastard!*'

The blind impulse was on her to hurt, *hurt* him, make him suffer too. Her hands flew over the surface of the chest of drawers, the dressing table . . . and found the glass.

When the echoes of the crash had died, he went on looking at her. In his eyes she read regret and pain behind the shock. And, undying, flaring for her still, she read love.

He said quietly—soberly—'I think I'd better go.'

She watched as he dressed. She realised, later, that a part of her had known then he wouldn't be back.

For some weeks she existed in limbo. Saying the word to herself, she thought, no, that's wrong. Limbo is where babies go if they die before they've been baptised. It doesn't imply any sort of suffering, other than the sadness of not being with God.

This, then, isn't limbo.

She waited daily for the blow to fall. She checked the post anxiously each morning for letters from the bank—how would they phrase it? 'Dear Madam, it appears your husband's pay-cheque has not been paid into your joint account this month and I am concerned in case this means he's boozed himself out of a job'? She dreamt, worryingly and repetitively, of being in desperate trouble and searching for Barry, only to discover him laughing and singing in some bar, so that in her anger and frustration she attacked him with bottles, ashtrays, whatever came to hand. Heard her dream self saying—crying—'I *hate* you! I could *kill* you!'

Late one night he came to see her. He looked—smelt—a shambles. His pinstripe suit was torn at the shoulder, and the trousers hung low on his hips—he must have lost weight—so that the bottoms were frayed and dirty from trailing on the ground. She suddenly remembered going to buy that suit with him. It had been his best one; he'd worn it to Sophia and Tom's wedding. With a carnation in the buttonhole. He'd brought her flowers, too, a huge bunch as lovely as Sophia's. 'For my bride,' he'd whispered in her ear. 'My lovely Fay.'

She pushed the memory behind the iron door.

He had collapsed on the sofa. Eyes drooping with weariness and hopelessness, he told her he'd lost his job.

'I've blown my last chance, Fay. They've been good to me, far more patient than I deserve. They sent me for counselling, and then for a fortnight at a drying-out clinic.' His face creased as if in pain. 'I was all right, in there. No problem. But—' He broke off, putting a hand over his mouth. 'God, it was so humiliating.' She could still make out the muffled words, and almost wished she couldn't. 'Soon as I got out. Fell at the first hurdle. Missed the fucking train, and went into the bar. Four whiskeys—large ones—and I fell over.'

Legs weak, she sank down to sit on the arm of a chair.

He had folded his hands in his lap, like a child about to recite a poem. 'I went out into the street when the barman refused to serve me any more.' He glanced nervously at her, eyes meeting hers then quickly sliding away. 'I suppose I was aiming for another bar. I can't remember. Then there was a police car, and a big policeman standing in my path. He asked me to stop, and when I did I fell over again.'

In her heart an overwhelming, pitying tenderness was growing, too fast for her to stop. She folded her arms tightly across her body, hugging herself before she should yield to the temptation to hug him.

'They arrested me, Fay. Put me in the cells till the pubs were shut, then managed to forget about me for a few more hours. When they let me out it was morning.' He drew in a shuddering breath. 'I spent a couple of days trying to get myself together, and when I finally went into work, somehow they already knew what had happened. They said they were very sorry, but they really didn't think there was anything more they could do for me. I'm being "retired on medical grounds", in their parlance. But everyone knows what it means. It's the end of me, Fay.'

She tried to take it all in. Having expected it to happen didn't seem to be any help at all; is this how people feel when someone dies after a long and predictably fatal illness? she wondered. They say things like 'I knew he was dying but it was still a shock when it happened.' Now I know what they mean.

No job. No prospect of him getting another. She said, 'What will happen to us?'

'To us?' His head shot up and he stared at her, a new light of hope in his eyes.

'To the boys and me!' Her voice was loud in fury. How could he have thought I meant him and me! She watched as the hope faded and despair came back. For an evil, sadistic moment, she enjoyed her power to hurt him.

'I don't know,' he said wearily. He hesitated. 'I'm thinking that maybe if I—' He broke off. 'I can't,' he whispered. 'I haven't the strength even for that.'

'What?'

He didn't answer. Instead, imploringly, said, 'Fay, couldn't we give it one more try? You've always been my strength. My best years were with you, me love. If I came back—if you'd have me back—I think I might be all right. I'd stop the drinking, if you loved me again. If you let me love you again. I do, you know, Fay. I do love you, I've never stopped. You and the boys, you're my whole world. I love you all, so much.'

She looked at him. Took in the pleading in his face. The cringing demeanour. The terrible, mutilating weakness. She thought clinically, if he'd only stopped at saying he loved me.

'You don't love the boys in any way worth having,' she said coldly. 'Nor me. Your trouble, Barry, is that you don't love anyone as much as you love yourself.'

'I do! I love you so much—'

'You love me?' She was on her feet, leaning over him, breathing in the stale-sweat, sour-drink smell. 'Mentally you're too concerned with where the next full glass is coming from, and physically—ha! You climb into bed with me, climb on top of me, move around for a few desperate minutes and then present me with something about as potent and interesting as a dead goldfish! You're useless, Barry, useless as a husband, as a father, as a lover. *USELESS!*'

She could no longer bear to be in the same room.

Slamming out, she went through into the kitchen. Began on the motions of making herself a cup of coffee, then realised she didn't want it. Heard the chink of bottle on glass from the living room. Heard, after a few minutes, his woebegone, mournful voice, singing softly.

'I'm drunk today and I'm rarely sober,
A handsome rover from town to town,
Oh but I'm sick now and my days are numbered,
Come all ye young men and lay me down.'

Abandoning him—for what else was there to do?—she went to bed.

In the morning he'd gone. There was a note in the kitchen, propped against the kettle. He must have remembered that the first thing she always did when she came down was to put the kettle on.

'I didn't want us to end this way. I'm sorry. Although I know I've had a poor way of showing it, Fay me darling, I do love you. I always have and I always shall.
For ever,
Barry.'

She stood for a long time, the note in her hand. All she could think of was the first note he'd sent her. Asking her to go to the pictures. It seemed ironic, that life with him had both begun and ended with a brief note on a tatty scrap of paper.

Hardening her heart, she screwed it up and threw it in the bin.

TWENTY-SIX

Cast from the Light

It was two months later that the phone call from Liam came. It came at midday, an incongruously level-headed hour of the day for such abandon. When she lifted the receiver and heard the husky Irish voice she thought at first it was Barry.

'Yes, I know it's you, Liam.' She interrupted the incoherent shouting. God, it's only twelve, and he's out of his tree! 'You said.'

'I gave him to you! You said you'd look after him! Loved him, said you loved him, promised it, in front of witnesses, in front of us! Said . . .'

She could hear another voice in the background. A man's voice, deep and authoritative. She couldn't make out the words, but he seemed to be trying to reason with Liam. To calm him, perhaps.

Then Liam was back, ranting, sobbing, loud in her ear so that instinctively she held the receiver away. The loudness of his anger was distorting his words: all she could make out was *'WHORE!'*

What was wrong? Had he heard that Barry had gone? Did he blame her for coming to the end of her rope and ceasing to be the long-suffering, all-suffering wife?

Sod him if he did!

'Liam, will you please stop shouting at me and—'

'Mrs. Leary?'

It was the other voice. The authoritative one. And for some reason she didn't understand, it shot her through with a cold foreboding.

'Yes?'

'Mrs. Leary, I'm Dr. Quirke. I am afraid I have bad news for you. Are you alone?'

'Yes.' A doctor? Was something the matter with Liam? Was this Dr. Quirke trying to contact Barry? Fat chance of that, ringing here!

'Ah.' There was a pause. 'Mrs. Leary, you should know that I tried to stop Liam from calling you, but unfortunately he was determined. The news we have for you is not best imparted over the telephone, but now that Liam has spoken to you, it seems I'm left with no choice. It's Barry.'

Not Liam. Barry. The vague foreboding coalesced into a hard block of ice in her heart.

'Barry?' she whispered.

'Mrs. Leary—Fay, isn't it?—I am very sorry to tell you he's had an accident. A very bad accident.'

'Will he be all right?'

'No, Fay. He died some time in the night.'

Died. In the night.

Barry was dead.

There must be a mistake! How did this man know? Where was he speaking from? Was he in Ireland, with Liam? Was Barry in Ireland? He didn't say he was going, I wonder what he's doing there?

He's not doing anything. This man says he's dead.

'Where are you?' she asked.

'What did you say?'

Perhaps he hadn't realised she was addressing him. She found herself smiling, then as suddenly stopped. 'Are you speaking from Ireland? Did he—did it happen—where did it happen?'

'Yes, yes, he came to stay with his brother. He—'

296

There was a great howl of anguish, and the dreadful sound of a big full-voiced man crying. 'I'm sorry, but I must look after Liam. He is taking it hard, you understand.' Was there a reproof there? A suggestion of, he's breaking his heart, why aren't you? 'You had better fly over, Mrs. Leary, as soon as you can. There are, of course, things you must see to, things we shall have to talk to you about.'

'Yes. I will.' Dublin, I'll book a flight to Dublin. Liam used to meet us, when Barry and I went together. Don't suppose he'll do that this time.

'Let me know when you will arrive,' the doctor was saying, 'and I will arrange for you to be met.'

It was so unemotional. They might have been arranging an appointment for her to have her hearing tested. 'Thank you,' she said politely.

Then, his voice suddenly full of sorrow and sympathy, he said, 'Go to a neighbour, or a friend. Don't be alone. Will you promise me?'

'I—'

'I knew Barry,' he said quietly. 'Believe me, I understand better than you can know.'

'I don't—' It was no good: if he'd stayed aloof, she thought wildly, I could have managed. 'I must go,' she said, voice shaking, 'make arrangements, before the boys come home.' The boys. Oh dear God, the boys.

'Call someone,' the doctor urged.

Yes. Who?

As soon as he'd rung off she dialled Sophia's number.

On the flight to Dublin the next morning she derived comfort from thinking about Sophia. What a friend. What a capable, supportive, loving friend. Sophia had given up being an air stewardess when marriage to Tom had resulted, within a couple of months, in pregnancy: with an overnight bag in hand, she moved

297

into Fay's house half an hour after Fay phoned her.

'It doesn't matter how long you're away,' she had said calmly. 'I'll be here. I'll stay till you come back. Tom can come and join us. We'll look after your boys.'

The boys. Rupert, just into his first term at primary school. Oliver, gone straight from his morning's finger-painting to a hastily-arranged lunch with a playschool friend. How in God's name was she going to find the words to tell them?

Sophia had advised *not* telling them, at least for the time being. 'It's enough for them to cope with you going away,' she said, 'even though Tom and I will do our best to make it fun. If they know why you've gone, they'll be desperate without you.'

She's right, Fay thought. And somehow she managed to get through the long afternoon, evening and night of pretence until at last it was morning and time to go.

A few rows behind her a child was giggling. He sounded just like Oliver. With a heavy heart, she wondered how long it'd be till Oliver giggled again.

In the Arrivals section, a priest stood holding up a card which said 'Mrs. Fay Leary'. She thought abstractedly, Leary alone wouldn't have done, there must be any number of Mrs. Learys arriving in Dublin this morning. Then she thought, a priest! They've sent a priest to meet me! Are the recriminations going to begin before I'm even out of the airport?

She walked up to the tall, broad figure. 'I'm Fay Leary,' she said.

He had blue eyes, Leary-blue, as blue as Barry's. For a few seconds she could read in them no expression at all. Then he held out his hand, grasping hers, and as he did so she realised he might be kind after all.

He took her out to his car, and drove her the twenty or so miles to Barry's home town. Apart from telling her his name was Father Flynn and remarking that this

298

was all very terrible, he barely spoke on the journey. She looked out at the familiar countryside—it was, quite suitably, she thought, pouring with rain—and felt her small amount of courage seep out through the soles of her shoes.

In the town he drove over the bridge and past the big hotel where she and Barry used to drink in the evenings when they came to see Liam, usually accompanied by Liam and whoever else was about and had nothing better to do. On the outskirts, a couple of hundred yards past the church, Father Flynn drew up outside a small bungalow. Ushering her inside, he showed her into a sparsely-furnished living room and called down the hall to some invisible presence in the kitchen for coffee.

A nervous-looking woman with dyed black hair and a wrap-around apron brought a tray of coffee and Marie biscuits, barely pausing to nod to Fay before going out again, closing the door firmly behind her. No doubt you learn to be discreet, Fay thought, if you keep house for a priest.

Without preamble Father Flynn suddenly announced, 'I am going to give you the facts, Mrs. Leary.' Right now? she thought wildly. When I'm in the middle of dunking a Marie biscuit in my appallingly weak coffee? 'You will hear much colouring of these facts over the time you are here, but I hope that, like me, you will close your mind to speculation and rumour and concentrate instead on what I am about to relate.'

I'm not ready for this! she pleaded silently. I need time, to come to terms with why I'm here, to field a bit of courage so that I can hear what you're going to tell me without wishing I were as dead as Barry. She looked at him, trying to put her request into her expression, but he was staring out of the window and would not meet her eyes.

'He was staying with Liam and the family,' the priest said. 'He had been here for a couple of months. Perhaps a little less.'

'I didn't know,' she said. I *should* have known, she berated herself. Should have known he'd run here. And I ought to have checked—he must have been waiting for me to phone them, to ask if they'd any news of him.

'Did you not?' Now he was looking at her. Thinking, no doubt, just what she was thinking. 'Liam, as you will have observed, was devoted to Barry, and welcomed him, although perhaps he was wrong to put his love for his brother above his duty to his wife and family, who were not quite so happy to have a deeply-troubled brother-in-law and uncle respectively thrust upon them. There were—' he paused, apparently searching for the diplomatic word, '—tensions, I understand.' I bet there were, she thought. Deeply-troubled. Oh, Barry.

'Barry was a bad influence on Liam, or so Liam's wife thought,' Father Flynn went on, 'and the pair of them spent most evenings in the bar. Including the evening before last, when they were there until Maureen sent her eldest son to fetch his father home. Left alone, Barry drank the harder, according to the barman, who reported that his mood was clearly sorrowful and lamenting.' What a choice of words, she thought, her mind fighting shy of taking in their meaning. A London barman would say he looked a bit pissed-off, or he seemed down. Only in Ireland would he be described as sorrowful and lamenting. 'He was the last to leave,' the priest was saying, 'and when Sean finally got him out it was after midnight and the streets were empty.

'We don't know for certain what happened next. He stumbled, possibly, or perhaps a car passed too close to him on that narrow bridge. Somehow he fell from

300

the bridge into the stream, and in the morning was found in the shallows, face-down in the water. He had been dead for some time.'

She tried to take it in. Tried to picture it. The bridge, and that friendly-looking water. Only shallow, it was, even out in mid-stream. And running gaily over stones. A clear browny-gold, like melted topaz. Barry, face-down. Handsome face, face she'd touched. Kissed. Loved.

She looked up at the priest. Had she expected compassion? If so, she was to be disappointed. Whatever else the priest had on his mind, pity for her wasn't up there with the front runners. He thinks it's my fault, she thought. Without waiting to find out my side of it, he's judged and found me guilty. Whatever happened to judge not that ye be not judged?

Barry. Was it my fault?

It was too much to cope with. Hurriedly she said, 'You spoke of colouring of facts. What did you mean?'

He spun round to face her, and for an instant, before he covered it up, she saw an offended surprise that she should have moved so soon to ask him that. If only you knew, she thought.

'There is an unkind and untrue rumour that he did not fall. That he jumped. Because, so the story goes, he was desperately unhappy and no longer felt he had a place in the world.'

She could hear the words he wasn't saying. You were the reason he was desperately unhappy. You kicked him when he was down and made him an outcast.

But perhaps she was wrong, for when he spoke again it was to say, quietly and vehemently, 'These rumours I will not countenance. Barry had too much to drink and he fell. He banged his head on a stone, and, unconscious and unable to help himself, he drowned.'

That, then, was the official version. Was he telling her it was the version she must accept? Was he, in fact, being kind? Warning her of the rumour of suicide but advising her—*ordering* her—to take no notice?

But it's too late, she thought. If he didn't want me to believe it, he shouldn't have put it into my mind.

I do believe it. The trouble is, it's all too credible.

He *was* unhappy. Of course he was! He was a hopeless alcoholic, he'd lost his job, his family, and his self-respect, and his wife, just to ram the point home, reminded him at their last meeting that he was impotent and useless.

Oh, yes. I believe it. If ever there were a likely suicide, then Barry was it.

Suddenly she remembered his words when she'd asked what would happen to herself and the boys. He'd said he'd been thinking of something, then said, I can't. I haven't the strength even for that.

Was this what he'd had in mind? Going home to Ireland and killing himself? On the grounds that he was no more use to her? To anyone?

Barry, oh, Barry, no! Please, not that! Because if it's true, then I am guilty. And I don't think I can live with that.

There was a sudden crash from outside, and voices, raised in anger. One in anger, anyway, and one quieter, pleading. The black-haired woman hanging on his arm, Liam threw himself into the room.

'You killed him!' he shouted, red face right above her, fine rain of whiskey-scented spittle falling on her. 'You took him from his family who loved him, you drove him to drink and then you threw him out! Whore! *Bitch!'* Tears streaming from his bloodshot eyes, he wiped at his face with a huge hand then, too fast for her to defend herself, with the same hand struck her across the mouth. Once, twice.

The priest was on his feet. She'd noticed he was tall,

but not how strong he was. Overpowering Liam in an instant, he got his arms up behind him, pulling him away from her. As if that had been his last throw, Liam collapsed against him and the priest helped him into a chair.

The housekeeper silently handed her a tissue, and she dabbed at her bleeding lip. The priest, kneeling at Liam's feet, was whispering, face intent, attention fully absorbed in him.

She thought, why is nobody offering *me* sympathy? For either my bereavement or my beaten face?

The truth dawned like two more blows. Because they agree with Liam. They think I killed him, too. Drove him to suicide. My Barry. My lovely Barry!

And, quietly, unnoticed, at last she started to cry.

Nobody mentioned suicide again. It was a small town, and the priest was a strong character: perhaps they always did what he told them. After the wild excesses of the funeral and the howling wake which followed, she found out that you were not allowed to bury your dead in hallowed ground if your dead was dead by his own hand. Was it all a conspiracy of silence? Were they saying, we know quite well he killed himself but we're never going to admit it?

She didn't know.

But the total annihilation of the suicide rumour had an unexpected spin-off, which, working so thoroughly in her favour, increased her growing sense of guilt. When she'd returned dazedly home, among the matters soon clamouring for her attention was the question of life insurance. Barry had insured his life under a scheme which not only paid out a substantial lump sum on his death but also paid off the mortgage. In a conditional clause, she noticed—probably because of her current preoccupation—it said that the policy would not pay out if the insured died by suicide.

But accidental death, now, that was all right. How sympathetic they were, the insurance company, just like everyone else. How they all came to help the grieving widow. Julie and family, Julie warm and fat, hugging, her eldest daughter temporarily taking over the care of Rupert and Oliver and, incredibly, making them hoot with laughter.

Fay's parents, even, coming up on the train for an afternoon of stiff condolences which everyone was heartily glad to see the end of. But, on leaving, her father had muttered something about letting him know if money got really tight and he'd see what he could do.

It was, she thought, awful that it took something as frightful as Barry's death to make him act like a human being towards her.

Sophia and Tom were her strength. She didn't know how she'd have managed without them. They were there for the worst moment—to hug and hold in the terrible half-hour immediately after she'd broken the news to the boys—and for the not-quite-so-bad times, when she was in dire need of people to talk to, to laugh with.

She heard nothing more, ever, from the Learys. Barry's mother at the funeral had been like a skull swathed in black robes, fierce accusing eyes boring into Fay like red-hot spikes. Liam, sodden, wailing, had missed out on the final blow she was sure he had lined up—the doctor whom she'd spoken to on the phone had come to her rescue and whisked her back to her hotel to pack up and be gone before Liam realised what was happening.

The Learys hate me because they know the truth, she thought bleakly. Just as I do. I did kill Barry. Drove him to his death, brought it about as surely as if I'd pushed him off that bridge and held his face down in the clear water. Words of a poem floated into her head

. . . something about killing the thing you love. It was suddenly very important to get it right, and, after quite a long search, she found in a volume of works by Oscar Wilde 'The Ballad of Reading Gaol'.

> Yet each man kills the thing he loves,
> By each let this be heard,
> Some do it with a bitter look,
> Some with a flattering word.
> The coward does it with a kiss,
> The brave man with a sword.

And I? she wondered. How did I do it?

That night she couldn't sleep. At two-thirty, in a sweat-twisted bed, she lay face to face with her guilt, and it was hot-eyed and hideous.

Pictures. Barry. The whole of her life with him flashed before her as she drowned. And the pictures were all joyous and full of love.

Then Barry, dead. It's he who has drowned after all, not me. His swollen face is turning up to the sky he can no longer see, and the firm tanned flesh that I loved to touch, to kiss, is white and pappy. His bright blue eyes are glazed over, the light and the love gone away.

I loved him, and I killed him.

In the morning a disturbed bed was the only sign of the quality of her night. She remembered, in a vague sort of way, that she'd been distressed. Unhappy. But the crystal-clarity of the thoughts was gone. Pushed underground, too painful to live with—and she must live—her guilt was buried deep, piled with a cairn of stones to keep it down.

And, around it, life went on.

TWENTY-SEVEN

The Rising of the Sun

The iron door had disintegrated. Where it had stood, a fastness which she'd thought would last for all time, now there was nothing. She couldn't close it again even if she'd wanted to.

Now a sweet wind blew, right into the darkest corners. Like a secret, crouching house which had been unshuttered and opened to the spring, there were no longer any hidden-away places. The forbidden things which the door had concealed were out now, mixing with everything else in her mind, and while their blackness was lightened a little by the mixing, at the same time the new malign influence already seemed to have started its pollution.

She didn't know what to do next.

Aaron beside her said, it is done. You have reached the depths, and so the only way now is up.

His quiet words stroked across her mind. She reached out, feeling for his hand, and he was there, holding her in a firm grip that seemed to pump fortitude into her. She was aware of how much she needed it.

'How am I going to cope?' she whispered. 'I don't think I can live with the knowledge that it was my fault.'

'You will not have to.' His tone was calm but quite incontrovertible. 'It was not your fault. You have been carrying this burden of buried guilt needlessly, and now you are going to set it down and leave it behind you.'

She saw herself setting down a heavy parcel by the roadside and walking away from it without a backward glance. She wondered if he had put the picture in her head.

But it wasn't as straightforward as that.

'You know the whole story now!' she cried, turning to him, trying to read his eyes in the darkness. She didn't allow herself to stop and ponder on the mechanics of *how* he knew, nor indeed why she was so sure of it: one thing at a time. 'How can you possibly conclude that I wasn't to blame?'

Instantly he answered with a counter-accusation: 'How can you conclude that you were?'

'I failed him!' she shouted. 'I was his strength, and I let him down! Liam said—'

'Each one must find his own strength,' he said, cutting across her anguish, 'for ultimately everyone stands alone. And you did not let him down. You supported him to the limit of your capability, which is all that could have been asked of you. You only gave up when you were faced with another, greater claim than his.'

'You mean the boys?'

'I do. Understandably, you could not allow them to suffer. Somewhere in you, perhaps unadmitted, was the knowledge that matters would get worse, and from it you drew the courage to say, enough.'

'But I don't know if that was right! He might have got better, if I'd given him that last chance he asked for! He might have stopped drinking and become the person he really was, underneath it all!'

'Do you really believe that?'

'Yes! Perhaps!'

He made no response. And in the end she had to admit, 'No. I don't.'

'Nor did he. And that was why he killed himself, because he knew that otherwise he'd go back to you, keep on going back to you, and that you wouldn't be able to abandon him, until in the end he dragged you—and your boys—down with him into the misery from which he couldn't escape.'

He was right. She knew he was right. After a moment she said, 'Then you do think he killed himself?'

'I know that he did. He had the mark upon him.'

'How do you—?'

As if she'd come up against a force field, her flaring curiosity was deflected. She thought she caught the word, later.

'Liam thought so too,' she said after a moment. 'They all did, the priest, the doctor, the relations. And they all put the blame on me.'

'They did not.'

'Yes they did! Liam said so! ''You killed him!'', he said to me!'

His grip on her hand tightened till it hurt. 'And did it never cross your mind that Liam was in terrible need of a scapegoat? That in his heart he carried the unbearable knowledge that he was as much to blame as anyone for his beloved brother's death? Who was it introduced Barry to alcohol in the first place? Who was it took him, underage, along with him to the rugby club, and proudly boasted that you'd think the lad was twenty-six, not sixteen, the way he carried his drink?'

'Liam?' Of course. She hadn't known that. But it was true: somehow she knew without a doubt that it was true. It fitted far too well with all that she knew about the two of them and their relationship with each other to be anything else.

'What about the priest? The doctor? His mother?'

'His mother didn't like you because you married her son. But hers was a general dislike of daughters-in-law; it was not directed specifically at you. The doctor did not blame you—if you will recall, he said he knew Barry and understood better than you could know. As for the priest—possibly he too required someone to share his guilt at losing a member of his flock to suicide. Despair is, I understand, the ultimate sin against the Holy Ghost.'

'And there I was,' she murmured, 'already half-accepting the blame before anyone had got as far as suggesting I should.'

'That,' Aaron said gently, 'is the only part of all this that is your fault. Your predisposition to put yourself in the wrong.'

In that clean, healing place, the brilliant stars looking down with benevolence and the universe holding out its arms to her, something moved over in her mind. And suddenly she saw herself from a different angle. Against her old, tired instinct to protest one last time, but it was my fault! came his quiet voice, no more.

After some time—for seeing herself in a new light was alarming and took some getting used to—she said, 'Why? Why did I drag the weight of blame on to myself so tenaciously?'

'I don't think you need to be told. Think.'

My fault. Mea culpa. 'Through my fault, my fault, my most grievous fault', knocking her fist against her childishly flat breast as the nuns did, accepting blame for some crime she barely understood and couldn't be sure she'd committed. Pray for the souls in Purgatory! Poor, poor souls, suffering torment the longer if you forget to pray for them, every hour, every *minute!* Forsake your sinful ways, for every time a little girl sins, Jesus suffers again the agonies of Crucifixion!

My fault. By my negligence, by my actions, making others suffer. *MY FAULT!*

She said, 'It was conditioning. Wasn't it? A conditioned reflex, like Pavlov's dogs.'

'The Jesuits, I believe, boast that if they are given a child before he is seven then he is theirs for life. Children are easy to condition, which makes the offence of the adult the worse if the adult does not—or will not—know when to stop.'

'They were so sure they were right!' Her brand-new clarity of vision seemed to apply to others besides herself. 'Never any question of, this is what *we* believe, but there are other creeds.'

'Of course not.' He sounded scornful. 'The followers of most religions believe emphatically that theirs is the only way and that anyone who does not agree is damned, but the Christian faith holds the distinction of inflicting more suffering in its name than any other.'

'Poor Jesus,' she said suddenly. 'What must he have made of the Inquisition, and witch-hunts, and wars in the name of religion, and bigotry, and hatred, when he told us we should love each other?'

'Who can speak for Jesus? But he came to earth as a human, and since we too are human, perhaps our own response may indicate what his would be.'

She felt tired, as if the weight of all that had been going on in her head were overcoming her. She let herself sag against the warm stone at her back, and, as if the revolution in her mind had made her at a stroke more receptive, felt the healing strength flow into her. She said in surprise, 'It tingles!'

He laughed. 'It does indeed. Earth power is the stronger, when you let it in and do not fight it.'

'Yes,' she said, remembering. 'I resisted, before. Didn't I? When we got here and you said the energy entered the body from the rocks, I was frightened.' It seemed so very long ago.

'And you are not frightened any more.'

'No.'

Then, feeling that he was waiting, she said, 'What is it?'

He didn't answer with words spoken aloud. Because that, she realised, would be impossible. Instead he put pictures, images, into her mind. The great ball of matter with which the universe in all its mystery began. Collections of atoms, spinning into spheres. Globes. Worlds, such as this one. The fire in the sky that gave life to what had been barren. And something of that creative energy treasured still within the Earth, awesome in its power but, to those who knew where and how to look, ultimately beneficial.

Although she knew she had a very long way to go, she felt that the first step to understanding had been taken.

Some time later he said, 'It has worked.'

She knew what he meant, but needed all the same to confirm she was right.

'Your master plan?' she said with a smile. 'The long circuitous route by which you've managed to make me see the error of my ways?'

'Precisely that.' She could tell from his voice that he was smiling too. 'The removal of your cage, I think, so that you walk free and see the world as it really is.'

'My cage.' A cage whose bars were made of childhood impressions, too deeply seared into her. A cage that held her tight in its singlemindedness, blinkering her to wider horizons. A cage in which she had inflicted upon herself her own punishment, so relentlessly that to remove it had taken someone as—as—as what?—as Aaron.

She thought, what *are* you?

And, again, he said, later.

Aloud he said, 'Now that you are free to look without prejudice, speak to me of Barry.'

311

Barry. Her heart filled with love, and she thought, I loved you, Barry, and I know that, to the best of your ability, you loved me too. She saw him as he once was, in his track suit, kit bag in hand. Clear-eyed, eager-faced. Handsomest boy she'd ever seen. Then she began to see beyond the perfection to the mutilated man who lay underneath. And, despite the weakness—perhaps because of it—knew that she loved that poor inadequate soul just as much. Possibly more.

When admitting to his flaws no longer triggered off her guilt because she hadn't managed to overcome them, she was left with nothing but pity. Love, and pity.

Grieve for him, Aaron said in her head. Grieve because you loved him. But finish there—responsibility for what he was and the manner of his death is not for you to bear, for he had set his feet on the path of self-destruction long before you met.

I know that, now.

Yes. You do. And there is no more to say.

She perceived, after a measureless time of sitting against her rock and merely absorbing, that in front of her the sky was not as black as it had been. And the stars were blinking out, dimmest first, brightest lasting a little longer as if staying for a final benediction.

Across the narrow sea, over the mainland mountains to the east, an orange glow was beginning. The start of a new day.

But it was more to her, so much more, than merely another day. Under the kind cover of the darkness she had been remade. Taken apart—not without pain—and reassembled, so that now as the rising sun poured itself once more on the earth, it shone down for the first time on a new being.

As if he knew what she was thinking—of course he

does!—he stood up, helping her to her feet, and said, 'Come with me.'

Holding her hand, he led her forwards across the plateau, stopping after some twenty or thirty paces. In the waxing light she saw that they were standing on the edge of a precipice. Gazing out over the valley below, she saw beyond it the sea, on whose restless surface the dawn was painting flashes of gold. As if the thought came from deep within and long ago, she thought of the people down there, asleep now but waking soon to begin the day. Working and squabbling. Loving and hating. Being petty and being magnificent. Discovering, perhaps, the ultimate truths.

The human race, with all its faults and all its strengths.

The glow over the mountains was increasing, shooting rays of orange and yellow into the lightening sky. The sun was coming! Lifted to wild exhilaration, she leaned forward, searching for the first sight. There was a feeling of wonderful inevitability, and she had a sudden strange insight into the minds of her distant ancestors, who still lived in ignorance and to whom the morning reappearance of the sun was a daily miracle.

It *is* a miracle.

She didn't know where the thought came from. It didn't matter: she agreed, wholeheartedly. Yes, yes!

Over the black silhouette of the land a bright light now shone. A pinpoint at first, with startling abruptness it spread sideways and was all at once an arc of brilliant orange. She was aware of Aaron speaking, in a soft monotone, words she didn't know but whose meaning was somehow quite clear. A hymn to the morning, a psalm of thanksgiving to the sun.

The arc was a semicircle now, orange turning to yellow, and it filled the dip between two mountains. As she watched, eyes fixed—unable to turn away, unable even to blink—the semicircle rose, lifting itself with effortless power ever up, up, and its lower curve came steadily into view.

Then it was a circle, complete, perfect, entire in itself. As it cleared the land and ascended into the pale sky, she thought, I have been inert, marking time. Alive, but not living. In the shadows. But now a faint star has gone nova. A sun has been born and it shines on me, calling me out of my darkness into its healing light.

She felt her soul fill with joy and gratitude. She turned to Aaron, wanting to share it with him, wanting him to know, to be with her in the excitement of rebirth.

She fumbled in the depths of her mind for the right words, for everything she could think of was so inadequate as to be useless.

He said in her head, as he had said before, there is no need of speech between you and I.

And as he put his arms round her and drew her to him, she gave herself up to the euphoria of being united with him in a moment out of time which, she had no doubt, would stay with her for ever.

TWENTY-EIGHT

The Legend of the Zodiac

They stood in each other's arms while the sun climbed steadily into the sky. After some time, she became aware that the total peace and stillness in her head was being interrupted by her thoughts beginning to stir again. Perhaps it's this glorious early morning. Or perhaps it's Aaron's body so close against mine.

She remembered yesterday—was it only then?—that she'd had an instant's disappointment when she worried that all they'd do together during the night ahead would be to go driving and visiting. And he'd sent her the thought, of course that won't be all!

It hadn't been all. Oh, God, it hadn't, but the other things which had happened were hardly what she'd had in mind. As if the thought were sparking-off a response in her body, she pressed herself closer to him.

Instantly she felt an answering movement in him, and into her mind flowed warmth and strength. She raised her head and he bent down to kiss her, gently, with affection rather than with passion. Before she could even begin on the thought, aren't we going to make love? he said into her mind, no, for we have been awake all night, I am far too tired, and so are you.

She laughed aloud, not minding now. She said, 'I don't believe that you ever get too tired to do anything.'

315

'Oh, I do, I do.' He cradled her head against his chest, his hand smoothing down her hair. 'And, in case you have forgotten, the night before last you and I made love throughout the darkness.'

'So we did.' The memory alone was sufficient to make her legs feel weak. She thought of her stiff thighs and sore jaw, and smiled. *So long, since I did anything like that. And such a man, to rediscover the joys with.* She said, for there was no point in hoping he hadn't picked up the thought anyway, 'I was a bit out of practice. It's been years and years since I did anything like that.' She added silently, *if ever.*

She felt at first his sympathy, although he didn't express it in words. Then, as if to lighten the mood, he said, 'And for me. Many more years than for you.'

'I don't believe that, either!'

'It's true.'

She couldn't tell from his tone whether or not he was serious. 'Go on, then, how long?'

He seemed to be considering. Then he said lightly, 'Hundreds of years,' and she realised he was joking after all.

'I shall take you home,' he announced, pushing her gently away from him and taking her hand. 'I shall put you to bed and leave you to sleep, and later in the day, when I too have rested, we shall be together again.'

There was no need for him to say what they'd do: she already knew.

Early-rising Corfiots were already about when they drew up outside The Twins' House. She felt like a naughty teenager, like an all-night reveller returning home in the morning still wearing last night's dishevelled evening clothes. But it didn't seem to matter.

He came with her up the steps, taking his spare key

from her and opening the front door. Silently they went upstairs, and, as before, she peeped into the twins' and the boys' rooms.

'Perfect peace,' he whispered in her ear.

He closed the door of her room behind them, and while she was in the bathroom, she heard him secure the shutters and draw the curtains against the bright morning light. She thought tiredly, no need to do that, my love, I would sleep now even with searchlights in my eyes, and he answered, perhaps, but the darkness is more restful.

She walked across to the bed, and, aware of his eyes on her, took off her clothes, reaching under the pillow for her nightshirt. As she was about to put it on, he took hold of her hand, stopping her, and, just for a moment, touched his fingers against her flesh: neck, breast, stomach, thighs. Then, hand under her chin, raised her head so that she looked into his eyes.

Are you really going?

He smiled. Yes. Put on your nightshirt and get into bed. I am sorry—I wanted to look at you, but I should have known I couldn't look without touching.

It was almost too much: she felt that, with the smallest amount of pressure, she could get him to stay. And she knew he didn't want to. She got into bed so quickly that she got the sheet in a twist and had to start again.

He sat beside her, pulling the sheet up to her chin. He said, 'Thank you. I will see you later,' and then bent down to kiss her forehead.

She said as he quietly padded away, 'It's I who should be thanking you.'

She wasn't sure he'd heard—perhaps he was already thinking ahead to his own bed. But at the door, just as he was going out, he turned and said softly, 'It is what I am here for.'

*

She woke at half-past one, with the urgent need to be with the boys. I feel new, she thought, I feel that suddenly things are going to be better, *I'm* going to be better, and I want to share my optimism with them.

Down at the lido they were standing with the twins discussing what to have for lunch. She put an arm round each of them and hugged them, sneaking in a quick kiss on both tanned faces before Rupert had time to protest. She saw the twins watching, smiling benevolently. Do they know? she wondered. And from somewhere—it didn't matter where—came the answer, of course! She went up to them, and hugged them both just as she'd hugged the boys, and as one they bent their beautiful golden heads and kissed her. Castor said, 'We are pleased to see you looking so happy.'

She replied, 'Me too!', and although that wasn't quite right, knew that he understood.

She wanted to celebrate—nothing was too good for today—and suggested they go into the town for a *real* lunch, somewhere nice. But the boys didn't look too keen—'We'd have to get dressed, and if we have a big meal it'll be ages before we can swim again,' Oliver said.

'But I—' She was about to protest, to say, I want this to be special. But she didn't. She seemed to have more wisdom that she'd had before, and it was saying to her, you want to celebrate, but if you impose on them your idea of celebration, they won't like it as much as you think they will, and you'll end up disappointed. 'All right,' she said cheerfully. 'We'll stay here and have the usual.'

And Rupert, as if he knew just what she needed to hear, said, 'This is the best, Mum. We like this better than anything,' and gave her a straight-from-the-heart smile.

They sat at their table in the shade, and she bought

them all the most lavish meal the snack-bar could provide, pushing the boat out further with a second Coke for the boys and two Amstels for the twins. After the regulation half-hour to let the food sink down, the boys went off with Castor to play about in the shallows.

Pollux stayed at the table with her. Feeling his eyes on her, she turned to meet his brilliant blue gaze. He said, 'It has gone. The shadow over you has gone, and you now look as you are meant to look.'

She was moved almost to tears. 'I know,' she whispered. 'I feel—I can't say how I feel.'

'You need not.' He reached out and took her hand, and his was warm and strong. 'It is apparent.'

She wanted to say, it's Aaron. And to a lesser extent, you and Castor. But mainly Aaron. She wanted to ask, what is he? How does he do it? How do you all do it? And why?

She held her peace. If Pollux was picking up her questions, he wasn't showing any sign. He certainly wasn't answering them. And somehow she felt that was right, that it would be against some strange sort of etiquette to grill him on the nature and the actions of his—his boss? His employer?

From somewhere was supplied, his master.

Pollux said quietly, 'He will tell you all that you need to know.'

Quickly, before she could stop herself, she said, 'All I need to know or all I want to know?'

And, laughing, he said, 'Possibly the one will be the same as the other.'

They sat for some time in a companionable silence, still holding hands. She wondered why he didn't go off and join the others in the water as he usually did. Perhaps he and Castor had arranged between them that one of them would stay with her, today. If they had, she was glad: it was lovely just having him close.

After a while, she asked tentatively—not sure if it counted as grilling—'Do you live in The Twins' House when it's not let to people like me?'

He gave her a long considering look. 'We do,' he said.

'Don't you mind having to move out? Where do you go?'

He smiled. 'We do not mind. When we are not in the house, we live on Aaron's boat.'

No wonder they didn't mind! she thought. They were young enough for living on a boat to be entirely wonderful.

'We take her out,' he confided suddenly, 'we sail her over the waters, far away, sometimes with the others, sometimes just us.'

She wondered who he meant by the others. She couldn't ask. She said, 'I should think it's best with just you and Castor.'

'It is.' He nodded fervently. 'The others are argue—argumative.'

'Argumentative.'

'Yes.' He flashed her a dazzling smile. 'Ar-gu-men-tative.' Then, apparently anxious not to have her suffering under a misapprehension, he added, 'Not Aaron. He is never argumentative. We like to go with him. But Virginia, Leo, Angelos—they like to tell everyone what to do, and everyone does not like to be told.'

They're part of this strange group, she thought. Just like that awful woman and the Bull man, the twins are Aaron's people. If they hadn't been childminding for me that first night, they'd probably have been in the restaurant with all the rest of them.

She counted in her mind. Aaron, Virginia, the Bull man, Leo whose birthday it was the other night. Who else? She thought back to the restaurant where she'd seen them all together. The man who ordered the wine, the sad-eyed woman next to him. The younger man who blew me a kiss. The crabby woman who poked my legs with her stick. There were a couple of others, too—a miserable, dark-countenanced man and the companion to whom he was muttering.

Ten. With the Twins, twelve.

Her mind leading her involuntarily down the path it had discovered, she thought, the Twins. And on Aaron's key, the sign of Gemini. Aaron, with the sign of Aries the Ram round his neck. A man called Leo, with a birthday in August, and a woman called Virginia, which is very close to Virgo. A man who may be called Angelos but whose new name of the Bull man is far, far more appropriate. Taurus the Bull.

Twelve people. Twelve signs of the Zodiac.

For an instant she believed she had stumbled on the truth. Then, as suddenly, she thought, there are only eleven signs, not twelve. The Twins count as one.

Immediately she felt silly and credulous for believing so readily in her own far-fetched ideas. She hoped Pollux hadn't picked up any of her fantasising. She glanced surreptitiously at him, but his pleasantly bland expression gave nothing away. Fleetingly she wondered why it was she couldn't read his mind or his brother's, when she seemed increasingly often to be able to read Aaron's.

I don't think he noticed. Thank goodness! I must push such thoughts out of my head.

She concentrated hard on the boys and Castor, who had got hold of an airbed and were trying to get on it all together, without much success. They appeared to be laughing too much to have any control, over either themselves or the wayward Lilo.

From the depths of her newly-liberated, free-flowing memory came a picture of a beach and a girl called Charlotte, who told her about the star signs and the gods that ruled them. Who asked her if she'd ever wondered why the names of the ruling planets were the same as the names of the old gods. Suggested, disturbingly, that perhaps the gods had been named after the planets and not the other way round.

What did it all mean?

She thought of what Aaron had said about the origins of the planets. How the great ball of original matter had exploded and blasted out its atoms, and how the mysterious laws that rule the universe had set the atoms spinning and whirling into the bodies which became, eventually, the stars and the planets. This sun, these nine planets. She'd helped Oliver compose a mnemonic for remembering the planets—how did it go? My Very Eager Mouse Jumps Swiftly Under Nuclear Power. That was it. He'd done a lovely illustration of a fat mouse daubed with the warning sign for radiation. Charming.

Mercury, Venus, Earth, Mars, Jupiter, Saturn, Uranus, Neptune, Pluto. Earth the home planet. Did the others have their own equivalent of earth power? They all came from the same source, so it was likely.

She thought again of Charlotte. 'The planets are alive,' she'd said. 'Pulsing with electro-magnetic energy.' How strange, that a chance conversation all those years ago should be so relevant now. And that she should remember it, word for word. Earth power. Mars power. Venus power.

She saw in her mind's eye the paintings on the wall of The Twins' House. Ares and Aphrodite. Mars and Venus. As if she were peering through a thick mist, getting tantalising glimpses of a picture whose full meaning she could only guess at, she tried to make the pieces come together.

What did it all mean?

Dazed by the profundity of her thoughts, she was aware of Pollux standing up. As she watched, he walked away and down the steps into the water. Don't

322

go! she cried silently. But it was all right: he waded up to Castor and, as if handing over to the next runner in a relay race, touched his hand, and instantly Castor set off for the shore, climbing dripping out of the sea and coming to take his brother's place at the table.

She stared at him. He was exactly the same as his brother. She had never seen two people so totally identical. Even now, after all the days spent with them, she found it uncanny.

He was smiling at her, his expression open and receptive. She thought, what the hell? It'll do no harm to ask. The worst he can do is say no.

She said, almost certain he already knew what she was going to say, 'Castor? Will *you* tell me?'

He looked at her, and in her mind she felt a gentle intrusion like searching fingers. Then he closed his eyes, and the fingers went away. Where had he gone? Was he communing with someone else? Pollux, perhaps? Then he was back, and, his eyes open again and fixed on to hers, into her head came the thought, some things I may tell you.

Without apparently having to stop and think, he began to speak. 'There is an ancient legend of this place which says that one day, one of the Old Ones came down from the mountain to be with the new young race which had supplanted him and his kind. He bore them no ill-will, for he was wise, and he understood that as the world evolves, so its inhabitants must evolve too. Watching from afar was no good, for him—he wanted to help, and he chose to leave the paradise to which he was entitled and descend to share in the world of men.

'He was benevolent and patient, this First One of the Old Ones, but he found mankind too headstrong to cope with alone. So he journeyed all around the central land-circled sea, searching the mountaintops, the far valleys and the secret unknown islands for others of his kind who might be willing to share the burden with him. Most sent him away and refused their help, but some did not. When finally he came back to his own beloved island, with him were twelve others. They divided the year into twelve moons, and one of the Old Ones—in the case of the midsummer moon, a pair of them—each agreed to rule one month. The First One—he was called Aare, which in time became Aries—took the first moon of spring, and his sign was the Ram, who wakes to power in the first warm month of the year.'

Aries the Ram, she thought. The First One.

'For a time,' Castor said, 'all was well, and Aare observed with joy how many of his companions worked in harmony with mankind and made great progress. Leo the Lion, who ruled in the late summer, Capricorn the Goat and Aquarius the Water-Bearer, who ruled the hostile winter months. But then he perceived that some of the others were growing too like the species they were meant to be educating— Taurus the Bull had become violent and selfish, Virgo the Virgin was learning from womankind the dubious arts of deception and flirtation. And one of the Old Ones went away, for among the Twelve she was the only one who could not settle on a persona that fitted in the world of humans. Her symbol was Libra the Scales, the only inanimate object in the twelve.'

My sign, she thought.

'Her companions—the Bull, the Twins, the Crab, the Lion, the Virgin, the Scorpion, the Archer, the Goat, the Water-Bearer and the Fishes—tried to persuade her to stay with them, for they loved her and knew that they would miss her. But her mind was made up, and one morning she was no longer there. The others mourned her, but the Ram grieved more deeply than any of them, for she was his opposite sign, ruling the second half of the year as he ruled the first, and he

324

did not know how he would manage without her. And just as his influence was from the planet Ares—Mars, you call it now—so hers was from Aphrodite, which you call Venus. Aphrodite and Ares of old were lovers, cleaving to each other with an enduring and a passionate love. Was it not therefore understandable that Aries should be incomplete without Libra, that he should search, go on searching through the millenia, until he should find her again?'

Her mind was reeling. Aries and Libra. Ares and Aphrodite. Mars and Venus. The god of war and the goddess of love, the original lovers, side by side on the wall in The Twins' House.

Was it all true?

She was floating in the blue of his eyes, seeing images of misty mountainsides, sparkling streams, great wide skies where eagles soared. What am I to believe?

He seemed to know that she was lost. Changing at a stroke from the chanting monotone he had been using to his usual voice, he said, 'But it is only a myth. A story, to entertain during the long winter nights by the friendly fire that drives back the darkness.' He put his hand on her forehead, soothing her anxiety, banishing her fear. 'I tell it to you to make you happy, on your special day.' He was getting up, preparing to go back into the water.

As he walked away, he turned back for a moment and said softly, 'You need not believe it if you do not want to.'

TWENTY-NINE

Past, Present and Future

The boys and the twins had already gone out that evening by the time Aaron was expected. She'd had the house to herself for over an hour, and would have been revelling in the unusual freedom were it not for a chance remark of Rupert's as he was leaving: he'd said they were meeting up with a family of two boys and a girl who were going home to England in two days, and added innocently, 'If they'd gone a couple of days later, we might have been on the same flight, mightn't we, Mum?'

As soon as she was alone she'd rushed to look in her diary. He was right: they went home in four days' time.

Where has the time gone? she wondered frantically, trying to keep at bay the awful thoughts of *leaving*. And why haven't I been keeping count of the days? I could have prepared myself, saved myself this, if I'd kept my head!

It was so unlike her, she thought, not to have noticed the weeks slipping by. Normally she was better-organised than that. It crossed her mind that perhaps this amnesia had been inflicted on her deliberately, as part of the cure. The thought made her feel a little better, for if it had been Aaron's doing, she was prepared to accept that there must be a good aspect to it.

Showered, she sat in her dressing-gown and thought back over the weeks, still unconvinced that there really had been almost four of them spent in this happy place. The first fortnight, when she'd been content to lie in the sun and do nothing. The night she'd decided to break out, and gone to the restaurant. The next night, when he'd taken her to the concert. All the lovely outings, which were either with him or made possible by him, like the trip with the twins to the beach and the day he'd taken her to the Museum. The days since the Bull man had attacked her, in the course of which she and Aaron had become lovers and everything had changed, for ever.

Yes. It added up to more than three weeks.

And in four days I must go home.

She was still sitting on her bed trying to come to terms with it when Aaron came in.

He said straight away, 'You have woken up. A part of you is already back at home.'

'No!'

'Yes.' He stood looking down at her, and she couldn't read his expression. Then he said, 'Do you wish to forget again?'

She thought instantly, I do! Then, realising that if she went back into oblivion she'd have to face returning to reality all over again, she said, 'No. It's all right. I can cope with waking up.' She managed a laugh. 'At least I think I can.'

He came to sit on the bed beside her, taking her hand in both of his. 'You can. You have always been stronger than you have thought.'

'Have I?'

'You have.'

She digested that. Then said, 'Now that we've brought the spectre of my imminent departure out into the daylight, can we not talk about it any more, please?'

He smiled. 'Not if you do not wish to.'

She stared into his eyes. She thought, I don't know how I can leave you. I—

Across her thought he said, do not worry. It will not be as you think.

And her mind suddenly filled with peace.

He said, getting to his feet, 'Perhaps you could get dressed. I am hungry, and I cannot take you out to eat in your dressing-gown, lovely though you are in it.'

Somewhere along the line, she thought vaguely, he's changed the subject. Why didn't I notice?

Following where he led, she said, reaching in the cupboard for a dress, 'Where shall we go?'

'I shall take you to a restaurant on the Listón, where none but the most privileged families dine.'

She put the dress back into the cupboard and instead got out her best one, hoping he wouldn't notice that she'd already worn it, when they went to the Museum and he'd said she looked like an English lady in her garden-party frock. Keeping her back to him, she stepped into it and did up the zip.

His hands moved hers away and he fastened the last inch for her. His fingers on her skin did strange things to her, setting in motion a surge of pleasure which swept through her and was gone almost before she'd had time to enjoy it. She turned, silently leaning against him, wrapping her arms round him, and he responded, pulling her close and touching his lips to hers.

After a moment he said, 'Later.'

It was, she thought as she picked up her handbag and put on her shoes, a word he seemed to have said to her rather a lot recently.

On the Listón, the tables under the colonnade were full of people drinking, laughing and commenting on the world passing by in front of them. Aaron led the way through an imposing-looking double doorway, over which was a wooden carving of some bird of prey. Inside, the décor was quiet but attractive, and instead of the usual white shirts the waiters wore black jackets. She realised the room was air-conditioned.

The head waiter approached, and bowed to Aaron. She thought, a while ago I might have been surprised at that. They were shown to a table in a corner, one of a couple on a low dais which gave them a good view over the room and everyone in it.

They ordered ouzo, and studied the menu. He asked her what she would like, but she found she could not concentrate on food. He said into her head, if you would not be offended, I shall order for both of us. She was just giving him a smile of thanks when he added, disconcertingly, then you may remain on the erotic paths in which you walk.

He had looked away and was talking to the waiter, and although she tried to get her own back, he had closed his mind to her and she couldn't get in. Under the table she felt his feet intrude between her own, sending a fierce shock of passion through her as if he were parting not only her feet but her legs as well. She lowered her head, praying that the waiter would hurry up with writing down the order and go away.

He seemed to take for ever: Aaron was engaging him in conversation, she was sure. Finally he went, and Aaron said: I am sorry.

She looked up at him. He seemed to be on the verge of laughter. Thinking—hoping—this was an indication that his defences were down, she sent out to him a picture of the two of them making love, his body on hers, her legs twined around him and her breasts crushed to his chest as her mouth opened to his.

Delighted, she saw his pupils widen in surprised reaction and knew she'd hit home. She said, shall we call it quits? and he replied—even in his thoughts he sounded slightly breathless—Yes.

She said conversationally, 'This is very nice. Thank you for bringing me here.'

'You are being polite again.' He sounded as if he hadn't quite forgiven her.

'I am. I suppose I'm just a polite person.'

He studied her. 'I suppose you are.' Then he smiled, and for some reason it made him look vulnerable. She found she didn't want to tease him any more.

She looked away from him and glanced around at the other tables. He was right about only the most privileged families, she thought. There are more diamonds down there than in Cartier's window. And that's only the men.

Something was nagging at the edge of her mind. A memory, intangible and evasive. She shook her head, and it went away. Then the waiter brought their first course, and she turned her full attention to mustering sufficient appetite to do it justice.

They talked easily throughout the meal, about the island, the twins, the boys. Undemanding topics. As if they were both saying, these things will do, for now.

He knows what it is, she thought in a flash of insight. He knows that something is tweaking at my mind, and he also knows exactly what that something is.

When they had finished eating and were on their first cups of coffee, she said to him, tell me. Please, tell me.

He replied, you went to Poros, you and Barry. On the last night of your holiday, you went to an expensive restaurant, a little like this one.

Yes. What of it?

From him she received the command, remember.

I got drunk. And I got depressed—I felt that Barry and I wanted different things. So different that I wondered what on earth I was doing with him. And

330

I wanted reassurance that it'd turn out okay, and instead got an awful vision of a bleak and despairing future which proved to be one hundred per cent accurate.

And I looked round the restaurant to see who could have put that thought into my mind.

When he gave her the answer, at first she couldn't accept it. She said, aghast, *you*?

Yes.

She felt sick with shock, and the room seemed to reel. She pleaded, I can't take it in. I can't think, here.

She was hardly aware of him calling the waiter and paying the bill. It all seemed to happen very fast, and then there he was, strong hand under her elbow, guiding her outside into the warm evening, supporting her as they walked the short distance to where he had parked the car. He helped her into the passenger seat, then quickly got moving and drove them out of town.

She noticed, without surprise, that he was driving her up the familiar roads to his house.

Apart from a light over the front door, all was in darkness. He led her round the path under the trees to the terrace where they had sat the first night, and said, 'Wait here. I will go inside and bring us a drink.'

She thought, I'm not sure that's wise. Then, oh, but a large brandy would be lovely. Barry, I'm depending on drink too, tonight.

Lights came on in the long room which faced on to the terrace, and she saw him moving around inside. He unlocked one of the French windows and stepped out between two of the Muses, a tray with a bottle and two glasses in one hand. It was, as she'd expected, a bottle of brandy.

He poured large measures into the two heavy cut-glass globes. Then, sitting down beside her on the marble seat, he said, 'Poros was where I first saw you.

Where I was distressed to see you, a woman like you, with a man whom you loved but who was nevertheless to bring you nothing but pain.'

'You said he had the mark on him. The mark of self-destruction. That was how you knew, because you'd actually seen him.'

'I had. It is no great achievement, for one like me, to recognise such a mark. It makes an aura, a greyish aura of despair. It is dreadful to see.'

She asked tentatively, 'Couldn't you have spoken to him? Couldn't you somehow have made things turn out differently?'

He sighed. 'No, Fay. It is one thing to see the future before it has happened—that is relatively easy, merely a matter of time mechanics—but to alter the future, that is not possible.'

'But if he'd *known*, if—'

'It would have not made any difference. In any case, a part of him did know.'

It was hard to accept that this man before her had actually seen Barry. Had sat across the room from him in a Poros restaurant and observed him, living, in the flesh. As the amazement subsided, she discovered that it made her feel happy.

He said, interrupting her pleasure, 'But it was not Barry who was my prime concern. It was you.'

'You tried to warn me. I felt you in my mind, and I looked round to see where the thoughts were coming from.'

'You did. You asked me a day or two ago, right here, upstairs in my bed, to name the occasions on which I had been surprised that you'd—"known I was there," I think was the phrase you used. That was the first time, in that restaurant, and I was more surprised than I have ever been. We did not know each other, but yet there you were, perceiving thoughts you could perfectly well have attributed to your own mind yet

332

knowing, *knowing*, they had been put there by someone else.'

She said wonderingly, 'I've no idea how I knew.'

He smiled briefly. 'Nor have I. But it made you special. Someone I—' He hesitated. 'Someone I didn't want to lose into the abyss of life.'

She said, after a long time, 'Did you make me come here?'

'You attribute to me more power than I possess. No. I could not do that. I merely waited, and hoped, and arranged things so that if you did come, I should not miss you.'

She wondered irrelevantly how many days and nights the Bull man had spent waiting at the airport. She thought, no wonder he didn't like me.

He said slightly abrasively, do not evade the matter in hand.

Penitent, she said, 'I can't remember what made me decide to come to Corfu.'

'Try.'

She let her mind relax. Quite soon, she saw herself at home, watching television. The Holiday Programme, or something, saying that Corfu was still a great holiday destination despite the tourist crowds. And something within her had told her, that's where to go.

He said, putting an end to further puzzling, 'You were brought here.'

Her mind slid away from that: it was too alarming. Brought here. Oh, I'm not sure I can handle that! Brought. And, once here, he arranged that I would be brought to the Corfiot Cultural Evening. Which wasn't.

She said with sudden urgency, 'The first time we met. Here, I mean, down in the town. I *knew* you! I recognised you. Was that because of Poros?'

It seemed, somehow, an anticlimax.

But, smiling, he said, 'No. What happened between

333

us that night was not of my doing. It is, I believe, something which happens once in a while to human beings.'

'What?'

He seemed to be considering. Then he said, 'It would be too easy to say it was love at first sight. And inaccurate, for what is felt is an awareness that something—love, perhaps—may come. An awareness, anyway, that the other will adopt a position of great importance in your life.'

It sounded plausible, and she knew she should believe him, in the light of her own experience. But still she said, 'I'm not sure I'm convinced.'

He leaned closer, taking hold of her hand. 'Fay, why not accept? That, although I already knew you and was therefore in a different position, that was the first time in your life that you had set eyes on me. Yet you knew me. How could that have been, unless you had a moment of precognition in which you foresaw all that we would become to each other?'

He seemed to sense she was still not convinced. He said, 'You are used to a world in which time moves, steadily and surely, in one direction, and that is forwards. You must open your mind to the concept that this may not be quite accurate. I am telling you, from my different vantage point, that there is a place at which past, present and future overlap and become one.'

Past, present and future. She was feeling weird, the brandy relaxing her, making her receptive to him, to his insistence. Her hand was still clasped in his, and she was very conscious of the warm touch of his skin. She raised her eyes, meeting his, and it seemed to her that she put her heart out for him to claim or deny.

She said, 'I love you. I love you more than I have ever loved anyone. I—' She didn't know how to go on without sounding dismissive. Then it didn't matter any more. 'I don't care how it happened, where or when. I only know that you are my world, and, if you want me, I'm yours.'

He went on looking at her. Then, almost as if it was torn out of him, said, 'I love you too. I have never felt about any woman the way I feel about you.' He leaned forward and kissed her, mouth firm against hers, tongue sliding along the inside of her lips sending through her a thrill of pleasure, a melting, dampening pleasure.

Through the joy she was aware he was saying more. Something about her not realising just what he was telling her.

But that didn't matter either. For he was taking her up in his arms, hands on her clothing, unzipping, unfastening, until she was naked and inspired to do the same to him. The heap of their garments cushioning her from the cold marble, she lay down, parting her legs, pulling him down on top of her, the cumulative effect of the whole evening making her wet and ready for him, more than ready, so that as he slid into her there was no resistance.

His hands held her face, and above her he said, look at me.

She met his eyes. Rose into him, met him, body, mind, soul.

Knew that, in every dimension, she loved him more than life itself.

THIRTY

Libra the Balance

Some time in the night he woke her, murmuring something which at first she didn't understand. She wondered if, half asleep, he'd spoken to her in the wrong language. Repeating himself, he said, 'We shall be together, for all of your last days. Here, at The Twins' House, at the lido. We shall not be apart.'

My last days, she thought. Only three of them, now. She turned to him in the darkness, face pressed to his chest. For a moment the strength in him she was trying to draw on wasn't there, and she knew, if she'd ever had any doubts, that the thought of parting affected him as deeply as it did her.

Then, as if weakness were an indulgence he only permitted himself for a second or two, she felt the strength come back. Like a tangible force, she felt it flow through him and into her. Absurdly, she had a vision of Popeye as he ate his spinach.

She whispered, 'I *still* don't want to leave you, even if we are going to be brave about it.'

Instantly he replied, 'Do you think I want to let you go?'

No. Of course you don't.

'You have your own life to lead,' he went on. 'You cannot uproot two lively and intelligent boys from all that they know and bring them out to a Greek island to live. It would not be fair.'

'I know.'

'And you, too, should be in England, for the time is now right—you are now right—for a resumption of your career.'

She thought, why didn't that occur to me? With Rupert already at secondary school and Oliver nearly there, it is time I turned my attention to myself. I could look for a job doing what I did before the boys were born. It made me happy then, so why not now?

Now that there's no longer a barrier to thinking of the past, I can see the present so much more clearly. Nothing's blocked off. I can remember the early days of working, and although that means remembering being with Barry too, that's no longer something that hurts too much to think about.

Aaron. See what you've done to me?

She said aloud, 'No more data-processing. No more fill-in jobs. Instead, something satisfying. Yes, why not?'

The vision of herself, capable, good at her job, well-dressed and in charge of her life, looked great, and for a little while filled her mind. Then, slowly at first and then with increasing speed, it began to crumble.

For there was something missing in this brave new world of hers. Aaron would not be in it.

He said into her mind, I cannot be in it. Not in the sense you are wanting. This is my place, and I must stay here, but for you the future lies elsewhere.

She asked, hardly able to form the thought, will it always be like that?

She didn't think he was going to answer. Then, holding her very close to him, his head against hers, she began to see a vague picture form in her mind. They were together, in the sunshine, aboard his boat.

He said aloud, 'Children grow up, and their mothers need no longer be there for them all the time.'

He didn't say any more. But then he didn't need to.

They arrived at The Twins' House in time for breakfast. Sitting at the kitchen table with the boys and the twins, she felt almost that she and Aaron were intruding. Watching the four of them managing quite satisfactorily without any help from her, she said quietly to him, 'Why do they get on so well? You'd think they'd known each other for years.'

He smiled. 'When are your boys' birthdays?'

'Rupert's is the sixteenth of June, Oliver's is the twenty-fifth of May.'

'What star-sign does that make them?'

'Gemini.'

'Yes. That explains the special affinity. The twins are looking after their own.'

She said, voicing a thought that had been on her mind for some time, 'The boys will miss them dreadfully, when we go.'

'They will. And Castor and Pollux will miss them, too.'

'How will I help them cope?' When I am also missing you?

'They will know, without any doubt, that they will be with the twins again.' As you will know that you will come back to me.

While the boys were gathering together all they would need for a day at the lido, Aaron spoke quietly to the twins, who appeared to be enthusiastically agreeing to whatever it was he was suggesting. He said to her, 'We think it would be nice to take you and the boys on the boat for a couple of days. They would enjoy, I think, a night at sea.'

'They'd love it.' And something so different would

338

remove from all their minds the thought that there were only three days left.

It was absolutely the right thing to have done. Coming back into the Marina the next evening, she watched the twins with the boys. They'd taught them the rudiments of sailing, and because they were who they were, had embued the whole business with the magic and the joy that was their hallmark. Looking at the beautiful faces, she thought, I love them too, not only because they've given so much to my sons but because they are good, and kind.

It had been an intimate thing to do, to sail off just the six of them on their own. The confined space had brought them closer, and seemed to have acted as a confirmation of the ties that existed between them. Last night they had anchored a little way off shore, in a sheltered bay, and she had seldom known such peace. The boys had gone exhaustedly to bed soon after supper, and the twins, with supreme tact, had followed half an hour later. She had sat in the darkness with Aaron, sharing thoughts, sometimes talking quietly, until he got up, taking her hand, and led her below. Silently, aware of the others so near, he undressed her and in his narrow bunk made love to her with a tenderness that brought her to tears.

He had said in the morning, 'We shall leave the boys and the twins to sleep on board, tonight. They can return to the house in the morning, to pack up in time for your departure.'

'And where shall we go?'

He looked at her, amusement in his face. 'We shall go to my house. Making love in a bunk is acceptable, once, but I prefer more space.'

Now it was evening. Their last evening. Don't think of that.

He took her to The Twins' House first, and she showered and put on clean clothes. Then they went into the town, wandering arm in arm through the lanes, past St Spiridon's church, along the Listón, and on to the Esplanade. A lot of people seemed to know him, and they all greeted him, many making a sort of bow.

They strolled past the bandstand, and she remembered the concert.

She said into his mind, I thought there was something supernatural about you, that night.

And what do you think now?

I no longer think. I *know*.

And his laughing response neither confirmed nor denied.

He asked her if she wanted to eat, and she said no. Instead they sat at a table on the Listón drinking coffee and brandy until it was time for bed.

Back in the car, driving out of town into the darkness of the minor roads. Up the track, through the green gates. To his house, porch light on in welcome.

Inside, he said, 'Do you want a drink? Something to eat?'

And she said, 'Neither. I want you to make love to me.'

They went upstairs to his cool and opulent bedroom, and with the evening air blowing gently through the open windows undressed and lay together on the wide bed. There was so much she wanted to say to him, but it was best to begin by communing without words, in a joining of their bodies that completed, as it always did, the trilogy. Mind, heart, body.

Some time later—she thought she might have dozed off for a while—she felt him stirring beside her, and realised he was getting up.

'Where are you going?' she asked drowsily.

He turned to smile at her. 'Not far.'

340

She watched him walk across the room. He had switched on a dim bedside light, and she could see him quite clearly. It gave her pleasure simply to look at him.

He had gone to a desk in the corner, and from a drawer he took out a small box. Coming back to bed he held it out to her. 'For you.'

She hadn't expected him to give her anything more. He had already given her back her life. She opened the box, and inside, hanging on a heavy gold chain, was a medallion. It was similar in design to his, except that where his bore the ram's head, this one had a set of scales. She held it up, and the precious metal glinted in the light.

On the reverse side some words were engraved. She didn't know what they said: they were not English words.

She remembered Pollux and his legend of Aries and Libra. For a moment she was tempted, then her common sense came back. He had, after all, said she didn't have to believe it if she didn't want to.

She said, 'It's beautiful. The loveliest thing you could have given me.' Because it's like yours, and that makes me think I'm linked to you.

You are linked to me. This merely serves as confirmation.

She asked, as she had done before, how will I leave you?

Calmly came his reply. You only leave me physically, and, as I have told you, that must be. You are healed, and the purpose of the healing is to allow you to pick up your own life and live it as you were meant to. But—The clear thought broke off. For a moment she perceived nothing, then he said: It has been different, with you. In walking with you through your past I have come to love you, and I cannot let you go as I should.

Her heart sang with joy.

341

There was a longer pause. Whatever he was trying to assemble, he wasn't finding it easy. Then he said: You will go from here, and your life will be good. And a part of me will go with you, because although I have tried to hold it back, I have not been able to help myself.

She said, I don't understand.

Where am I now?

You're in my mind.

And where are you?

I am in yours.

That, Fay, cannot be reversed. Once there, we stay with each other for ever.

She let the thought filter down into her, throughout her consciousness. We stay with each other for ever. It was a good thought.

After quite a long time, another thought occurred to her, suggested, she imagined, by thinking of a part of him being in her. She asked him, will I have a baby?

Do you want to have one?

At first she thought, yes! Yes! Your baby, yes! Then she saw herself at home. Managing with two sons approaching adolescence—and, she had to admit it, almost off her hands—and a new small addition. Who would, apart from the fact that he would put her returning-to-proper-work schedule back by five years at the least, take a bit of explaining.

And anyway she had been through her baby days. With Barry.

She said, I suppose I don't.

And he replied, then you shall not have one.

She laughed, and said aloud, 'You can arrange it, just like that? After all these times we've made love, with no precautions whatsoever, you can lie there and calmly tell me, you shall not have one?'

He said seriously, 'You are not pregnant at this moment. If you wanted to be, that would be something

342

for us to think about. But as you don't, there is no need for you to be.'

She thought, I'm not going to question him. I trust him with my life, so I certainly trust him over this.

And then, I don't need a baby to keep his presence with me. I'll have that anyway. He's just told me so, and I know without a doubt he's right.

She was reluctant to come down from the mystical plain on to which they seemed to have climbed, but could not stop herself. She said, trying to make her voice level, 'I could write to you, if you gave me your address. Or phone you sometimes, perhaps.'

'You could. Although perhaps you will find you neither want nor need to.'

She wished he hadn't answered like that. It didn't exactly encourage what she wanted to say next. 'I really meant it might be an idea if I could write when I'm—when I thought I could come out here again. To let you know, so that we can see each other.'

'Why would you have to write?' He sounded genuinely puzzled.

'To make sure you're here!' Because I'd only be coming to see you! Can't you see?

He said with total serenity, 'I am always here.' He turned to her, gathering her in his arms, his mouth against her hair. 'And I shall know.'

'When I'm coming?'

'Yes.'

'But—' It still seemed so chancy.

He pulled away from her and sat up, reaching out to the bedside cabinet for his wallet. He found a piece of paper, and wrote a few lines on it. She looked at what he had written: a P.O. Box number, and what was presumably a Corfu sort code. Then a five-figure phone number, with a three-figure prefix. He said, 'You will have to find out the international code for Greece,' and handed the paper to her.

Feeling that he was laughing at her, she hastily leaned out of bed to retrieve her bag and tucked his address safely away inside. Turning back to him, she saw he was smiling, a lazy, indulgent smile.

He said, 'Are you happy now?'

And, with honesty, she said, 'Yes.'

The Twins' House in the morning was a sombre place. She was glad their flight went in the morning, since it meant fewer hours of this inescapable sadness. Rupert, she noticed, wore his surly expression, which she knew from twelve years' experience of him meant he was hurting and trying not to show it.

Castor and Pollux were, as she would have expected, perfect. They knew exactly what tone to adopt. Half-joking, half-sorrowful, they stayed close to the boys and kept their spirits up.

They had a succession of visitors while they finished the packing, and each time there was a knock on the door, from upstairs in her room she heard Aaron go to let the visitor in. His friends came, and she recognised faces she'd met that first night in the restaurant. They all wanted to see her, and they all bade her pleasant goodbyes. Virginia came, to her great surprise, with the tawny man whom she learned belatedly was Leo. Virginia caught her on her own as she was seeing her out, and whispered, 'He is different, you know. No longer ours.'

Fay thought she saw the suspicion of a tear in the glittering dark eyes.

At the last minute, when they were stuffing their luggage into the back of Aaron's car, another caller arrived. And this time she could hardly believe her eyes, because it was the Bull man.

Aaron was standing at the front door, refusing to let him in. But she saw something in his face—a sort of pleading—and, going to stand behind Aaron, she said, 'What is it?'

He handed her a melon. He said, 'I give you present.' She took it, reluctantly, for it was an absurd gift and she knew she'd ditch it long before they got to Gatwick. Holding her eyes, his own full of distress, he muttered, 'I am sorry. Please forgive me.'

She didn't know what to say. Aaron right in front of her kept silent: no help from *there*.

She thought, we all have to ask forgiveness, some time. And if we're lucky, we get it. She said, 'You're forgiven.'

As she hurried back upstairs to fetch the last of her bags, she had the distinct feeling that Aaron approved.

The Twins said they would not come to the airport but would say goodbye there. In the hall they hugged, Rupert, Oliver, Castor, Pollux, Fay, each trying to kiss all of the others. She thought, they have been a part of it, these wonderful twins, and I shall always be grateful for what they've done. For my beloved boys and for me. Into her head one of the twins—perhaps both of them—said, we know. For the first and only time she kissed both of the beautiful mouths, and a small cheeky part of her said, idiot! Why didn't you do that ages ago?

She went down to join Aaron in the car, leaving the boys to make the final break on their own. They came down the steps, Oliver first, Rupert a slower second. She looked at her elder son, who was taking the parting far more deeply, as he always took everything. Always would, probably. As he got in Aaron turned to him, and for a moment put his hand across Rupert's forehead. Rupert managed a smile.

As they drove out of the square the twins stood at the top of the steps, not waving, hardly smiling. She

345

said, as much to comfort herself as her sons, 'We'll see them again.'

And Rupert said aggressively, 'I know!'

He didn't stay, once he'd helped them into the long queue for the check-in. It was better that way. He said goodbye to the boys and, leaving them guarding the luggage, she went outside with him.

Briefly he hugged her to him, intensely. She didn't think she could bear it if he kissed her, and he didn't. Into her head he said, I have no words to say. And she said, nor me. Except, I love you.

And I you.

He let her go, abruptly, as if he were tearing himself from her. Turning, he walked quickly to his car and drove away.

She watched until she couldn't see him any more. Then she went back to the boys.

Boarding passes in their hands, they went through Passport Control into the Departure Lounge. An hour to go—the flight was, thank God, on time. She didn't let herself think of him. Not yet, when it still hurt so much.

The flight was called. Sheep-like, they boarded, stowed their hand-luggage, sat themselves down for the long journey home.

As the airplane lifted up and circled over the town, Oliver peered out. 'I can't see The Twins' House,' he remarked. Rupert gave a sort of snort. Realising that perhaps anything to do with the twins wasn't the best topic of conversation, Oliver muttered, 'Sorry.'

Then, a few minutes later, he spoke again. Lovely, cheerful, tactless Oliver, he said to her, 'Ma, wasn't Aaron nice?'

And, ignoring his unwitting use of the past tense she said, laughing and crying at the same time, 'Yes, my love. Very nice.'

December

She sat in the late evening writing Christmas cards. The boys had gone to bed, and in the calm of the silent house she worked with a lighted Advent candle on the table in front of her.

It was a happy house. No more ghosts, no more black corners. They talked of Barry now, for she no longer feared to think about him and it was natural, after all, to keep alive the memory of someone you'd loved.

She'd suggested tentatively to the boys that, one day, the three of them might go to Ireland together to see Barry's home town, and perhaps put some flowers on his grave. Oliver had said yes straight away—but she suspected it was more for the thrill of going overnight on the ferry—and Rupert had looked at her thoughtfully and said eventually, 'I think I'd like to, too.'

She found a photograph of Barry and put it on the desk in the living room. Quite often, as she passed, she would smile at him. Gently touch his cheek.

She stretched, arching her back and rotating her shoulders. It had been a hard day, but ultimately satisfying because the Nativity play at her special school had gone off with hardly a hitch, and parents, teachers and most of all children had been delighted. One of the mothers had come up to her afterwards for a quiet word: her son had been a Wise Man, and, overcoming the handicaps of a brain that couldn't recognise words and an appalling stammer, had reeled-off his rote-learned five lines without a mistake.

His mother said to her, eyes very bright, 'You don't know how much this means to me.'

And Fay, swallowing the lump in her throat, said, 'Oh, yes I do.'

There was a stack of signed, sealed and stamped cards on the table. She had worked her way through the long list, and was now thinking if anyone she'd met since last Christmas warranted a card.

Aaron.

He moved to the forefront of her mind. A position in which he was often to be found, for if he were not the next thought, then he was the one after that. Pushing the cards away and capping her pen, she gave herself up to him.

Coming back had been awful. The only way to cope had been to throw herself into life at home, dragging the boys with her. Their school term had started almost immediately, and quite soon she'd been happy to see that normal life was reabsorbing them.

For her it was more difficult. The temptation was there to give up, give in to her misery and think, I lost one man, now I've lost another. But even right down in the depths she didn't believe that was true. Sometimes she would hear Aaron's voice—you are healed—and sometimes it was purely her own common sense that ordered her to stop feeling so sorry for herself.

She wrote numerous letters applying for jobs, not allowing herself to be discouraged when people failed to answer, and she went for a few interviews. Then out of the blue came an offer: stand-in teacher at a

348

school for five to elevens with learning difficulties, replacing a woman who, to Fay's great good fortune, had slipped while decorating and broken her hip.

It was a start.

Having a job—a *worthwhile* job—to go to every morning helped her so much that she could hardly believe it. For a time she seemed to forget about him, so far in the back of her mind had she pushed him.

But then, as if her unconscious were saying, enough!, she began to dream of him. And one night heard his loved, unique voice say, I told you life would be better.

Hardly knowing if she were asleep or awake she had answered, with love, with joy, sending all her feelings to him in a great wave. He heard, she was quite sure, and in that delirious, semi-conscious border between waking and sleeping she thought, now I know why he laughed when I asked for his phone number.

. In the daytime, working right up at the sharp end of life with children to whom every little challenge was a major hurdle, there wasn't a moment for mystical imaginings. And Aaron seemed to slip out of focus, so that if during some hasty coffee-break she had been called upon to explain him to a colleague, she would have said, oh, it all seems impossibly unreal, now! I expect I dreamt most of it. Or perhaps I had too much sun!

But in the peace of the evening and the night, he reclaimed her.

She picked up a card. One of the more expensive ones which she'd bought to send to special people. Now that she was alive again, there seemed to be a growing number of those. From her writing-case she drew out the piece of paper on which he had written his address.

But something held her back. It seemed sort of— mundane, she thought, to communicate with him by means of a Christmas card. Even if it was a special one. It put him on a par with everyone else.

Turning the slip of paper over, she noticed he'd written on the back of a bill. Two coffees, two brandies. And printed at the top, the name of the café on the Listón.

She could see it all, vividly. See that long row of graceful arches, see the pretty lamps, see the lively, attractive people chatting in the evening light. She could see him, close beside her. See his dark eyes full of humour. Full of love.

I'll be back, she said vehemently to him. I promise. In the spring. Perhaps I'll come alone, just for a week, if I can make arrangements for the boys. I'll tell them I'm going out to fix up our summer accommodation. Another month in The Twins' House?

But, however, whenever, I'll be back.

She heard his voice. Quite clearly, he said, I shall be waiting.

She held the slip of paper in her hand. Deliberately, she tore it in half and, one after the other, held the pieces into the candle flame until they had charred and crumbled to nothing.